CHARTER SCHOOL OUTCOMES

EDITED BY

MARK BERENDS
MATTHEW G. SPRINGER
HERBERT J. WALBERG

Ann Primus
Vanderbilt Managing Editor

Lawrence Erlbaum Associates
Taylor & Francis Group

New York   London

Lawrence Erlbaum Associates
Taylor & Francis Group
270 Madison Avenue
New York, NY 10016

Lawrence Erlbaum Associates
Taylor & Francis Group
2 Park Square
Milton Park, Abingdon
Oxon OX14 4RN

Printed in the United States of America on acid-free paper
10 9 8 7 6 5 4 3 2 1

International Standard Book Number-13: 978-0-8058-6222-5 (Softcover) 978-0-8058-6221-8 (Hardcover)

Library of Congress Cataloging-in-Publication Data

Charter school outcomes / editor, Mark Berends.
    p. cm.
  ISBN-13: 978-0-8058-6222-5 (alk. paper)
  ISBN-10: 0-8058-6222-6 (alk. paper)
  1. Charter schools--United States--Evaluation. 2. Charter schools--Accountability.
3. Educational accountability--United States. I. Berends, Mark, 1962-

LB2806.36.C518 2007
371.01--dc22
                                 2007012766

Visit the Taylor & Francis Web site at
http://www.taylorandfrancis.com

WITHDRAWAL

CHARTER SCHOOL OUTCOMES

Contents

Preface

Since the school reform movement began in 1991, the percentage of students in elementary and secondary schools who attend a "chosen" public school has increased significantly. So, too, have the attention to and debate about various choice options (e.g., charters, magnets, vouchers, homeschooling). Charter schools comprise one of the largest growth areas in the choice sector; there are now over 3,000 and about 1 million students attend them. Thus, it seems appropriate that a new Research on School Choice (RSC) series begins with an edited book on charter schools. Our series, however, will hardly be restricted to charter schools. In the coming years, we envision that it will feature important research on private schools; public and private voucher programs; magnet schools; homeschooling; Internet-delivered programs; supplementary educational services and providers; and other options that offer educators, parents, and students more choice than traditional neighborhood public schools do.

The RSC series will examine these forms of school choice from multiple perspectives: economic, political, sociological, psychological, historical, and legal. It will also include work on the governance, structure, process, effectiveness, and costs of choice schools. It will feature much domestic research but also draw upon international and comparative studies of choice in foreign countries. As in the present book, the work included will report on the methodology of research, substantive findings, and the policy and practice implications. We intend to solicit the best research on school choice for the series, wherever it is done.

The series' sponsor is Vanderbilt University's National Center on School Choice (NCSC), directed by Professor Mark Berends. The NCSC is one of only ten such centers supported by the U.S. Department of Education's Institute of Education Sciences (IES) (Grant# R305A040043). Its location alongside the National Center on Performance Incentives in Vanderbilt's Learning Sciences Institute makes Vanderbilt the only institution to house two national IES centers. NCSC partners are the Brookings Institution, Brown University, Harvard University, the National Bureau of Economic Research, the Northwest Evaluation Association, Stanford University, and the University of Indianapolis.

Preliminary versions of the chapters in this volume were presented and discussed at the NCSC's National Conference on Charter School Research at Vanderbilt University in September 2006. These chapters are intended to provide education researchers, practitioners, policymakers, and the general public with access to cutting-edge research findings and their implications for education research, practice, and policy. Each chapter is published in the name of the author(s) and the views expressed do not necessarily reflect those of the NCSC, its partner institutions, or sponsoring agencies.

We gratefully acknowledge Ann Primus, managing editor of this volume. We also acknowledge Susanne Jackson, who supervised the planning, logistics, and conduct of the National Conference on Charter School Research. We thank both for their attention to detail, patience, calmness, and good humor. Without their participation, the conference and volume would not have been possible.

We welcome your comments and suggestions.

Mark Berends

Matthew G. Springer

Herbert J. Walberg

Contributors

June Ahn
Rossier School of Education
University of Southern California
Los Angeles, California

Dale Ballou
Department of Leadership, Policy and Organizations
Vanderbilt University
Nashville, Tennessee

Mark Berends
Department of Leadership, Policy and Organizations
Vanderbilt University
Nashville, Tennessee

Robert Bifulco
Department of Public Policy
University of Connecticut
West Hartford, Connecticut

Dominic J. Brewer
Rossier School of Education
University of Southern California
Los Angeles, California

Richard Buddin
RAND Education
Santa Monica, California

Xiu Cravens
Department of Leadership, Policy and Organizations
Vanderbilt University
Nashville, Tennessee

Ellen Goldring
Department of Leadership, Policy and Organizations
Vanderbilt University
Nashville, Tennessee

Paul T. Hill
Daniel J. Evans School of Public Affairs
University of Washington
Seattle, Washington

Caroline Hoxby
Department of Economics
Harvard University
Cambridge, Massachusetts

Helen F. Ladd
Department of Public Policy Studies and Economics
Duke University
Durham, North Carolina

Robin J. Lake
Center on Reinventing Public Education
University of Washington
Seattle, Washington

Sonali Murarka
National Bureau for Economic Research
Cambridge, Massachusetts

Anna Nicotera
Department of Leadership, Policy and Organizations
Vanderbilt University
Nashville, Tennessee

Paul E. Peterson
John F. Kennedy School of Government
Harvard University
Cambridge, Massachusetts

Michael Podgursky
Department of Economics
University of Missouri
Columbia, Missouri

Mark Schneider
National Center for Education Statistics, Institute of Education Sciences
U.S. Department of Education
Washington, DC

Francis X. Shen
Harvard Multidisciplinary Program in Inequality and Social Policy
Harvard University
Cambridge, Massachusetts

Sheree T. Speakman
WCLS Group, Ltd.
Highland Park, Illinois

Matthew G. Springer
Department of Leadership, Policy and Organizations
Vanderbilt University
Nashville, Tennessee

Bettie Teasley
Department of Leadership, Policy and Organizations
Vanderbilt University
Nashville, Tennessee

Peter Tice
National Center for Education Statistics, Institute of Education Sciences
U.S. Department of Education
Washington, DC

Herbert J. Walberg
Hoover Institution
Stanford University
Stanford, California

Caroline Watral
Department of Leadership, Policy and Organizations
Vanderbilt University
Nashville, Tennessee

Kenneth K. Wong
Department of Education
Brown University
Providence, Rhode Island

Tim Zeidner
Learning Sciences Institute
Vanderbilt University
Nashville, Tennessee

Ron Zimmer
RAND Education
Arlington, Virginia

Introduction

MARK BERENDS, MATTHEW G. SPRINGER, AND HERBERT J. WALBERG

A charter school is a publicly supported school governed by a private board under performance contract with a "charter authorizer" for a defined term. In the process of forming a charter school, the board submits a proposal to a school district, state, or other authorizer such as a mayor's office or university. If the proposal is approved, the school's board is issued a charter (or contract) to operate the school for a fixed period (typically, 5 years), unless the school fails academically, attracts an insufficient number of students, or violates the terms of the charter or the law.

Although charter schools are public institutions and thus responsive to the democratic processes offered by public institutions, they are free from many of the regulations that traditional public schools face. Thus, they can take advantage of their autonomy to be innovative in their organizational and educational approaches. For instance, charter boards may appoint their own staff or hire nonprofit or for-profit management organizations to operate the school for them.

Charter schools face their share of challenges, however. Despite their advantage of a fresh beginning, charter schools may have all the start-up difficulties of new organizations, as well as the imposition of heavy regulatory and other burdens, such as requirements to hire union employees. Their actual per-student funding, moreover, is apparently less on average than that of nearby traditional public schools.

THE GROWTH OF CHARTER SCHOOLS

Charter schools have grown from 1 school in the 1992–1993 school year (the City Academy in St. Paul, Minnesota) to 3,613 in 40 states and the District of Columbia, serving 1,040,536 students in the 2005–2006 school year (National Alliance of Public Charter Schools, 2006). Both the number of charter schools and the number of students in them are limited—not as much by parent and student market demand as by enrollment caps in the charter contracts and caps on the number of charter schools by school districts, states, and other authorizers.

For this reason, many charter schools have student waiting lists. These limits on the size and number of charter schools may be attributable to the reluctance of some public authorities to allow extensive competition with the traditional public schools for which they are responsible and which they may have attended.

PRIVATIZATION

Charter schools are part of a worldwide privatization trend in which formerly government-provided services are subject to competitive bidding by private organizations. Privatization has been growing because studies of "contracting out" services to private nonprofit organizations and for-profit firms suggest that, on average, these entities respond swiftly, accurately, and efficiently to citizens' desires (Savas, 2000). Though objectionable to some, the metaphor is the challenge that private restaurants would offer public restaurants owned and operated by government entities.

An analysis of dozens of privatization study results in the United States and other countries shows that, other things being equal, private organizations on average perform substantially better at lower costs and are more satisfying to their staffs and customers (Wolf, 1988). The studies cover airlines, banks, bus service, debt collection, electric utilities, forestry, hospitals, housing, insurance sales and processing, railroads, refuse collection, savings and loans, water utilities, and weather forecasting. In the United States, units of government are even beginning to privatize prisons, police and fire protection, and public pension systems. A quarter of a century ago, few might have believed that Americans would employ privately governed and managed roads and bridges. Yet, Chicago recently sold concession rights to operate the Chicago Skyway toll bridge, a 7.8-mile elevated highway, for $1.8 billion. The city also sold, for $563 million, rights to operate the city's parking garages beneath Grant and Millennium Parks, which are thought to be the most extensive single set of enclosed garages in the nation (Spielman, 2006).

Although many see the benefits of increased privatization—viewing it as the panacea for the nation's education problems (e.g., Chubb & Moe, 1990), others see privatization as the mechanism that undermines the public education system in the United States (Apple, 2001). Still others are agnostic, emphasizing the *conditions* necessary for privatization to work well and the need for additional evidence (Belfield & Levin, 2005; Henig, 1994).

CHARTER SCHOOL PURPOSES

Following privatization in other areas, charter schools are seen as a means of bringing effectiveness, efficiency, innovation, and diversity to public education. The public, particularly legislators and parents, is concerned with the high costs and poor performance of American schools. Although American high school students rank poorly compared to those in other economically advanced countries, the per-student costs of American schools rank near the top (Walberg, 1998). Can charter schools achieve equally or better at lower costs?

Advocates see charter schools as a means to promote entrepreneurship and innovations that yield better outcomes, lower costs, and greater public and parent satisfaction. They also believe that privately governed schools can better respond to the variety of parental and student preferences than do traditional public schools. Furthermore, some maintain that charter schools offer challenges and competition to traditional public schools that can induce them to improve.

Charter school skeptics who favor different strategies to improve traditional public schools tend to discount accomplishments of charter schools. They argue that they have merely "skimmed the cream" (the better students) from the traditional public schools. Voucher advocates criticize charter schools on the grounds that they threaten to take students from independent and parochial schools. They also have reservations about charter schools since they remain under the ultimate control of the state rather than leaving school choice to parents themselves.

In principle, all charter schools should be successful since failing ones are to be closed, but some critics have argued that authorizers have failed to carry out this central responsibility. A primary driver for empirical research represented in this book is to begin to provide factual answers to test such assertions and provide sound evidence to guide U.S. educational policy and practice.

INITIAL ACCOMPLISHMENTS OF CHARTER SCHOOLS

In addition to their rapid growth, charter schools have attained considerable diversity of education offerings; it is misleading to speak of them as homogeneous. Charter schools reflect the varying philosophies, goals, and programs of their boards and staffs, and they often serve diverse student populations. Some charter schools focus on at-risk students, others on gifted students, and still others on pregnant teenagers. Some concentrate on the teaching of dual languages and others on the arts and vocations. Some are founded on a particular curriculum, such as the academically focused Core Knowledge program. In fact, some researchers have argued that because of the variety of the approaches for organizing and operating charter schools, there may be no single charter school effect (Zimmer et al., 2003).

Some of the most interesting charter schools employ new technologies. In "cyber schools," for example, parents supervise partly self-paced Internet- and computer-based instruction, and teachers serve as daily coordinators, consultants, and assessors of individual student progress. Cyber schools employ resource centers for proctored testing, parent–teacher conferences, and curriculum and equipment stock rooms. Students may participate in teacher-led, specialized lessons at resource centers, but the majority of instruction takes place online in students' homes. Cyber charter schools may be particularly appropriate for severely handicapped students who must remain at home, for students who live in isolated areas far from traditional public schools, and as a supplement to the efforts of homeschoolers.

Charter schools have arguably had a constructive influence on the states' school accountability systems and the 2001 No Child Left Behind (NCLB) Act. The momentum for school reform had been growing since the 1983 publication of *A Nation at Risk,* which first informed citizens about the poor achievement of American schools. But the central idea of charter schools in 1990 was the performance contract and accountability for measured results, consistent with privatizing other public services.

In theory, most parents of public school students today should know where their children and their children's schools stand with respect to state standards, since the release of such information is required by both state legislation and NCLB. It seems likely that such accountability may have occurred, in part because of the rapid growth of and demand for charter schools, which set the pace for accountability.

Indeed, one of the distinctive features of charter schools—that they could be threatened by or even closed for poor performance—has been made generally applicable to all public schools. NCLB menaces poorly performing traditional public schools. In the most recent school year, the percentage of traditional public schools failing to make "adequate yearly progress" under the NCLB increased from 13 to 17% (Olson, 2006).

These schools must inform parents that their children are in failing schools. Repeatedly failing traditional public schools face escalating sanctions such as transferring funds from their budgets to private agencies to provide tutoring and other supplementary services. Continuing failure means that parents may transfer their children to successful schools. Ultimately, continuously failing schools must be "restructured." They may have to replace their staffs or be forced to close. Thus, traditional public schools increasingly face the pressures of charter schools—a change that charters have apparently induced.

ORGANIZATION OF THIS BOOK AND QUESTIONS RAISED

These issues remain at the nexus of the charter school debate, and more research is needed on all of them. In that spirit, the authors in this volume raise questions and provide some answers. We organized the chapters into three broad sections in the areas of assessing teaching and learning in charter schools; charter school finance, governance, and law; and charter school effects on achievement. Within each section, the chapters address some critical questions about charter schools.

Section 1: Assessing Teaching and Learning in Charter Schools

- What research designs can best answer questions about the relative performance of charter and traditional public schools?
- What answers do specific new studies provide to the preceding question?
- What features and practices of successful charter schools set them apart from other charter schools?
- How do the teaching staffs at charter and traditional public schools compare?

Section 2: Charter School Finance, Governance, and Law

- Do charter schools receive less funding per student than traditional public schools?
- What are the principal forms of charter school governance and how do they work?
- How do state laws differ and how do they affect the mission and operation of charter schools?

Section 3: Charter Schools' Effects on Achievement

- What do prior studies reveal about the effects of charter and traditional public schools on how students learn?
- What are the comparative effects of charter schools in California, North Carolina, and Idaho?
- What further, ongoing research will examine the mediating effects of organizational and instructional conditions in charter schools?
- What opportunities are there for the study of charter and other forms of school choice in the databases of the National Center for Education Statistics?

An independent scholar introduces each of these three sections, summarizing and synthesizing the section's findings. Authors, commentators, and editors do not claim final answers to these and other questions raised in the book. But it can be said that the chapters contain much of the best, most recent research on charter schools. The authors not only describe present findings important for policymakers and educators but also discuss the best methods of research to answer these and other questions in future research on charter schools.

REFERENCES

Apple, M. (2001). *Educating the "right" way: Markets, standards, God and inequality.* New York: Routledge and Farmer.

Belfield, C. R., & Levin, H. M. (2005). *Privatizing educational choice: Consequences for parents, schools, and public policy.* Boulder, CO: Paradigm Publishers.

Chubb, J., & Moe, T. (1990). *Politics, markets, and America's schools.* Washington, DC: Brookings Institution.

Henig, J. R. (1994). *Rethinking school choice: Limits of the market metaphor.* Princeton, NJ: Princeton University Press.

National Alliance of Public Charter Schools. (2006). *A state-by-state look at the number of charter schools and the number of students they serve.* Washington, DC: Author. See http://www.publiccharters.org/content/publication/detail/1170/.

National Commission on Excellence in Education. (1983). *A nation at risk.* Washington, DC: U.S. Department of Education.

Olson, L. (2006). As AYP bar rises, more schools fail. *Education Week,* September 20, 2006, 1, 20.

Savas, E. S. (2000). *Privatization and public–private partnerships.* New York: Chatham House Publishers.

Spielman, F. (2006). Daley sells off four city parking garages. *Chicago Sun Times,* October 13, 2006, p. 1. See also http://www.suntimes.com/news/metro/95870.garage101306.article.

Walberg, H. J. (1998b). Uncompetitive American schools: Causes and cures. In D. Ravitch (Ed.), *Brookings papers on education policy* (pp. 173–206). Washington, DC: Brookings Institution.

Wolf, C. C. (1988). *Markets or governments: Choosing between imperfect alternatives.* Cambridge, MA: MIT Press.

Zimmer, R., Buddin, R., Chau, D., Gill, B., Guarino, C., Hamilton, L., et al. (2003). *Charter school operations and performance: Evidence from California.* Santa Monica, CA: RAND.

Section 1

Assessing Teaching and Learning in Charter Schools

HERBERT J. WALBERG

The three chapters in this section provide excellent perspectives on past research on charter schools, offer guidelines and models for future research, and help set the stage for scientifically based charter school policy and practice. This commentary successively highlights key points from each chapter and points out their significance. The last section synthesizes the highlights and significance of the chapters as a set.

CAROLINE HOXBY AND SONALI MURARKA, "METHODS OF ASSESSING THE ACHIEVEMENT OF STUDENTS IN CHARTER SCHOOLS"

This first chapter sets forth ideas for understanding and improving research methodology not only on charter schools but also on a wide variety of causal topics within the social sciences. Philosophy and theology—ancestors of the social sciences—were and are concerned with the moral value of ends and the ethical justification of means, issues that today rest with individuals, organizations, and governments as decision makers. But the equally difficult issue is causality: Do the means indeed causally affect the ends? This question is particularly difficult to answer with respect to social (including education) policy because any valued end is usually a product of many causes changing over time, and the causes and ends are often unreliably measured. For these reasons, the causal effects in question for policy are often small and difficult to detect. The authors Hoxby and Murarka provide many insights for detecting such effects of charter schools. Two are highlighted in this commentary: experiments and value-added measures.

Experiments

The social sciences—anthropology, economics, political science, and sociology—are perhaps a half-century behind the applied natural and human sciences in drawing causal inferences necessary to base policy and practice decisions on scientific conclusions. The gold standard of causality is the random assignment of units to experimental and control or contrast conditions (or "treatments"); they are most greatly valued in agronomy, medicine, public health, and the most rigorous parts of psychology and education research. Experiments require that the units of analysis be randomly assigned to alternative conditions purely by chance—for example, a coin toss or, more often, randomly generated numbers. Thus, there is no reason to think that groups initially differ (though this possibility should be investigated rather than assumed).

In research on schools of choice, "randomized field trials" compare the academic achievement and other measurable outcomes of applicants who were lotteried into an oversubscribed charter school or voucher program to those who were lotteried out and attended a traditional public school. Since whether an applicant is admitted or not is determined by lottery, any statistically significant difference between the two groups of students is attributable to chance and, more probably, the effectiveness of the treatment, in this case the school type. Hoxby herself has carried out just such an experiment on students who were lotteried in and out of the Chicago International Charter School. Similarly, Paul Peterson (see his introduction to section 2 in this book) has contrasted students lotteried in and out of a voucher program.

Over-Time Measures

Hoxby and Murarka also emphasize the importance of measures taken on at least two occasions, which help detect effects in both experiments and in quasi-experimental research that contrast the gains of nonrandomly assigned students in charter and other schools. Measuring "value-added" gains or "over-time" growth in achievement during intervening periods increases the sensitivity of the study, reduces possible biases attributable to pre-existing differences among students, and makes the findings more creditable. Such prior information helps take into account the powerful influence of families and helps estimate the separate and distinct contribution of the school to a student's achievement.

Having information on many occasions, for example, 6 prior years of test scores, can add even more precision since it allows investigators to estimate the "trajectory" of a student's achievement and see if a change in circumstances makes for a detectable change in achievement. Behavioral psychologists make much use of this methodology, even in studying single subjects, since they can easily administer and withdraw a treatment such as rewarding "reinforcement" and plot the change in the subject's behavior (Subotnik & Walberg, 2006).

Internal Versus External Validity

In line with their purpose, Hoxby and Murarka appropriately focus on causality. In addition, the range of circumstances in which the findings apply is an important question. Even if we can establish that a set of charter schools causes higher achievement in a given locality—say, a city or state, the effect may or may not generalize to other circumstances. Beginning in the early 1960s, psychologists carrying out school research have distinguished these ideas of causality and generalizability and called them internal and external validity, respectively. In medical research, "multisite" experiments are carried out in hospitals in several states to determine both the efficacy and generalizability of a treatment in question.

To my knowledge, two national experiments in school research have been reported (Cook & Walberg, 1985; Walberg & Welch, 1972). These concern education effects in health and physics, fields with long experimental traditions. Multisite experiments might greatly increase the scientific foundations of education policy and practice. Short of this ideal, which would be admittedly difficult to attain, investigators might look for consistency of effects among a diversity of students in many locations.

ELLEN GOLDRING AND XIU CRAVENS, "TEACHERS' ACADEMIC FOCUS ON LEARNING IN CHARTER AND TRADITIONAL PUBLIC SCHOOLS"

Goldring and Cravens take up a related question—not whether charter schools achieve more, but rather whether the conditions in charter schools make for greater degrees of academic focus. They begin with a review of prior research on the school factors likely to raise academic focus that should prove useful for education leaders who would like to know what factors make for charter and traditional public school success.

Conceptual Model

The authors condense previous research findings in a useful graphic, conceptual model of the probable external and internal precursors of teachers' academic focus, which is hypothesized to lead to higher levels of achievement. Among the internal factors—that is, "in-school organizational enabling conditions"—are principal leadership, professional learning community, teacher decision-making authority, and teacher efficacy. The model is likely to be valuable in their own and others' research.

Findings and Discussion

Goldring and Cravens' analysis of national sample data leads the authors to conclude that charter school teachers did not differ from others in academic focus. They explain, and I agree, that all schools—charter and traditional public—are under increasing pressure to raise their academic focus and achievement, which may account for the lack of difference in the two types of schools. One of the original ideas about charter schools is that they would be issued a performance contract, typically for 5 years, which could be sustained and renewed provided their students achieved well. Now, as the authors point out, traditional public schools may have similar pressures to increase academic focus to perform well. In addition, many charter schools are new and may not have had time to develop the academic focus that was intended for them. It would be interesting to find out if older charter schools have greater academic focus than newer ones.

The authors' positive findings are valuable and should be taken seriously by education leaders since they corroborate previous research. In-school conditions associated with higher achievement—namely, principal leadership and professional learning community—lead to greater academic focus.

Next Research Step

Goldring and Cravens plan to analyze the relation of academic press to academic achievement. This step should be valuable since schools must foster not only the conditions for achievement but also achievement itself. This is the criterion by which both charter and traditional public schools will be judged and, if found persistently lacking, "reconstituted" or closed under the provisions of the federal No Child Left Behind Act.

MICHAEL PODGURSKY, "TEAMS VERSUS BUREAUCRACIES: PERSONNEL POLICY, WAGE SETTING, AND TEACHER QUALITY IN TRADITIONAL PUBLIC, CHARTER, AND PRIVATE SCHOOLS"

As a labor economist, Podgursky points out that more regulatory freedom, decentralized wage setting, and a competitive environment are expected to promote effectiveness and efficiency in charter and private schools. Accordingly, they can respond to market conditions and employ merit-, shortage-, and performance-based pay to respond to competitive market forces.

Unlike traditional public schools, schools of choice can pay physics teachers more because they are scarcer than those in other fields, and teachers whose students perform better can be rewarded with merit bonuses or raises. In addition, these schools can hire teachers with the most promising credentials—that is, mastery of their subject matter fields, which predicts their students' success rather than does having education degrees or state certification. These ideas corroborate labor market studies and the facts about charter and private schools. They also support the basis of two studies that follow from these ideas: a merit pay experiment and new examinations for licensing beginning teachers and identifying master teachers.

A Multisite Merit Pay Experiment

Three investigators associated with the National Center on School Choice, which is sponsoring this book—James Guthrie, Dale Ballou, and Matthew Springer—are carrying out a multisite, randomized field trial of merit pay in several school districts. This study follows the experimental design and over-time guidelines suggested by Hoxby and Murarka and may turn out to be the most important labor market analysis ever conducted in schools.

Though merit pay is the norm in most U.S. nonunionized industries, it is rare in traditional public schools. Many traditional public school educators and some psychologists have argued that merit pay would be destructive of school morale, but much human behavior can be parsimoniously explained by the common characteristics of humans both to compete and to work for recognition and compensation. A study that reveals the facts should be valuable for formulating future education policy.

A Scientifically Based Beginning and Master Teacher Examination

Educational, industrial, and organizational psychologists hold statistical validity as a key criterion for employment, college admission, and other tests. Tests should statistically predict or correlate with job performance. Oddly, the validity of teacher licensing examinations has never been firmly established. Rather, the usual traditional public school teacher licensing depends on completing education courses or a degree and passing a test without established statistical validity. But studies show that subject matter mastery—high scores on a subject matter examination or a degree in the subject being taught—predict teaching success as defined by teachers' student gains. In addition, there is experimental and value-added evidence that some teaching techniques are measurably more effective than others.

For the American Board for the Certification of Teacher Excellence (ABCTE), these two areas—subject matter and pedagogical knowledge—form the basis of its examinations. A passing score does not guarantee good teaching but rather the prerequisites for it, which many teachers lack. Podgursky sits on the scientific advisory group, which I chair, and has helped plan and evaluate studies of the examinations' statistical validity. Two studies have been made thus far to see whether the students of teachers who pass the examination do better than others. All were in-service teachers paid to take the examinations and, to induce motivation, paid more for higher scores. In both cases, the passing groups' students gained more than others.

Our group also chose the research firm Mathematica, among other applicants, to randomly assign students in several districts to teachers who pass the examination and to those who do not, and contrast their achievement results. Continuing good results should enable educational leaders in public and private to select more confidently teachers most likely to succeed in helping students learn.

CONCLUSION

These three chapters as a set seem fundamental in arriving at recommendations for further research on charter schools and, even now, for better understanding their causal effects. Each of the chapters contributes toward that end, and the section as a whole helps set the stage for the remaining sections of this book.

REFERENCES

Cook, T. D., & Walberg, H. J. (1985). Methodological and substantive significance. *Journal of School Health, 55,* 340–343.

Subotnik, R., & Walberg, H. J. (Eds.) (2006). *The scientific basis of educational productivity.* Greenwich, CT: Information Age Publishers.

Walberg, H. J., & Welch, W. W. (1972). A national experiment in curriculum evaluation. *American Educational Research Journal, 9,* 373–384.

1

Methods of Assessing Achievement of Students in Charter Schools[1]

CAROLINE HOXBY AND SONALI MURARKA

A CHALLENGE FOR ASSESSMENT

Policymakers wish to have evidence on the effects of charter schools on their students' achievement. Such evidence has two potential uses. First, a policymaker who is considering expanding or contracting the availability of charter schools in his state may wish to know whether parents' desire to send their children to charter schools is based on their observations of achievement or based on other criteria. That is, a policymaker may say to himself, "Unless it can be shown that charter schools have X effect on achievement, I do not want to allow students to attend them even if the students and their parents desire it." (The policymaker has no question in front of him unless he is willing to impose his judgment on parents and

[1] The authors wish to thank the Chicago Consortium on School Research, the Chicago Public Schools, the Chicago International Charter School, the New York City Center for Charter School Excellence, and the New York Department of Education for data, information, cooperation, and help. None of these organizations or their staff members is, however, responsible for the content of this chapter. For comments that made the project stronger, the authors also wish to thank anonymous reviewers for the Institute for Education Sciences, Mark Schneider and Phoebe Cottingham of the Institute for Education Sciences (NCES and NCER, respectively), Jonah Rockoff, and seminar participants at Mathematica, RAND, UCLA, Harvard University, and the National Bureau of Economic Research.

unless there are more parents who want to send their children to charter schools than there is space available. Changing the legal availability of charter schools is a meaningless act unless there are parents who want to enroll their children in the places that become available or unavailable.) A policymaker's second potential use for evidence on charter schools' effects on achievement is very different: He may wish to discover what works in public education and he may view charter schools as laboratories in which interesting educational experiments often occur.

If the policymaker's need for evidence is of the first type, he should be supplied with evidence on how the average charter school in his state affects the achievement of students who wish to attend them. Even better, if he is considering expansion, he should be supplied with evidence on the achievement effects generated by the charter schools that are most in demand on the students who want to attend them. If he is considering contraction, he needs evidence on the achievement effects generated by the charter schools his policy is most likely to shut down.

If the policymaker's need for evidence is of the second type, he should be supplied with evidence on which charter school characteristics, if any, predict that the school has significant positive or negative effects on student achievement. This is a much more demanding evidentiary requirement because characteristics must vary substantially among charter schools, must be measurable with objective metrics, and must vary fairly independently. Intuitively, this last requirement means that clumps of characteristics are problematic. If a long school day is always found in conjunction with a long school year, guided instruction, and certain curricula, researchers will be unable to identify the independent effect of a long school day.

Because researchers find it challenging simply to produce credible estimates of the average effect of charter schools on achievement, they have thus far mainly attempted to generate the first type of evidence and left the second type for future studies. In this chapter, we will largely follow this approach and will focus our discussion on methods for estimating the average achievement effect. We will, however, briefly turn to the second type of evidence in the final section. Note that in no case are we interested in how charter schools might affect the achievement of students who do not want to attend them. This is because the charter school idea is inherently voluntary; there is no version of charter schools that students are forced to attend.

Readers should understand that this chapter is primarily about methods, not about results. There is a need for serious discussion of methods at this time, given the large number of studies, recently completed or in process, that purport to estimate the achievement effect of charter schools. Some of these studies are wholly out of touch with modern evaluation methods; others are simple, but somewhat credible; others are apparently sophisticated, but actually misguided; and a very few are rigorous and credible. We target this chapter toward the community of serious researchers sincerely interested in credibly evaluating charter schools.

Most of the evaluation problems and solutions that we discuss are *known*, even if they have not been well described in the context of charter schools. We are drawing upon more than 20 years of methodological work that developed around the question of whether training programs positively affected youths' outcomes—the "program evaluation problem." It is a matter of concern that the community of researchers interested in charter schools is apparently ignorant of much of this work. A thorough knowledge of it is essential for expert analysis of the evaluation of the effects of charter schools and many other educational interventions. For instance, the program evaluation literature describes many of the failings inherent in value-added analysis for applications akin to charter school evaluation. If researchers who have attempted to use value-added analysis had been expert in program evaluation, they might have avoided some pitfalls. Similarly, the program evaluation literature provides considerable guidance on the relative merits of various comparison-with-controls methods. This chapter refers to the program evaluation literature throughout, but it cannot substitute for the sort of deep knowledge of that literature that any aspiring evaluator of charter schools should acquire.[1]

SELF-SELECTION INTO CHARTER SCHOOLS

To the layman, it is perhaps surprising that researchers find it so difficult to answer the narrow question, "What is the effect of charter schools [in area Y, of type Z] on the achievement of students who wish to attend them?" There are two serious problems, however: selection and general equilibrium. The general equilibrium problem occurs when charter school enrollment is so pervasive that it substantially affects the peers, locations, or finances of regular public schools or private schools. That is, charter schools might affect achievement not only by their direct effect on learning but also by indirectly altering students' main alternative schooling options. In the long run, researchers will find that the general equilibrium problem is extremely hard to address. For now, charter schools account for so little enrollment that researchers can ignore the general equilibrium problem unless they are gathering evidence on one of the very few areas, such as certain counties in Arizona, where charter schools are prevalent.

---

[1] An aspiring evaluator who is unfamiliar with the program evaluation literature should preferably obtain graduate training in the subject because having an instructor who can integrate the many findings is important. However, a determined autodidact might begin with the following reading list: Imbens and Wooldridge (forthcoming); Heckman, Lalonde, and Smith (1999); Angrist and Krueger (1999); Dehejia and Wahba (1999); LaLonde (1986); Ashenfelter and Card (1985); and Heckman and Hotz (1989).

Unfortunately, the opposite is true of the selection problem: It plagues researchers now, and there is every reason to believe that it is as serious today as it will ever be.

In a nutshell, the selection problem occurs because families self-select into charter schools for numerous reasons and many of the reasons have their own effects on achievement. Self-selection is highly prevalent at present because charter schools are an unusual, new option. Therefore, when parents submit a charter school application, they are diverging more from their inertial or default behavior than they will be years from now, when charter schools will be less novel and probably more ubiquitous (judging from their growth thus far).

Why might students self-select into charter schools and how might the selection destroy the credibility of some evidence? A parent who switches her child to a charter school may do so because she sees that child starting to struggle academically in his regularly assigned public school. Alternatively, she might feel that the child is "getting in with the wrong crowd" or otherwise beginning to display problematic behaviors. A parent might make the switch because she wishes to give her child a clean start after a troubling event such as bullying or being taught by a prejudiced teacher who took an unjustifiably dim view of the child's ability. Another reason for choosing a charter school may be a child's failure to make the cut for a selective magnet or exam school in the regular public system. As reasons for switching, all of these examples, as well as many others like them, would lead us to expect negative self-selection into charter schools.

Self-selection into charter schools may also take positive forms. For instance, families who apply to charter schools may be those who are better able to process information about the educational system. Such information processing could be helpful in any number of ways that would improve a child's trajectory: more productive parent–teacher conferences, more accurate parent supervision of homework, and so on. Positive selection may also be triggered by an event. For example, a child may have a second grade teacher (in the traditional public school) who rates him highly or tells his family that he is underchallenged. His family may therefore seek out a charter school that promises more homework, more frequent testing, or more opportunities for advanced learning. The child's second grade experience and the family's evolving expectations for him would presumably improve his achievement regardless of his school.

Finally, there are forms of self-selection that are difficult to classify as positive or negative. Consider parents who disagree with the special education diagnosis their child has recently been given in his regular public school. They might enroll him in a charter school in an attempt to get a fresh diagnosis. Some commentators might see this as negative self-selection: poorly informed parents trying to ignore expert opinion. Other commentators might see this as positive self-selection because only parents who are very invested in their child's education are likely to go to the trouble of contradicting the diagnosis of an expert. In any case, it is important to realize that there are plausible forms of self-selection that could lead either to upward or downward biases in estimates of charter schools' effects. As a result, researchers must take care to eliminate all forms of self-selection that they possibly can. This is not a case where, if a researcher eliminates some forms of selection bias and finds that the estimates go in a certain direction, he can reasonably project that the estimates would continue to go in that direction if he were to eliminate all forms of selection bias.

For evaluating charter schools, a researcher must distinguish between two forms of self-selection. "Innovation-based self-selection" occurs when a student self-selects into (or out of) a charter school based on an event or information that arises once the student is in school. "Fixed self-selection" occurs when a student self-selects into (or out of) a charter school based on a factor that is effectively fixed for his entire school career. The factor need not be inherently fixed (like genes), but it should be predetermined at kindergarten entry and should stay the same through high school graduation. Fixed self-selection can cause a student to choose regular public schools or charter schools in the first place. It can also cause a student to plan a trajectory such as "charter school through grade 8, after which there is no local charter school, and regular public school for grades 9–12."

However, fixed self-selection will not cause a student to switch between charter and regular public schools midstream because an initial decision about schools based on fixed information does not change unless some new event or information arrives. Innovation-based self-selection accounts for switches. To illustrate, consider race, which is generally regarded as a fixed characteristic. A student's race may cause fixed self-selection, but not a switch. On the other hand, a student who is a racial minority may have a bad experience with a prejudiced third grade teacher who takes an unjustifiably dim view of his ability. This experience would be an innovation that could cause a switch into or out of charter schools.

Both forms of self-selection pose challenges to the researcher. With fixed self-selection, a researcher will observe the student in only one environment (or only one preordained sequence of environments). In such circumstances, finding an appropriate control group may be difficult because control students must match charter school students on all fixed characteristics that affect achievement, yet control students must not have selected into charter schools. With innovation-based self-selection, the researcher does observe students in both the regular public and charter school environments, but this is not as helpful as a naïve researcher might think because a student's pre-event trajectory is not a good guide to his trajectory after the event.

This problem is known as "Ashenfelter's dip" in the program evaluation literature. The "dip" refers to the fact that people do not apply to training programs for no reason. They apply because some event or new information has arrived—for example, the industry in which they are employed is facing new international competition, a machine has been invented that makes their skill useless, or they have discovered that they have abilities previously unknown to them. In the charter school context, the equivalent of Ashenfelter's dip might be a negative event, such as a prejudiced third grade teacher, or a positive event, such as a family learning that their child is of higher ability than previously suspected. The essential consequence of the dip is that a student's previous trajectory is not a good guide to his future trajectory *even if he does not shift his program.* Any method that relies on a student's pre-charter-school achievement to predict his achievement if he had not gone to charter school will be useless in the presence of innovation-based self-selection. Put another way, a control student must not only match the charter school student on all fixed characteristics that affect achievement but must also match him on any innovations that affect self-selection and achievement.

Thus far, we have provided examples of self-selection based on phenomena that are hard for researchers to observe: a bullying episode, a teacher's prejudices, a family's ability to process information, a child's getting in with the wrong crowd. This is because, to the extent that selection is based on readily observable variables, researchers can statistically account for the selection so that it poses a limited challenge to generating evidence. This point can best be illustrated with an example. For numerous reasons (cost, safety, neighborhood friends), most parents prefer not to send their young children to schools located at a great distance from their homes. It is no surprise, therefore, that the distances from a child's home to the nearest charter schools affect selection; parents tend not to apply to charter schools if the nearest ones are far away. If researchers could not observe home and school locations, this selection phenomenon would be problematic. A researcher might have a hard time explaining why children from the suburbs were not reasonable controls for central city students enrolled in a charter school.

With locations being fairly observable, the problem is mitigated. The researcher may model how distance from a charter school affects the probability of applying. To the extent that he models the relationship correctly or simply matches students with control students who live at the same distance, he surmounts the challenge created by self-selection on the basis of distance. In short, although self-selection on the basis of observable variables occurs and requires a researcher's attention, the most troubling forms of self-selection are those that are not readily observable to the researcher.

Given that much self-selection is not readily observable, can be either negative or positive, and has both fixed and innovation-based forms, what more can we say about it? There are three important things.

First, the more novel a charter school is, the more parents are going out of their way when they choose it. Parents who send their child to a novel school are necessarily accepting a degree of uncertainty that does not exist in their regular public school. Put another way, when a charter school starts up and has no track record, a family needs to feel more strongly about the match between its child and the school before the family is pushed over the threshold and applies. The match could be strong for a negative reason (the child needs to escape a very bad crowd) or a positive reason (the family is extremely interested in a heavier homework load). Novelty intensifies all forms of self-selection. When we say that the selection problem is intensified, we mean formally that there is a greater difference in characteristics, observed and unobserved, between those who apply to the charter school and those who do not.

Second, the later self-selection occurs in a student's career, the more information the family uses when it makes its decision. For example, a family with a child who is about to enter kindergarten knows a lot less about their child and what his experience will be in his regular public school than does a family with a child who has already attended kindergarten through fourth grade. A family cannot learn that their child is struggling academically or getting in with the wrong crowd until he does it; a family cannot have an experience with a prejudiced teacher until their child enters her classroom and cannot decide that the homework assigned falls short of their expectations until they see what homework is assigned.

This point is obvious, but its important implication is often overlooked: The self-selection problem intensifies over a student's career simply because the family has more private information (information observable to them but not to the researcher) on which to base their decision to apply to a charter school. That is, the researcher is always at an informational disadvantage relative to the family. The disadvantage is smallest at kindergarten entry and grows dramatically over time as the family accumulates knowledge about their child's school experience but the researcher's knowledge remains quite fixed. (He knows a few demographic variables, a few socioeconomic variables, and perhaps some test scores.) In short, the forms of self-selection that are most worrisome intensify over time because of the growth in the information gap between researchers (who do not observe the basis for selection) and parents (who do).

Third, self-selection tends to intensify over a student's career because of the *relative* novelty of the charter school or—put another way—the relative inertial pull of the regular public school. Consider a parent with a child entering kindergarten. The charter school may be more novel than the regular public school, but the child will find either school's kindergarten quite novel. He will have to meet new peers, learn his way around a new building, adjust to a new culture, and otherwise become acclimatized. The difference in uncertainty is there, but it is less extreme than it is for, say, a prospective fourth grader. He will likely face little or no adjustment if he keeps attending his regular public school; he will face considerable novelty and acclimatization if he switches to a charter school.

No reader will be surprised to hear about the relative inertial pull of the regular public school increasing over time (and being particularly great when the child would stay by default in the same building with the same set of peers). We are all aware of parents who would like to move for their own reasons, but are wary of school switches; who "save" a school switch for a year in which the child must change buildings anyway; or who delay a career change until it can occur without a school switch. Yet, readers may be surprised by the serious implications of increasing relative inertia: The self-selection problem becomes increasingly intense over the course of a student's career, and it is particularly intense between any two grades where a school switch does not occur in the regular public system.

METHODS FOR ASSESSING CHARTER SCHOOLS' EFFECTS ON ACHIEVEMENT

In this section, we consider the three main forms of analysis used to evaluate the achievement of students in charter schools: comparison with controls based on observable variables, value-added analysis, and lottery-based comparisons. For each method, we ask: Which forms of selection bias does this type of analysis eliminate?

Comparison With Controls Based on Observable Variables

Comparison with controls based on observable variables comprises a large set of methods that can be very good at eliminating forms of selection based on observable variables. The methods under this heading include everything from fully nonparametric matching to linear multiple regression.

It is now fairly widely agreed that, within the comparison-with-controls set of methods, the most credible evidence is obtained using fairly nonparametric methods if they are feasible. These methods are most feasible if the observable variables are categorical[1] and, more importantly, if a great number of student observations are available. We will start with nonparametric methods because they also have a purely expositional advantage: They clearly illustrate the key strengths and weaknesses of comparison with controls.

In a fully nonparametric comparison, we take each student enrolled in charter school and match him with a student who is identical to him based on all of the predetermined, observable variables available to us. In a realistic application, students might be put into "cells" based on their gender, race and ethnicity, free- and reduced-lunch status, age, grade, census block of home residence, limited English proficiency at school entry, permanent disability if any, and so on. Thus, a cell might be kindergarteners who are black, non-Hispanic, male, eligible for free lunch, native English speakers, born in a certain period, not disabled, and living in census block X. Within

---

[1] Gender, for instance, is a categorical variable, while family income is often a continuous variable.

each cell that contains a charter school enrollee ("treatment student"), we hope to see one or more control students who do not attend charter school. We compute the treatment minus control difference in achievement within each cell and average across the cell differences to obtain evidence on the effect of charter schools.[1] That is, the estimated effect of charter schools is some average of within-cell differences in achievement between treatment and control students.

In the preceding example, the students were kindergarteners, so it was plausible that selection was based on fixed factors. Thus, the treatment and control students were matched on fixed characteristics. Suppose, however, that the students were midway through elementary school. Then it would be implausible that selection was based on fixed factors; it would be essential to match treatment and control students not only on fixed characteristics but also on the events or new information that trigger charter school applications. In practice, such matching can be extremely challenging—even if the needed information is available (and it is usually not).

All other comparison-with-controls methods are essentially variants of the simple procedure described before. Without going into technicalities, the other methods add parametric restrictions to the procedure in the hope of gaining efficiency without introducing bias. If there are many observable variables or if some observable variables are quite continuous (family income might be measured in dollars, for instance), some cells that contain treatment students will probably not contain control students. The researcher can overcome this problem and potentially gain efficiency by modeling the relationship between the observable variables and selection into the charter school. Such modeling may lead to nearest-neighbor and propensity score-based matching methods (where each treatment student is essentially matched with the control students who are the closest match to him based on their modeled propensity to select into charter school), a variety of regression methods (where researchers control linearly for the propensity to select into charter schools or control for a variable that is a transformation of the propensity), and methods such as local linear regression that combine matching and regression.

The advantage of comparison-with-controls methods is that they can eliminate large amounts of selection bias based on observable variables, such as selection based on a child's proximity to the nearest charter school. In addition, comparison-with-controls methods can often be applied to less than ideal data such as achievement data available only by group—

---

[1] See Imbens and Wooldridge (forthcoming) for comments on the optimality of various weighting schemes used in computing the average. Their article also provides a helpful review of several other techniques discussed here, including matching on the propensity score and local linear regression.

for instance, the ethnicity by grade by school by year groups for which reports are mandated under the No Child Left Behind Act.[1]

Unfortunately, there are substantial disadvantages of comparison-with-controls methods. First, they do not eliminate selection problems based on unobserved variables and can actually exacerbate biases associated with unobservable variables. To see this, consider two children who appear to be a perfect match for one another: They live next door and they have the same grade, race/ethnicity, gender, free and reduced-lunch eligibility, English proficiency, and so on. One applies to charter school; the other does not. We ought to ask ourselves why two neighboring families made different decisions. It seems unlikely that the families would not communicate or would together flip a coin about which child should apply to the charter school.

Therefore, we must suppose that the two families had some reason for making different choices when they appear to have identical circumstances and are offered identical opportunities. Perhaps one child has been bullied and the neighboring child *is* the bully! More formally, by focusing on families who appear identical on observable variables but who make different schooling choices, we automatically focus on a sample of families who are disproportionately *un*alike on the unobservable variables.[2] As a result, the potential for bias from unobservable variables can grow as the researcher tightens the matching on observable variables. Indeed, in the case of the neighbors described previously, a researcher might be well advised to loosen up the match on location so that his treatment and control families are less likely to know one another. He might decide to match only on census block or school attendance zone, not on street address.

This leads us to the second disadvantage of comparison-with-controls methods: If they are to generate good evidence, they must be practiced by researchers who exercise considerable good judgment. A researcher must have a deep understanding of the strengths and weaknesses of various

---

[1] In order to use grouped data, a researcher must find the analog to the procedure he would obtain if he performed comparison with controls and subsequently aggregated. This is best illustrated with an example. A charter school's grouped data might be put into cells with data for the same group from each of the regular public schools from which the charter school draws students. After achievement differences were computed based on the grouped data, a weighted average would be computed across the cells with weights based on the share of the charter school's students who were from that particular cell.

[2] More precisely, they are disproportionately unalike on unobservable variables among families with their observable characteristics. The point we are making has been made previously in the context of identical twins being used to estimate the rate of return to education. If one identical twin decides to go to college and the other does not, there must be *something* unobservable that is different about the two of them. An important decision like enrolling in college is not made by the flip of a coin, and it is extremely unlikely that the twins did not communicate and thus had randomly different information on the costs and benefits of college. See Neumark (1994) and Bound and Solon (1999).

statistical methods, and he must also have a strong intuitive sense for likely behaviors and sources of bias. In the hands of a researcher with the best training and judgment, the comparison-with-controls methods tend to converge because they are deeply related. In other words, a researcher should be able to start at either end of the parametric spectrum (fully non-parametric matching or multiple linear regression) and, through specification testing and logic, arrive at similar estimation procedures. However, comparison-with-controls methods are not "dummy proof" and not even proof against modest deficiencies in training, analytic ability, data sense, or attentiveness. All too often, comparison-with-controls methods are exercised by researchers who have only the foggiest idea of the strengths and weaknesses of the method they are using and who make empirical choices out of habit or in imitation of someone else.

Fortunately, there is sometimes a practical way of selecting the appropriate comparison-with-controls procedure: Researchers can select the one that is best at generating "gold standard" evidence when such evidence is available.[1] We shall return to this point because it is very important: The disadvantages of methods based on comparison with controls may be mitigated if gold standard evidence is available for some of the data.

Comparison of Gains With Controls Based on Observable Variables

It is worthwhile saying something about the method of comparing achievement *gains* with controls based on observable variables (hereafter, "comparison of gains with controls"). This method is often confused with value-added analysis (discussed later), in part because conventions of nomenclature are not strict. However, comparison of gains with controls is logically separate from value-added techniques: The two methods start from fundamentally different assumptions and should not be lumped together.

Comparison-of-gains-with-controls methods are similar to comparison-with-controls methods except that the outcome variable is a student's *gain* in achievement in a grade, rather than his level of achievement in a grade. In its most extreme form, the comparison-of-gains method is based on the assumptions that (1) all student characteristics are fixed, (2) the fixed characteristics affect only a student's initial level of achievement at school entry, and (3) all students would make the same progress each year if given the same school treatment. Under this assumption, we should be able to compare achievement gains across all kinds of schools without worrying about whether the children have backgrounds that are at all comparable. The assumptions needed for the extreme version of the method are violated by the data, however. Obviously, not all student characteristics are

---

[1] This is the essence of the line of applied econometric research which began with the influential paper by Dehejia and Wahba (1999).

fixed. Also, background variables *are* correlated with rates of gain, not only with initial achievement. This fact will be known to many readers because some well-known achievement gaps, such as the black–white achievement gap, grow with age.[1] An achievement gap could not change systemically with age if background only affected initial achievement.

Because the extreme assumptions do not hold, researchers generally use observable variables to find control students who attend regular public schools but who should otherwise make the same gains as students who attend charter schools. Thus, we return to the issues discussed under comparison with controls. Should we put students into cells and use fully nonparametric methods? Should we impose some parametric structure on the decision to select into charter schools and match on the propensity to apply? Should we use linear regression and control for the propensity to apply? The sole difference between this and the previous discussion is that the outcome variable is the achievement gain.

Does using the gain reduce bias due to selection? Does it reduce the amount of judgment required of the researcher? Arguably yes. However, there is no *logical* reason why the problems of comparison with controls are reduced when we use comparison of gains with controls. For instance, there is no logical reason why a child's getting in with the wrong crowd should not affect his future rate of gain. There is no logical reason why a child from a more motivated family should not gain achievement faster, not merely start with a higher initial level of achievement.

Hereafter, we will lump comparison of gains with controls with the methods of comparison with controls. These methods have the same essential advantages and disadvantages.

Value-Added Analysis

Value-added analysis starts with a simple logic: if a student attends first a regular public school and then a charter school (or vice versa), then his own prior self can be a good control for his later self. That is, if we compare a child's achievement before and after he attends a charter school, we can potentially estimate the charter school's effect. Value-added methods obviate the necessity of our finding an appropriate control student for each treatment student because each student is his own control. This logic (which is entirely separate from comparison of gains, a method that does not require students to be switchers) has intuitive appeal, and value-added analysis can be useful for evaluating certain educational interventions. We shall show, however, that the appeal of value-added analysis is entirely superficial when it comes to estimating charter school effects. Value-added analysis generates serious and intractable biases when used in the charter school setting.

---

[1] See Phillips and Jencks (1998).

Before delving into the nitty-gritty of value-added analysis, consider the essential logic. The fundamental assumption of value added methods is that we can use prior information on a student to *forecast* his future achievement. Thus, we can compare a charter school student's actual achievement to the achievement we would have forecast for him had he remained in the regular public schools. We make this forecast by examining his achievement while in the regular public schools and projecting it into the future, using some assumption about the relationship between past and future achievement (in the absence of school switches).

This leads us to the only major decision involved in value-added analysis: Do we have sufficient information for the forecast if we use just the student's prior *level* of achievement, just his prior *rate of gain* in achievement, both (the prior level and rate of gain), or both interacted with some student characteristics such as race/ethnicity and free-lunch eligibility?[1] For instance, if we need only his prior rate of gain to forecast his future rate of gain, then we end up with a value-added analysis of the form:

$$(A_{it} - A_{i,t-1}) = \alpha_0 + \alpha_1(A_{i,t-2} - A_{i,t-3}) + \alpha_2 I_{it}^{charter} + \varepsilon_{it} \qquad (1.1)$$

where A_{it} is the achievement of student i in year t, $A_{i,t-1}$ is his achievement in the previous year, and so on, and $I_{it}^{charter}$ is an indicator variable for his being enrolled in a charter school in year t. We must have data on switchers to estimate this equation; otherwise, the charter school effect (α_2) is not identified. Researchers familiar with value-added analysis will observe that the preceding equation nests a variety of more restricted equations also based on pre- and post-charter-school rates of gain.[2]

If we need information on a student's prior rate of gain and his initial level to forecast his future rate of gain, we end up with an analysis of the form:

$$(A_{it} - A_{i,t-1}) = \beta_0 + \beta_1(A_{i,t-2} - A_{i,t-3}) + \beta_2 A_{i,t0} + \beta_3 I_{it}^{charter} + \upsilon_{it}^3 \qquad (1.2)$$

---

[1] This question should be interpreted in a strict statistical sense: Which combination of variables is a sufficient statistic for the child's future achievement?

[2] The restricted-coefficient versions of this estimating equation are $[(A_{it} - A_{i,t-1}) - (A_{i,t-2} - A_{i,t-3})] = \beta_0 + \beta_1(I_{it}^{charter} - I_{i,t-2}^{charter}) + \varepsilon_{it}$ and $[(A_{it} - A_{i,t-1}) - (A_{i,t-1} - A_{i,t-2})] = \gamma_0 + \gamma_1(I_{it}^{charter} - I_{i,t-2}^{charter}) + \upsilon_{it}$. These restricted specifications are nearly always rejected by basic specification tests that reject the hypothesis that the coefficient on the prior rate of gain should be one. The second of these specifications is even more likely to be rejected than the first because it suffers badly from mean reversion: The observation for the year $t–1$ is used twice, generating automatic negative serial correlation between the two gains in the presence of mean reverting test scores.

[3] When we say *both* the level and rate of gain, we mean a specification in which these variables are allowed to have effects that are independent and in which the coefficient on neither variable is restricted to being one.

where t_0 must be prior to $t-3$. Which value-added equation to use is itself an interesting question, but—given our limited space—we prefer from now on to focus on Equation (1.1), the form favored by most analysts of charter schools.[1] We turn our attention to more important problems.

Does value-added analysis help with self-selection into charter schools? It does not. If we believe that that self-selection is based on fixed characteristics, then value-added analysis should not be performed because it should logically not be available. The fixed characteristics (being fixed) would necessarily have influenced a student's first choice of school and there will be no pre-charter-school achievement to use. If we see a student switching from regular public to charter school (or vice versa) after having established a record of achievement, then self-selection is almost certainly innovation based (put another way, fixed selection is implausible) and value-added analysis is inappropriate because the new event or information makes the student's old achievement a poor predictor of his future achievement. That is, in an Ashenfelter's dip situation, value-added analysis is methodologically unsound. In short, the case in which value-added analysis is useful for charter school evaluation does not logically exist. We are either in the fixed self-selection case, where it is unavailable, or in the innovation-based self-selection case, where it is inappropriate.

Let us put this in more intuitive terms. Suppose that a student has parents who have a fixed taste for the curriculum provided by the local charter school—they might be "true believers" in Core Knowledge, for instance. If this taste is sufficient to make them enroll their child in the charter school as a kindergartener and keep him there, then value-added analysis is unavailable. If the taste is insufficient to make them enroll him in charter school, then the only way in which the researcher will later see him enter charter school is through an innovation—the student performs unexpectedly badly, for instance. Any such innovation would make value-added analysis inappropriate because it would make the student's postinnovation achievement trajectory differ from his pre-innovation achievement trajectory even if he stayed in the regular public school. There is simply no way—using just information on the student himself—to predict how his trajectory would change after an innovation important enough to make him switch schools. (It might occur to the reader that the researcher could use information on other students; in that case, we are back to comparison-with-controls methods.) Unfortunately, value-added analysis does not plausibly cure any form of self-selection associated with unobserved variables.

If value-added analysis dealt with selection bias as well as, but no better than, comparison with controls, we might find it appealing for its simplicity. That is, we might be grateful for the fact that the method effec-

---

[1] Equation (1.1) is favored largely because it requires less data to estimate than Equation (1.2) does. In other respects, Equation (1.1) is more restrictive and thus less appealing than Equation (1.2). For examples of the use of Equation (1.1), see Bifulco and Ladd (2004), Hanushek, Kain, and Rivkin (2002), and Sass (2004).

tively chooses the control students for us, thus eliminating an otherwise complex decision. Unfortunately, value-added analysis has problems that comparison with controls does not have, and—unlike the problems with comparison with controls—the problems with value-added analysis are intractable when it is used to evaluate charter schools.

Value-added analysis does not solve self-selection and it exacerbates estimation problems. To see this, consider Equation (1.1). In order to estimate it, we must have data on students who switch from regular public schools to charter schools after having been tested in the regular public schools at least twice.[1] The typical district does not test before third grade. Thus, we can only use data only on students who switch after the fourth grade or later. This is highly problematic for several reasons.

First, as noted earlier, the self-selection problem is more intense among late grade switchers than among students who enter their chosen school at kindergarten or first grade. This is because the inertia effect grows and because the parents' private information grows dramatically relative to the information the researcher observes. Intuitively, if there are two children who make identical gains between the third and fourth grades but one child is pulled out of the school where he knows his peers, the building, the culture, and the curriculum, then the two children are *necessarily* very different on unobservable variables. Not only is a researcher not curing selection bias, but he is also discarding children for whom selection bias is not severe and is focusing exclusively on children for whom selection bias is severe. Since the bias is based on unobservable variables, he can do nothing about it even though he knows he has exacerbated it.

One might think that this problem can be mitigated greatly by earlier testing. Perhaps if all kindergarteners and first graders were tested, value-added analysis could work with children who switch as early as second grade. Unfortunately, this is not the case because kindergarten and first grade tests have much less predictive power than third and fourth grade tests. The assertion on which value-added analysis is founded is that we can forecast future achievement with past achievement. We do not merely need test scores, therefore; we need test scores that are highly informative about future achievement.

The second problem with value-added analysis is power. The researcher is throwing away most of the data—typically, all of the observations on students who enter charter schools before fourth grade. He will thus find it hard to identify effects of policy-relevant size simply because his sample is so small and his standard errors are so high. He is likely to produce estimates that are so noisy that substantial positive, substantial negative, and zero effects all remain likely. That is, positive effects of policy-relevant size will be in the confidence interval but so will be zero and negative

---

[1] We could also use data from the vice versa situation: switching from a charter school to a regular public school. To avoid clumsiness, vice versa may hereafter be assumed.

effects. Such estimates are virtually useless. Although people sometimes misinterpret noisy estimates and say that they mean that the effect is zero, such an interpretation is strictly wrong and should be firmly squelched.

The power problem is serious because it is not tractable. One might think that one can escape it simply by waiting for more years of data on the charter schools in question. Waiting does not help, however, because, as charter schools become more established, they admit fewer and fewer students in grades that are not typical entry grades. That is, in its start-up year, a charter school may admit students in every grade that it offers— kindergarten through sixth grade, say. In the first year of admission, there will be a certain number of students (those who enter in the fifth grade) on whom value-added analysis can be performed. Unfortunately, that number will not be much amplified by successive years of operation, in which the charter school admits a student to its upper-level grades only if some student has vacated a seat. There will be just a trickle of late grade entrants after the first couple of years, and the power problem will not disappear.[1] Moreover, even if one can get sufficient power by relying on data just from charter schools' start-up years, estimates generated in this way are highly problematic. Start-up years are not representative of charter schools in general, so estimates based exclusively on them are hard to interpret and impossible to extrapolate. In addition, as discussed before, self-selection problems are at their most intense in start-up years when parents who choose a charter school must accept a high level of uncertainty.

The final problem with value-added analysis is that a child's prior achievement is endowed with tremendous importance because it alone is used to predict future achievement. Still, we do not have the child's true prior rate of gain; we merely have an erroneous measure of it. This error will, at a minimum, exacerbate power problems; it may cause bias as well.[2] In order to reduce the measurement error substantially, as in Equation (1.1), we would need four observations of prior test scores. (Four observations would allow us to average two independent measures of gain.[3]) However, a researcher who requires four prior test scores can only use data on students who switch after the seventh grade. In other words, we cannot do anything about the measurement error without greatly exacerbating the selection bias that arises from relying on late switchers.

---

[1] Indeed, because the new students enter in different years than the remainder of their classmates, they absorb degrees of freedom (for years of treatment by grade effects, for instance) even as they add observations. Their net contribution to power is therefore negligible.

[2] Bias caused by measurement error in a multivariate setting is hard to predict, even supposing that parents do not react to the error in test scores but only react to their child's true achievement.

[3] There is only a trivial gain in forecasting power from adding only one observation (to make a total of three). This is because the middle observation is used twice, and serial dependence, such as reversion to the mean, makes the second gain highly dependent on the first.

To demonstrate some of the facts we mention above, we offer Table 1.1, which shows the number of students who apply to charter schools in each grade of entry in Chicago and New York City. This table shows that the vast majority of students enter charter schools in kindergarten or grade 1: Of Chicago students admitted to charter schools, 55% enter in these grades and 46% of New York students do the same. Yet these data, if anything, exaggerate the extent of late-grade entry because both cities' charter schools include numerous recent start-ups. In New York, there is a slight bump up in entries in grade 5 (schools in the Knowledge Is Power Program [KIPP] begin in that grade) and grade 9 (when high schools begin), but otherwise the applications drop off with each grade. The data on grade of entry demonstrate just how peculiar are the switchers on whom value-added analysis exclusively relies. Value-added analysis forces a researcher to focus on a small sample, disproportionately plagued by selection bias.

In summary, value-added analysis is not a useful method for generating evidence on charter school effects. It does not credibly reduce the problems of selection bias that also plague comparison-with-controls methods. Instead, it exacerbates selection biases and reduces the power of the estimates. Unlike comparison-with-controls methods, where better judgment may improve the estimates, better judgment is not helpful with

TABLE 1.1
Student Admissions by Grade

	Chicago charter schools	New York City charter schools
	Grade accounts for this percentage of all admitted students	Grade accounts for this percentage of all admitted students
Kindergarten	45.4%	30.8%
Grade 1	9.8%	15.4%
Grade 2	7.1%	10.1%
Grade 3	6.3%	7.4%
Grade 4	7.0%	5.9%
Grade 5	6.9%	13.8%
Grade 6	6.5%	4.7%
Grade 7	6.3%	1.7%
Grade 8	4.7%	0.8%
Grade 9	~0%	4.6%
Grade 10	~0%	4.1%
Grade 11	~0%	0.6%
Grade 12	~0%	0.1%

Notes: See Hoxby and Rockoff and forthcoming reports on New York City by Hoxby and Murarka for details regarding schools and data.

value-added analysis. The problems of value-added analysis are intrinsic: They stem from the nature of the decision to send a child to a charter school. The unobserved force that causes otherwise identical parents to apply to a brand-new charter school (susceptible to value-added analysis) is larger than the force needed to make them apply to a mature charter school (not susceptible to value-added analysis). As a child progresses in his school career (and becomes susceptible to value-added analysis), the unobserved event that will shock his other identical family into making a switch grows larger. Similarly, as a child progresses in his school career (and becomes susceptible to value-added analysis), the parents' informational advantage over researchers grows, thus reducing the likelihood that prior achievement is sufficient for predicting future achievement.

Lottery-Based Analysis

The foundation of lottery-based analysis is fundamentally different from that of either comparison-with-controls or value-added analysis. In fact, its foundation is purely statistical. Randomizing students between two groups will produce groups that are balanced on both observable and unobservable characteristics if the sample being randomized is sufficiently large. That is, randomization over a large number of students who apply to a charter school eliminates all forms of self-selection bias, whether from observable variables such as prior achievement or unobservable variables such as parental motivation. This is a statistical property, not an assumption. Therefore, an analysis that is based on comparing students who are "lotteried" in and out of a charter school requires only two things to generate useful, valid estimates: The lottery must actually be random, and the number of students must be large enough to generate balanced samples.

Fortunately, we can do more than hope that these requirements are met. They can be checked. (We will return to this point.) If the two requirements are met, all other problems associated with self-selection are tractable. This is not to say that there are no data or other concerns that affect lottery-based analysis, but the remaining concerns equally affect comparison-with-controls and value-added analysis and have not been of sufficient importance to enter our discussion thus far.

Another way of understanding why lottery-based analysis solves selection problems of all types is that all children in a lottery have already selected to apply to a charter school. Comparison-with-controls and value-added methods always make us ask, "If these children and their families are so alike, then why are they making different choices about an important thing like the school they attend?" The lottery-based method eliminates all such questions. The children and their families *are* making the same choices; a random number is turning the same choices into different school experiences. Because lottery-based analysis computes effects using the difference between lotteried-in and lotteried-out applicants, its evidence has a straightforward interpretation. The effect computed is the effect we should expect the charter school to have on students who wish to attend and therefore go through the application process. Since charter schools are strictly voluntary, this is exactly the estimate we need for policy purposes.

Ideally, lottery-based analysis proceeds as follows. Students apply to a charter school, and it holds a random lottery among the applicants. The lottery should be held in a fashion that generates prima facie validity (for instance, drawing chits from a box or using a random number generator), but the randomization can also be checked ex post by testing whether the lotteried-in and lotteried-out students who participated in the same lottery have observable characteristics that significantly differ statistically. This is not a full check, of course, but it can be made arbitrarily extensive using "no-stakes characteristics" such as the number of times the letter "k" occurs in a child's street address.[1] If a lottery is random but too small relative to the variation in the population, it may generate random but unbalanced lotteried-in and lotteried-out groups. Thus, the next check is for balance on the observable characteristics of students. Again, this is not a full check because we cannot actually check unobserved variables. Nevertheless, the check can be made arbitrarily extensive using no-stakes characteristics. We describe another, and more important, check for balance next.

In our Chicago and New York City charter school evaluations, we collect each charter school's lottery information—that is, the set of applications along with the lottery number assigned to each student. Nearly always, lotteries are grade specific for each school, a point that is important to remember. Schools do not always hold lotteries for every grade. A start-up school might, for instance, have lotteries for its kindergarten, first grade, second grade, and third grade, but be able to accommodate all applicants for its fourth, fifth, and sixth grades. We collect application information even if a lottery was not held. Later, we discuss how we can use such information. Our Chicago sample includes nine charter schools that together enroll most of the charter school students in the district. Our New York City sample includes 42 of the 46 charter schools in operation by 2005–2006. The application information is matched to the district's

---

[1] No-stakes characteristics are variables that are readily available for students in the lottery but that are not supposed to have the power to predict achievement. For instance, the number of times that the number 3 appears in a student's home address is a no-stakes characteristic. As the number of characteristics being checked for differences becomes large, we should find that the percentage of characteristics that appear to differ statistically significantly converges on the level of statistical significance being employed. We can make the number of characteristics being checked arbitrarily large by using no-stakes characteristics in addition to those that are expected to have explanatory power: race, gender, and so on.

database, and information is retrieved not only on a student's postlottery achievement (used to compare outcomes) but also on his prelottery characteristics, including his prior achievement scores if any. Prelottery data allow us not only to check for randomness and balance, but also to investigate whether a charter school draws applicants who are particularly high or low achievers relative to other local students.

In Hoxby and Rockoff (2004) and forthcoming reports on New York City charter schools, we show checks for randomness and balance. We have never found evidence of a nonrandom lottery, but we often find a lack of balance in small lotteries held for seats in grades that are not typical entry grades. For instance, if there are two sixth grade seats available and 20 students participate in a lottery for the two seats, the lotteried-in and lotteried-out groups typically are not balanced. Later, we discuss how information from unbalanced lotteries can be used, but unbalanced lotteries cannot be used to generate lottery-based estimates.

Lottery-based estimates are generated by computing the lotteried-in versus lotteried-out difference in achievement for each postlottery year for each lottery that did not fail the balance criteria. This leaves us with a large number of estimates—one for each group of students who participated in a lottery for a particular grade in a particular school in a particular year. Such a large number of estimates is not terribly informative, so we compute aggregates of them that we believe to be interesting. For instance, if one wants to know just the average effect of charter schools for a student in the sample, one takes a weighted average of all the lottery-specific effects, where the weights are the number of students used to compute each effect. If one wants to know the average effect of a charter school for a student who enters in the first grade, one takes a weighted average of the lottery-specific effects in which the first grade is the entry year. If one wants to know the effect of attending a charter school that has been in operation for 3 years when the student enters, one takes a weighted average of the lottery-specific effects for students who entered in the school's third year of operation, and so on. Because one cannot show all aggregates, it makes sense to show those that are most relevant to policy.[1]

The only aggregates we cannot compute reliably are those for which we lack an adequate number of balanced lotteries. This brings us to the second, and more important, test of balance. Randomization over a sufficient number of students automatically generates observed and unobserved characteristics that are balanced in a statistical sense. Therefore, the charter school effect we compute should not depend on whether we control for student characteristics or not. This is the beauty of randomization. It is

---

[1] Experienced researchers will realize that we do not actually compute effects for each lottery and then aggregate them later. Instead, we compute the desired aggregates while simultaneously computing individual lottery fixed effects. It is easier to calculate the correct standard errors for the aggregates using simultaneous estimation.

also good intuition for why randomization obviates concerns about self-selection associated with unobservable variables.

We can test whether a lottery is balanced by adding and subtracting observable characteristics from the estimation and seeing whether the estimated charter school effect varies to a statistically significant extent. In practice, we should not only carry out this test statistically; we should also see whether the estimated charter school effect varies to an extent that would confound a policymaker trying to make laws. If the charter school effect varies as we control for different sets of observable characteristics, then the lotteries on which it is based are insufficiently balanced to produce useful estimates.

Not all students who are lotteried in (offered a place) when they participate in a charter school lottery actually take the place they are offered. In practice, this occurs most often because a family has moved or its circumstances have changed, because a sibling who also applied was lotteried out, or because the student was simultaneously offered a place in magnet school or another charter school. Regardless of the reason, a student who is lotteried in was "intended to enroll" at a charter school. When social scientists and medical doctors perform lottery-based analysis, it is standard to compute not just the effect of actual enrollment, but also the effect of being intended for enrollment. In our studies, we compute "intention-to-treat" results for completeness, but the effect of being intended for enrollment has little or no policy relevance in the charter school setting. This is because attending a charter school is always meant to be voluntary.

Put another way, a student who does not comply with the lottery's "intention" for him is not doing anything wrong; he is not like a patient who does not comply with a doctor's intended treatment. The effect that *is* relevant for policy is the selection-bias-free effect of attending a charter school (the "treatment on the treated effect"). Because some students who are lotteried in do not actually attend, we compute this effect by instrumenting for the indicator for attending charter school ($I_{it}^{charter}$) with an indicator for the lottery "intending" the student to attend charter school ($I_{it}^{lotteried\ in}$). In fact, all along we have been describing these treatment-on-the-treated effects as the charter school effects computed based on the lotteries. We have delayed describing the instrumental variables procedure purely for expositional purposes.

An interpretative issue for lottery-based analysis is late offers. A late offer occurs when a place opens up a charter school after the lottery (usually held in the spring). The charter school then takes out its list of applicants and contacts the student whose lottery number was just below the threshold for being lotteried in. If he does not accept the place, it is offered to the student with the subsequent lottery number, and so on. The reason that late offers pose an interpretation problem is that a parent who has meanwhile made other arrangements for his child may refuse a late offer even if he would have accepted an on-time offer. Thus, it is not clear that we ought to lump on-time offers and late offers together in a single indicator

and assume that they have the same effect. Rather than attempt a definitive answer to this interpretation problem, we prefer to show estimates of
charter school effects that are for on-time offers only and for all offers.[1]
In practice, these effects have turned out to be so similar that it does not
seem worthwhile wrestling further with the interpretation problem.

When it is available, lottery-based analysis is strictly superior to comparison-with-controls methods or value-added analysis. Some estimation
problems, such as missing data and attrition (students who are lost to data
cachement altogether because, for example, they move out of the district),
pose problems for all three methods. However, lottery-based analysis
solves all selection problems much more credibly than the other methods
and does not aggravate any estimation problems. Thus, when they are
available, lottery-based estimates are the "gold standard."

COMBINING METHODS FOR MAXIMALLY COMPREHENSIVE
EVALUATION OF CHARTER SCHOOLS' EFFECTS ON ACHIEVEMENT

The creation of a gold standard suggests a remedy for the one deficiency of lottery-based analysis: the fact that it is not always available.
The small lotteries for atypical entry grades are often not balanced and
therefore not susceptible to lottery-based analysis. Some charter schools
can accommodate all applicants in their first year or two of operation and
only hold lotteries after they have been in business for a few years. Some
charter schools, particularly those located in rural areas, almost never
hold lotteries.

The best way to illustrate the use of the gold standard is to provide
a practical example. In our work, we often find unbalanced lotteries for
students who apply to atypical entry grades. Such students are susceptible to comparison-with-controls analysis. The difficulty with this type of
analysis is that it requires considerable judgment from the researcher, and
even a researcher who exercises brilliant judgment may have that judgment questioned by others. The availability of gold standard estimates
for the other grades of entry in a charter school allows a researcher to test
empirically his comparison-with-controls specification. That is, he should
be able to demonstrate that his specification closely replicates the lottery-
based estimates for the data for which both are available. Whether a sufficiently accurate comparison-with-controls specification can be found is,
of course, an empirical matter.

---

[1] Formally, there are three possible indicators for being lotteried in: being lot-
teried in at the time of the lottery ($I_{it}^{lotteried\text{-}in\,on\,time}$), being lotteried-in late ($I_{it}^{lotteried\text{-}in}$
^{later}), and being lotteried in regardless of timing ($I_{it}^{lotteried\text{-}in}$, which is the sum of the
previous two indicators). We compute estimates using the first and third indica-
tors as instrumental variables. There are an insufficient number of students who
are lotteried in late to compute a separate estimate for them.

Readers may derive intuition from an alternative logic about the relationship between comparison-with-controls and lottery-based analysis. The latter works because there is a group of students outside the charter school (the lotteried out) who are good controls for the students attending the charter school. Lotteries make it easy to find the appropriate control group of students but, in return for this ease, they do not always identify appropriate controls even when they exist. This is because lotteries depend on the law of large numbers and have no special way of picking the appropriate controls out of the crowd when the lottery is not large enough to provide balance. In contrast, comparison-with-controls methods create a rule for picking appropriate controls out of the crowd. We can even think of a superb comparison-with-controls specification picking out exactly the lotteried-out students without knowing that they had participated in the lottery. Therefore, a comparison-with-controls specification can, in principle, pick out the appropriate control for a charter school student who, say, participated in a lottery too small for balance.

In the event that a researcher is able to identify a comparison-with-controls specification that replicates his lottery-based results, he may then reasonably speculate that if he applies the same comparison-with-controls method to the data on *all* students who attend the charter school in question, he will obtain fairly credible, comprehensive results.

Thus far, our example has been grades with small lotteries, but using lottery-based results to validate a comparison-with-controls specification may also work for a charter school that does not hold a lottery in its first year of operation but thereafter does. Far more caution is needed if a researcher wishes to use lottery-based results from one school to validate a comparison-with-controls specification that he plans to apply to other schools. Extrapolating from one school to another is a speculative exercise unless there are a priori reasons—such as one school being a branch or offshoot of the other—to believe that selection into the schools is inherently similar.

In short, comparison-with-controls methods (including those that use gain scores) are deficient because it is difficult to verify whether they have solved selection problems when they are used. Indeed, such methods may be unable to solve selection problems even if used well, and they may aggravate selection problems if used poorly. The availability of lottery-based estimates may allow a researcher to address this deficiency empirically, thereby opening the door for estimates of charter school effects that are comprehensive—that is, estimates based on every charter school student's achievement. Combining lottery-based and comparison-with-controls methods is a sound overall strategy for generating comprehensive estimates, so long as researchers are aware that comprehensive estimates may remain unobtainable. We are better off having only credible lottery-based estimates than having a mixed bag of credible lottery-based estimates and noncredible comparison-with-controls estimates.

We can think of no justification for mixing value-added analysis with the other methods for analyzing charter school effects. This is because the problems with value-added analysis are inherent. Put another way, demonstrating that value-added analysis and lottery-based analysis produce similar estimates for students for whom they are both available does *not* allow a researcher to argue by extension that value-added analysis is valid for those students for whom lottery-based analysis is unavailable.

It may be easiest to explain this point with a concrete example. KIPP schools usually cover grades 5–8. Therefore, they admit most of their students in grade 5 lotteries. A typical KIPP school also enrolls a trickle of students to its later grades. Suppose that a KIPP school has a large fifth grade lottery and operates in a district where testing occurs in all of grades 3–8. Then, its fifth grade entrants will be susceptible to both lottery-based and value-added analysis. Even if the two methods produce similar results for the fifth grade entrants, one cannot conclude that value-added estimates for later grades will not suffer from substantial selection bias. This is because value-added analysis exacerbates selection bias precisely for students who enter in atypical grades. The fact that the value-added analysis on the typical grade entrants (grade 5 for KIPP schools) did not produce much selection bias tells us nothing about whether value-added analysis will suffer greatly from selection bias in atypical grades.

Readers may be interested in an important distinction between comparison-with-controls and value-added analysis. The latter always compares a student to his former self. This comparison is problematic precisely because some event must have precipitated the student to switch schools, and we cannot argue credibly that the event has no effect on later achievement. In contrast, comparison-with-controls methods seek the right control students among the possible controls. In principle, there could be a control student who experienced an equivalent event but was—for some arbitrary reason (most obviously a lottery)—unable to attend a charter school. This control student, who can generate unbiased estimates, may be extremely difficult to find in practice but does at least possibly exist.

SOME ILLUSTRATIVE ESTIMATES FROM OUR EVALUATIONS

This is primarily a methodological chapter, but readers may find it helpful to consider a few concrete results that illustrate some of the points discussed earlier. For more extensive results, see Hoxby and Rockoff (2004) and forthcoming reports on New York City charter schools.

Table 1.2 shows computations of a simple average charter school effect for Chicago. To compute the results, we included all balanced lotteries. The basic result is shown in the left-hand column: the average treatment-on-the-treated effect of attending a charter school. The average effect of charter school attendance is about 6 percentile points in math and about 5 percentile points in reading for Chicago students. The average Chicago student in

TABLE 1.2

Average Effect of Attending Chicago Charter Schools on Math and Reading Achievement: Treatment on the Treated Effects

	Basic estimate	Control for observable prelottery student characteristics (except prior achievement)	Control for observable prelottery student characteristics (including prior achievement)	Use all lottery offers (not only on-time offers)
Effect on math percentile score	5.61	5.66	6.20	6.31
	(2.85)	(2.65)	(2.10)	(2.45)
Effect on reading percentile score	4.82	5.00	5.33	5.97
	(2.78)	(2.57)	(2.00)	(2.36)
Observations	2701	2701	2701	3060

Notes: See Hoxby and Rockoff for details regarding schools and data. All estimations include a full set of estimated effects for individual lotteries (which are grade and school specific). The aggregate effects shown also include grade-by-year effects to account for variation in the tests from year to year and from grade to grade. The average student in this sample had attended charter school for 2 years. Standard errors are in parentheses.

the data has attended charter schools for 2 years, so 1-year effects in math and reading are 3 percentile points and 2 percentile points, respectively.

The fact that the lotteries are balanced is demonstrated in the second and third columns. There, we control for various sets of observable student characteristics, and the estimates of the charter school effect do not change to a statistically significant effect. Moreover, they do not change to an extent that would be relevant for policymakers. In the fourth column of each panel, we show results based only on all students who are lotteried in, not just those who receive on-time lottery offers. This change creates differences in the results that are neither statistically significant nor of a size relevant for policy making. The similarity of the estimates for on-time and all lottery offers suggests that families who receive late offers react in the same way that they would have reacted had they received an on-time offer.

Table 1.3 deliberately shows invalid results based on lotteries that are too small to be balanced. Otherwise, this table has a similar format to that of Table 1.2. Notice that the number of observations in Table 1.3 is much smaller than that in Table 1.2. This is because the vast majority of applicants to the charter schools are in balanced lotteries. Any large flow of students into a typical grade of entry will normally end up in a balanced lottery. Therefore, as a mechanical matter, most students will be

TABLE 1.3

Invalid Estimates Based on Unbalanced Lotteries: Invalid Treatment on the Treated Effects of Chicago Charter Schools on Math and Reading Achievement

	Basic estimate	Control for observable prelottery student characteristics (except prior achievement)	Control for observable prelottery student characteristics (including prior achievement)	Use all lottery offers (not only on-time offers)
Effect on math percentile score	−4.30	−7.24	−4.78	−2.47
	(3.68)	(3.63)	(1.83)	(4.10)
Effect on reading percentile score	−0.87	3.44	−3.11	−1.18
	(3.10)	(3.06)	(1.81)	(3.57)
Observations	573	573	573	649

Notes: See Hoxby and Rockoff for details regarding schools and data. All estimations include a full set of estimated effects for individual lotteries (which are grade and school specific). The aggregate effects shown also include grade-by-year effects to account for variation in the tests from year to year and from grade to grade. The average student in the Chicago sample had attended charter school for 2 years. Standard errors are in parenthteses.

in balanced lotteries. Notice also that when we control for various sets of observable student characteristics, in the second and third columns of each panel, the estimated charter school effects jump around to an extent that would be very problematic for policymakers. Put another way, when selection bias is present, as it is when lotteries are too small to balance, estimated effects are not reliable. This lack of reliability is not something that standard errors can reveal because it is result of uncontrolled biases, not merely noise in the data.

Finally, Table 1.4 shows a comparison of lottery-based and value-added results for Chicago. The left and middle columns both show lottery-based results, but the left column shows the lottery-based result that uses all of the balanced lotteries. The middle column, in contrast, uses only the *much smaller* sample of students whose achievement is susceptible to value-added analysis. This sample of late grade movers is less than 10% the size. The late grade movers also appear to be an unusual bunch: The lottery-based estimate for them has a large standard error and is quite different from the estimate based on all students (although not significantly different statistically owing to the large standard error). In the right column, we show the value-added estimate for the small sample of late grade movers who are susceptible to value-added analysis. For each city, this estimate is

TABLE 1.4
Lottery-Based and Value-Added Estimates, Compared: Effects of Chicago Charter Schools on Math and Reading Achievement

	Lottery-based estimate for all students in balanced lotteries	Lottery-based estimate that relies solely on students susceptible to value-added analysis (*not representative or valid*)	Value-added estimate that relies solely on students susceptible to value-added analysis (*not representative or valid*)
Effect on math percentile score	6.31	–1.38	1.03
	(2.45)	(5.92)	(7.02)
Effect on reading percentile score	5.97	–0.75	–1.35
	(2.36)	(5.29)	(8.64)
Observations	2701	562	562

Notes: The two methods are described in the text. The sample in the two right-hand columns is limited to students for whom value-added estimates can be computed. All students who apply to charter schools in balanced lotteries are included in the estimates shown in the left-hand column. The lottery-based estimates are treatment-on-the-treated effects. Standard errors are in parentheses.

radically different from the gold-standard lottery-based estimate, indicating the amount of selection bias present in—even exacerbated by—value-added analysis.

While the point estimates based on lotteries and value-added analysis for late grade movers in Chicago appear to be similar, this similarity is *not* meaningful. The standard errors show that it is mere coincidence. The actual effects could be as many as 28 points apart and still be within the 95% confidence interval. In other words, the point estimates do *not* imply that value-added analysis is a good substitute for lottery-based analysis on late grade switchers. We conclude that value-added analysis is not a reliable method for estimating charter schools' effects on achievement.

LEARNING WHAT WORKS FROM CHARTER SCHOOLS

As we noted at the outset, a policymaker may reasonably want evidence on what works in public education and may view charter schools as laboratories in which interesting educational experiments occur. In order to deliver this kind of evidence, a researcher must first compute credible estimates of each charter school's effect and then relate the effects to charter school characteristics. As we have seen, computing a credible estimate

TABLE 1.5
Some Characteristics of New York City Charter Schools

School characteristic or practice	Share of New York City charter schools
Operated by a charter management organization (CMO)	27%
Operated by an education management organization (EMO)	17%
Operated by a community grown organization (CGO)	56%
Long school day	89%
Long school year	62%
After-school program available	56%
Saturday school (mandatory for all or certain students)	51%
Long English/language arts period (1 hour or more)	54%
Saxon math curriculum	19%
Open Court reading curriculum	11%
Core Knowledge curriculum	22%
Internal assessments regularly administered	65%
Parent contract	38%
"No broken windows" discipline philosophy	22%
Uniforms required	76%
Teachers unionized	14%
Merit pay or bonuses for teachers	30%

Note: This table is based on 37 New York City charter schools that have provided and confirmed their descriptive information.

of each charter school's effect is a significant challenge and may not be possible in the case of new schools, small schools, and schools that do not run substantial lotteries. Assuming, however, that such estimates have been created, the next logical step is using multiple regression or a similar method to relate effects to school characteristics that are quantifiable. Researchers undoubtedly aspire to provide this sort of evidence. Unfortunately, producing such evidence is not as easy as many policymakers believe.

Consider Table 1.5, which shows 17 quantifiable or classifiable characteristics of New York City charter schools in our sample. The first thing to observe is that there are some substantial educational experiments taking place in the schools. Eighty-nine percent have a long school day, with a few having days of 8 hours or more. Sixty-two percent have a long school year, with some having years with more than 200 days. In about half of the schools, children attend Saturday school and study language arts (reading) for more than 1 hour per day. About three quarters require children to wear uniforms, 65% regularly administer internal assessments (in addition to the state tests), and 30% offer substantial merit pay to teachers. Table 1.5 also shows some management types and curricula used. In addition to the characteristics shown, we could easily observe variables such as the number of years a school has been in operation; which New York authorizing organization granted the charter; or whether the school has a dedicated school building, shares a building with a regular public school, or uses facilities not originally intended for a school.

Despite its length, the list in Table 1.5 contains only a small subset of the interventions about which researchers are asked to provide evidence. Yet, we have selected the list with some care to include the educational strategies that are used by multiple schools and that can be quantified. (We allow the schools themselves to classify their strategies if the school description is unclear. Thus, only strategies that the schools themselves find impossible to classify are excluded.) We must exclude strategies that resist classification because they are so dependent on implementation that they cannot be separately identified from particular management teams. We focus on policies employed by multiple schools because we *cannot* identify the effect of a strategy employed by a single school, and we are very unlikely to be able to identify the effect of a strategy employed by only a few schools.

To create the list in Table 1.5, we reduced the detail on various characteristics. For instance, rather than include an identifier for each charter management organization (CMO), we have lumped them together. Rather than include information on the detail of each merit pay plan for teachers, we have lumped them together. It is necessary to reduce detail to ensure that a characteristic is not associated with a single or only a couple of schools (in which case its effect cannot be separately identified). Moreover, even though we do not have the space to show a full correlation matrix, it is the case (and should be fairly evident) that collinearity among certain characteristics is likely to be an issue. For instance, we typically do not find the long school year or the long reading period in schools that do not also employ a long school day. Some characteristics come in clumps and thus cannot be examined individually.

Summing up: Individual charter school effects are estimated with error, school characteristics tend to be collinear, even a very modest list of characteristics (with deliberately reduced detail) numbers one third the number of charter schools in New York City. It is evident that we face a formidable estimation challenge. Moreover, we have so far not mentioned the fact that there is substantial variation in charter schools' locations, buildings, and student demographics. These variables could easily have independent effects or effects that interact with the strategy variables listed previously. For instance, researchers are often asked whether school uniforms work equally well with black students as with Hispanic students (school uniforms are traditional in many of the home countries from which Hispanic parents emigrate). Researchers are asked whether particular disciplinary policies work better when a school has a stand-alone building than when it shares a building with a regular public school (which may not have the same disciplinary policy).

In short, the fact that charter schools operate in different environments means that researchers must be cautious about ascribing achievement effects to school strategies unless they have, at a minimum, simultaneously controlled for a number of school environment variables. This just makes the estimation problem more difficult. Differences in environment also limit the benefits associated with increasing the sample to include, say, charter schools in New York state but outside New York City. A charter school in Utica (a small city in upstate New York) might add variation in school effects and school characteristics, but it would also add such a large amount of variation in school environment that its contribution to evidence on "what works" would be small at best.

We conclude with the hope that the effects of characteristics like those shown in Table 1.5 may be identifiable, but we also conclude with caution regarding the immediate promise of charter school research for discovering "what works" in education. Until we have dramatically greater availability of gold standard evidence on individual charter schools' effects, claims about identifying the effects of educational interventions should be extremely modest.

REFERENCES

Angrist, J. D., & Krueger, A. B. (1999). Empirical strategies in labor economics. In O. Ashenfelter & D. Card (Eds.), *Handbook of Labor Economics* (Vol. 3a). Amsterdam: Elsevier.

Ashenfelter, O., & Card, D. (1985). Using the longitudinal structure of earnings to estimate the effect of training programs on earnings. *Review of Economics and Statistics, 67*(4), 648–660.

Bifulco, R., & Ladd, H. F. (2004). The impacts of charter schools on student achievement: Evidence from North Carolina. Unpublished manuscript.

Bound, J., & Solon, G. (1999). Double trouble: On the value of twins-based estimation of the return to schooling. *Economics of Education Review, 18*(2), 169–182.

Dehejia, R., & Wahba, S. (1999). Causal effects in nonexperimental studies: Reevaluating the evaluation of training programs. *Journal of the American Statistical Association, 94*(448), 1053–1062.

Hanushek, E. A., Kain, J. F., & Rivkin, S. G. (2002). The impact of charter schools on academic achievement. Working paper, The Cecil and Ida Green Center for the Study of Science and Society.

Heckman, J., & Hotz, V. J. (1989). Choosing among alternative nonexperimental methods for estimating the impact of social programs: The case of manpower training. *Journal of the American Statistical Association, 84*(408), 862–874.

Heckman, J., Lalonde, R., & Smith, J. (1999). The economics and econometrics of active labor market programs. In O. Ashenfelter & D. Card (Eds.), *Handbook of Labor Economics* (Vol. 3a). Amsterdam: Elsevier.

Hoxby, C., & Rockoff, J. (2004). The impact of charter schools on student achievement. Harvard University manuscript.

Imbens, G. W., & Wooldridge, J. M. (forthcoming). Recent developments in the econometrics of program evaluation. *Journal of Economic Literature.*

LaLonde, R. (1986). Evaluating the econometric evaluations of training programs with experimental data. *American Economic Review, 76*(4), 604–620.

Neumark, D. (1994). Biases in twin estimates of the return to schooling: A note on recent research. National Bureau of Economic Research Technical Working Paper No. T0158.

Phillips, E. M., & Jencks, C. (1998). *The black–white test score gap*. Washington, DC: The Brookings Institution.

Sass, T. (2004). Charter schools and academic achievement in Florida. Unpublished manuscript.

2

Teachers' Academic Focus on Learning in Charter and Traditional Public Schools[1]

ELLEN GOLDRING AND XIU CRAVENS

INTRODUCTION

Research on school effectiveness continues to indicate that those aspects of schooling that are closest to the student—namely, teaching, instruction, and curriculum—have the greatest impact on student learning (see Gamoran, Nystrand, Berends, & LePore, 1995). Furthermore, the available evidence suggests that schools that cultivate particular in-school processes and conditions, such as developing a shared vision and instructional norms and taking collective responsibility for students' academic success, are better able to meet the needs of all students (Bryk & Driscoll, 1988; Newmann & Wehlage, 1995; Purkey & Smith, 1983). In contrast, much of the research on charter schools has focused on governance structures (Kirst, 2006; Levin, 2006), access and equity (Laciroeno-Paquet, Holyoke, Moser, & Henig, 2002; Schneider, Teske, & Marshall, 2000), and parent preferences and choice processes (Schneider & Buckley, 2002).

The rationale behind charter schools is that increased levels of autonomy and flexibility, and market-like competition among schools should propel them to operate more effectively. In other words, charter school supporters expect that schools of choice will be more able to develop the

[1] This research was supported by the National Center on School Choice, funded by the Department of Education's Institute of Education Sciences (Grant # R305A040043). We acknowledge the generous assistance of Mark Berends, Anna Nicotera, and Marc Stein.

in-school processes, conditions, and characteristics of effective schools. However, we do not know that this is the case. From a policy perspective, as noted by Hess and Loveless (2005),

> Choice-based reform is not a discrete treatment that can be expected to have consistent effects.… While some of the changes produced by choice-based reform are a consequence of choice qua choice, many others are only incidentally related to choice and may or may not be replicated in any future choice-based arrangement (p. 97).

A recent consensus panel of prominent researchers on choice concluded that researchers should seek to distinguish among schools of choice in terms of effectiveness, and to distinguish the reasons for those differences (Betts & Hill, 2006). Many researchers and policymakers advocate looking inside the black box of schools to better understand the conditions under which schools of choice have, or do not have, effects on achievement (Betts & Loveless, 2005; Gill, Timpane, Ross, & Brewer, 2001; Loveless, 2003; Zimmer et al., 2003).

More charter school research is needed on the important in-school conditions related to student learning and achievement. In this chapter we ask the following questions.

- Do charter school teachers indicate higher levels of academic focus on learning than traditional public school teachers (choice qua choice)?
- To what extent is the level of teacher academic focus on learning associated with in-school organizational conditions linked with effective schools, such as strong instructional leadership?
- Are charter schools more likely than traditional public schools to implement the in-school organizational conditions associated with teachers' academic focus on learning? In other words, as noted by Hess and Loveless (2005), do in-school organizational conditions predict levels of teacher academic focus on learning, irrespective of school type—charter or traditional public?

We posit that for charter schools to enable positive student outcomes and affect student achievement, they must implement the core components of schooling that are related to effective organizational conditions, curriculum, and instruction.

MARKET AND INSTITUTIONAL THEORIES

There are two competing theories about the possible impact of charter schools on teaching and learning and in-school organizational conditions: market theory and institutional theory. Many reformers argue that market-style mechanisms of consumer choice and competition between autonomous schools will encourage diverse and innovative approaches (e.g., Finn & Gau, 1998; Leonardi, 1998). The assumption is that with efforts intended to undercut bureaucratic political control of public education, educators in charter schools are given the opportunity and motivation to experiment with new instructional strategies for improving student achievement (Allen, 2001; Budde, 1988).

Reformers argue that allowing parents to choose their child's school will result in market-like competition and the decline of bureaucratic structures, thus providing parents with greater opportunities for home–school interaction and schools with greater openness to parents' demands (Chubb & Moe, 1990). Supporters of de-bureaucratization claim that parents, especially low-income and minority parents, will be less intimidated by the school and more willing to make their needs known to school personnel (e.g., Cookson, 1993; Rinehart & Lee, 1991), resulting in school processes that will lead to higher achievement. Based on the supply-and-demand supposition of market theory, we can imagine a situation in which school administrators have almost complete control over the mix of services they provide and the approaches they use, as well as a situation in which parents have many choices of schools available for their children (Betts, 2005).

Critics of the market model, however, raise questions about the empirical validity of its key assumptions about parent–consumers (demand side), school (supply side), and the products that a market in education would generate (Henig, 1999). An alternative theory about the consequences of school choice rests with institutional theory. This predicts that choice will not result in innovation and the alteration of organizational conditions, curriculum, and pedagogy (Goldring & Sullivan, 1995). Institutional theory emphasizes the "powerful institutional rules" held by public opinion, important constituents, and the laws and regulations (Dimaggio & Powell, 1983; Meyer & Rowan, 1977) that contribute to conformity and congruency between schools of choice and traditional public schools in terms of teaching and learning. From the institutional perspective, the structure of schools under recent reform movements is a response to institutional processes rather than a response to technical needs for efficiency and change (Goldring & Sullivan, 1995). The institutional process tends to be "ritually defined meanings and categories" (Scott, 1992, p. 279) that may include the rhetoric and legislation surrounding ideas such as teacher empowerment and school site management, but often do not involve the next steps—for example, implementing changes in the classroom through new knowledge of teaching and learning.

Institutionalization is tied to legitimacy; organizations facing uncertain environments and outcomes tend to adopt strategies and practices that others have used and view as legitimate (Meyer & Rowan, 1977; Scott, 1992). Thus, wide-scale innovation is rare. The result is that schools and schooling processes look much more alike than different (Elmore, 1996). Institutionalism provides an explanation for maintenance of a status quo and would predict that charter schools would not exhibit different in-school conditions from those of traditional public schools.

The limited empirical research is mixed on improved and differentiated instruction and in-school organizational conditions, curriculum content, and pedagogy in charter schools. It supports neither market theories nor institutional theories (see, for example, Bruno, Chester, Louann, & Gregg, 1998; Finn, Manno, & Vanourek, 2000; Hoxby, 2002; Lubienski, 2003).

IN-SCHOOL ORGANIZATIONAL PROCESSES AND TEACHERS' ACADEMIC FOCUS

There is considerable support for the notion that academic press is an important aspect of school improvement. Lee and Smith (1999) suggest that press toward a common goal, focus, and purpose serves to "set a normative environment that motivates its members to behave in desirable ways" (p. 912). Academic press is linked to the idea of high expectations for all students and is often considered an organizational property of schools. A school's level of academic press is a measure of the extent to which teachers focus on academic excellence and to which the school's professional and academic standards support learning. A school that is focused on student learning and achievement includes a maximization of instructional time, high expectations for all, and a normative culture or climate focused on learning (Lee, Smith, Perry, & Smylie, 1999).

We test the conjecture that, given market press and flexibility, charter schools should exhibit more academic press for learning and more of the in-school conditions that support teachers in their efforts to improve instruction, as noted in our conceptual model in Figure 2.1.

In this study, we refer to teachers' academic focus on learning in terms of four concepts: instructional program coherence, academic instructional innovation, time on task, and focus on achievement.

Instructional program coherence means the degree to which the interventions and programs a school has adopted fit together in terms of their demands on teacher attention and other resources; the alignment of classroom content with external standards and assessments; the consistency of the content taught among teachers of particular grades or courses; and the appropriate sequencing of content across grades (see Newmann, Smith, Allensworth, & Bryk, 2001). Newmann and colleagues define *instructional program coherence* as "a set of interrelated programs for students and staff that are guided by a common framework for curriculum, instruction, assessment, and learning climate that are pursued over a sustained period" (p. 297). Examining whether charter schools are able to foster greater program coherence may be critical for understanding achievement differences that occur among school types.

Academic instructional innovation refers to the related idea that a school's instructional innovations are focused on student learning, are aligned with goals, and have a high expectation for academic learning.

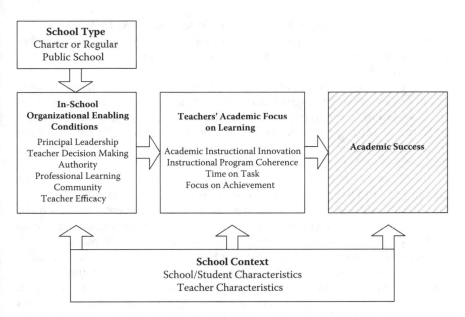

FIGURE 2.1 Conceptual model of relationships between in-school organizational enabling conditions and teachers' academic focus on learning.

Time on task focuses on how engaged teachers are on the core activities of teaching and learning. This concept is one of the seven effective school correlates, which include instructional focus, high expectations, school climate, monitoring of student progress, and school–community relations (Garrison & Holifield, 2005).

Focus on student achievement means the extent to which teachers strive for high levels of student learning; dedicate themselves to the quality of curriculum content, accuracy, and precision in teaching practices and student performance; and emphasize an in-depth understanding of instructional practice and student achievement (see Newmann & Associates, 1996; Newmann & Wehlage, 1995). Although effective schools have a shared mission and goals focusing on student learning, the focus is not on any type of student learning. Rather, effective schools concentrate on achievement goals that are aimed at a shared understanding of and continuous commitment to challenging academic standards for what students should know. Specifically, principals' influence on instruction is indirect through shaping the context within which teachers teach and work.

School effectiveness research indicates that particular in-school organizational processes or conditions both support and enable student achievement and teachers' efforts to improve instruction. In this study we explore the extent to which charter schools are more likely to implement the in-school organizational conditions that are associated with teachers' academic focus on learning. Specifically, we look at four in-school enabling organizational conditions: principal leadership, teacher professional community, teachers' sense of efficacy, and their influence over school decisions.

The importance of *principal leadership* for school reform and improvement has been well recognized in educational research. Several studies have shown its value in establishing effective school improvement efforts in terms of setting the school's vision and mission as well as providing instructional direction (Edmonds, 1979; Louis, Marks, & Kruse, 1996; Purkey & Smith, 1983).

Teacher professional community—the extent to which teachers cooperate, coordinate, and learn from each other to improve instruction and develop the curriculum—is an important feature of any school embarking on the path of improvement (Louis et al., 1996). Respectful, professional debate within professional learning communities is critical for continuous self-assessment of one's own teaching practice, of one's own management of the school and classroom, of the school-wide commitment to and engagement in furthering professional development and alignment to challenging instruction, and of coherence of schooling activities with the school's mission and goals (Newmann, 2002). Moore-Johnson (1990), for example, found that teachers discussed the importance of school-based collegiality and community to meet personal, instructional, and organizational needs. Consistent with this premise, Bryk and Driscoll (1988) found that teachers in communally organized schools—that is, schools with close collegial relations among teachers—reported high levels of morale and satisfaction. McLaughlin and Talbert (1993) in their studies found that "teachers' responses to today's students and notions of good teaching practice are heavily mediated by the character of the professional communities in which they work" (p. 8).

Efficacy refers to teachers' perceptions that their teaching is worth the effort and can lead to success for students (Newmann, Ruter, & Smith, 1989). In his seminal study, Lortie (1975) concluded that those teachers who perceive that they are achieving success with students report higher levels of commitment. "Conversely, teachers derive few rewards from teaching apathetic students" (Bryk, Lee, & Smith, 1990, p. 183). We suspect that teachers with a high sense of efficacy are more likely to feel committed to their schools because they are more likely to invest in their profession and their students. Research has found that high school teachers who have greater control of classroom practices are more efficacious (Lee, Dedrick, & Smith, 1991). Other studies report a positive relationship between teacher efficacy and student achievement (Ashton & Webb, 1986).

Teacher influence over school decisions is an important hallmark of charter schooling and other reform efforts. The rationale for this is twofold. First, it is argued that moving decisions closer to those with technical expertise will result in more informed decisions than those made by administrators who are further removed from students. Second, reformers claim that teachers who have a voice in decisions will take greater ownership in those decisions and therefore invest more in their implementation.

The logic for greater teacher autonomy is grounded in the conception of the teacher as expert. If teachers were only freed from bureaucratic schools, critics suggest, they would be autonomous to innovate, diversify the curriculum, offer varied instructional strategies, and meet the needs of their students (Chubb & Moe, 1990). In a survey of charter school teachers across 10 states, the large majority indicated that having more teaching authority and less bureaucracy were factors in their decision to teach in a charter school (Vanourek, Manno, Finn, & Bierlein, 1998). Similar findings are reported from research comparing private and public school teachers. In their study of San Antonio's private and public schools with students from a privately funded voucher program, Goodwin, Kemerer, and Martinez (1998) report that private school teachers "have greater autonomy and influence in their schools" (p. 289).

In this chapter we explore whether teachers in charter schools are more likely than teachers in traditional public schools to indicate higher levels of academic focus on learning. Are charter schools more likely to implement in-school processes associated with effective schools or, as noted by Hess and Loveless (2005), do in-school organizational conditions predict levels of teacher academic focus on learning, irrespective of school type— charter or traditional public?

METHODOLOGY

The research reported here is based on survey data collected in the spring of 2006 from teachers in a matched paired sample of charter and traditional public schools in four states. This is one of the ongoing research projects of the National Center on School Choice. Our selection of charter schools and matched traditional public schools made use of the sample of schools tested by the Northwest Evaluation Association (NWEA) during the 2004–2005 academic year. NWEA contracts with states, districts, and schools to provide computerized adaptive student assessments aligned to the academic standards of the state. Currently, NWEA tests students in over 1,200 districts in 40 states across the nation. We began our selection frame with NWEA because part of the ongoing research of the National Center on School Choice is to analyze student achievement in charter and traditional public schools.

We identified four states with the largest number of charter schools in NWEA's database as cluster states for analysis. NWEA tested 14 charter schools in Colorado, 16 in Idaho, 18 in Indiana, and 28 in Minnesota. In total, these 76 charter schools comprised our sample of charter schools for matching with a sample of NWEA-tested public schools in these four cluster states.[1]

We used school zip codes to identify a list of public schools tested by NWEA within a 5-, 10-, 15-, or 20-mile radius of each charter school. Geographic proximity was our initial criteria for inclusion in the matching process so as to improve the overall match by garnering a list of potential comparison schools as similar as possible before matching (Shadish, Cook, & Campbell, 2002).

The matching began by sorting the public schools by the charter school's grade level configuration. Those with more than a basic elementary, middle, or high school grade configuration (e.g., K–8, 7–12) were matched on all grade spans in the school. After the grade level configuration of the charter school was matched, we examined the total number of students tested and the percentage of the school tested to select public schools with large testing populations.

Once the testing population of schools was examined, we looked at school-level demographic data. NWEA collects student-level demographic data, including eligibility for free and reduced-price lunch and race/ethnicity. However, given that many schools do not test 100% of the student body with the NWEA assessment due to their grade configurations or testing contract with NWEA, aggregating the student-level information may not have provided accurate school-level demographic data. Therefore, we relied on the 2004–2005 Common Core of Data (CCD) for demographic information for the charter and traditional public schools. We collected data on the percentages of free and reduced-price lunch and race/ethnicity. We used the demographic data to sort the traditional public schools based on the closest data to the charter school, starting with free and reduced-price lunch and then race/ethnicity.

With the public schools sorted by grade configuration, testing population, and school-level demographic information, we used the geographic proximity information as a tie breaker to select two to three traditional public schools closest to the charter school for each grade configuration. If a charter school did not have a traditional public school within the 5-, 10-, 15-, or 20-mile radius, we looked at the list of traditional public schools identified as potential matches for other charter schools in the state and chose a match based on grade configuration, testing population, and school-level demographic data. For this nongeographic group of traditional public school matches, preference was given to schools that shared a district that we had already identified as having other schools to match. The matching process resulted in a list of charter schools and comparison traditional public schools to be contacted for participation in the study.

---

[1] According to the U.S. Charter Schools Website (http://www.uscharterschools. org/), the total number of charter schools in the four states is as follows: Colorado: NWEA tests 14 of 113; Idaho: NWEA tests 16 of 24; Indiana: NWEA tests 18 of 21; Minnesota: NWEA tests 28 of 102.

Of the 43 matched traditional public schools, 24 (56%) were schools matched based on our original matching criteria of grade configuration, testing population, demographic data, and geographic proximity. The remaining 19 schools agreed to participate and completed the survey, but the charter school that they were originally matched to did not participate in the study. Thus, they were matched after the survey to a charter school that was missing a traditional public school match, using the same criteria of grade configuration, testing population, demographic data, and geographic proximity. A total of 29 charter schools and 43 traditional public school matches is included in the analyses. The average teacher response rate for the final sample of schools in this analysis was 67.6%, with a range of 20–100%. The total number of teachers in the study is 851.[1]

VARIABLES

The survey scales and items of the constructs measured in this study are created from several well-established surveys with well-known psychometric properties and have been linked with student achievement in the literature. Four core constructs, as discussed earlier, are selected to gauge teachers' academic focus on learning based on research and theory of our understanding of school improvement processes.

Academic instructional innovation is based on nine items ($\alpha = 0.92$) developed by the NCSC, measuring teachers' perception on the improvement efforts in school on a Likert scale from 1 to 6. For example, teachers are asked if the school uses innovative strategies to improve student learning, if the instructional program is considered unique, and if the instructional approaches used are based on research evidence. Our measure expands the concept to focus on innovates that are related to learning and fit the programs and practices already in place in the school.

Instructional program coherence is measured by eight survey items established by the Peer-Assisted Learning Strategies Research Program (Fuchs, 2005) ($\alpha = 0.81$) on a scale from 1 to 6. This scale measures the degree to which the interventions a school has adopted fit together in terms of their demands on teacher attention and other resources, the alignment of classroom content with external standards and assessments, the consistency of the content taught among teachers of particular grades or courses, and the appropriate sequencing of content across grades.

Time on task is a six-item scale ($\alpha = 0.73$) with responses on a 6-point Likert scale that measures how engaged students and teachers are on the core activities of teaching and learning. The particular concept was used by Garrison and Holifield (2005) as one of the seven effective school correlates, which include instructional focus, high expectations, school climate,

---

[1] As evident from Table 2.1, we were not successful in matching the schools in terms of black enrollment.

monitoring of student progress, and school–community relations. Questionnaire items ask if the school uses a multifaceted approach to maintain a high level of student attendance, if teachers and administrators practice management and supervisory techniques that keep students on task and minimize disruptions, and if students are engaged during the vast majority of class time.

Focus on achievement is based on surveys used by the National Institute of School Leadership (NISL) study (National Institute of School Leadership, 2004) with four items ($\alpha = 0.86$) on a scale from 1 to 6. Teachers are asked if they expect students to complete every assignment, if they encourage students to keep trying even when the work is challenging, and if they set high expectations for academic work. Charter schools are coded as 1; traditional public schools are coded as 0.

School characteristics are obtained from the 2004–2005 CCD for demographic information for the charter and traditional public schools. Included in the analyses are total number of students enrolled, percent of students on free and reduced-lunch program, percent of black students, and percent of Hispanic students. We also added a dummy variable for elementary school status: If a school has at least one elementary grade from K to 6, it is coded as "elementary"; otherwise, it is coded as "nonelementary."

For *in-school organizational enabling conditions*, four constructs are used. *Principal leadership* is based on surveys used by the NISL (2004) with 12 items ($\alpha = 0.95$) on a scale from 1 to 6. Some of these items were adapted from the Consortium on Chicago School Research (CCSR). Teachers are asked to think about the leadership the principal has provided at the school in terms of vision for academic success and instructional guidance. For example, the teachers are asked whether the principal carefully tracks student academic progress, encourages teachers to raise test scores, works directly with teachers who are struggling to improve their instruction, and monitors classroom instruction to see that it reflects the school's goals.

Teacher decision making authority is based on surveys used by the NISL (2004), the Schools and Staffing Survey (SASS), and the CCSR, with seven items ($\alpha = 0.86$) on a scale from 1 to 5. It measures the influence that the teachers have over school policy in areas such as hiring professional staff, planning how discretionary school funds should be used, establishing the curriculum and instruction program, and determining the content of in-service programs.

Professional learning community is based on surveys used by the NISL (2004) on 10 items ($\alpha = 0.87$) on a scale from 1 to 6. This scale is adapted from the CCSR and the Study of Instructional Improvement (SII). Teachers are asked to what extent they agree that in their schools teachers respect other teachers who take the lead in school improvement efforts, may openly express their professional views at faculty meetings, are expected to learn and seek out new ideas continually in this school, and typically go beyond their classroom teaching to address the needs of students.

Teacher efficacy is also based on surveys used by the NISL (2004) with seven items ($\alpha = 0.71$) on a scale from 1 to 6 and adapted from the SII. Teachers are asked to what extent they agree on statements such as "I am capable of making the kinds of changes expected in this school"; "If I try really hard, I can get through to even the most difficult and unmotivated students"; and "Most of a student's academic performance depends on the home environment, so I have limited influence on my students' achievement."

ANALYSES

The research presented here employed ordinary least squares (OLS) regression. The analyses focused on three sets of independent variables: school sector (charter or traditional public school), school and student background characteristics (i.e., percent black and Hispanic students, school size), and in-school organizational enabling conditions (i.e., principal instructional leadership, teacher efficacy). In addition, we tested if charter schools status would mediate the influence of the in-school organizational enabling conditions on teachers' academic focus on learning by including the interaction between charter and the in-school condition variables. Separate regression analyses were conducted on each of the four indicators of teachers' academic focus on learning.[1] Because teachers are clustered within schools, all estimates are adjusted with clustering at the school level, taking into account that observations within schools are not independent and accounting for possible commonalities shared by teachers in the same school.

RESULTS

Descriptive statistics comparing charter and traditional public schools (Table 2.1) show that charter schools are smaller than their traditional public school matches on average, where traditional public schools also have a much bigger range in sizes. We also notice that charter schools in the study enroll higher average percentages of black students and those that are on free or reduced-lunch programs. As for Hispanic students, the averages are similar, but traditional public schools have a bigger range, where some schools have close to a 50% Hispanic student body. When comparing the means of teacher-reported measures on teachers' academic focus on learning—our dependent variables—charter schools have slightly higher averages in all four indicators that are statistically significant. However, the magnitude of the average mean differences is not very big, ranging from 0.19 for *academic instructional innovation* to 0.11 for *time on task* on a

---

[1] Multiple imputation was done for missing values in the variables by using switching regression, an iterative multivariable regression technique.

TABLE 2.1
Descriptive Statistics Comparing Variables Between Charter and Traditional
Public Schools

Variables	Charter school		Traditional public school	
Elementary/nonelementary	Elementary	Nonelementary	Elementary	Nonelementary
No. of teachers (no. of schools)	248 (22)	59 (7)	317 (27)	227 (16)
	Mean	Range	Mean	Range
School characteristics				
Total school enrollment	221	39–696	664	57–1,549[a]
Percent receive free/ reduced lunch	49	0–83	27	3–82
Percent of black students	49	0–99	7	0–49
Percent of Hispanic students	5	0–24	7	0–56
	Mean	SD	Mean	SD
Teachers' academic focus on learning				
Academic instructional innovation	4.62	0.84	4.43	0.85[a]
Instructional program coherence	4.40	0.80	4.25	0.69[a]
Time on task	4.51	0.77	4.40	0.76[b]
Focus on achievement	5.10	0.76	4.98	0.81[b]
In-school organizational enabling conditions				
Principal leadership	4.62	0.99	4.66	0.94
Teacher decision-making authority	3.47	1.03	3.59	0.70
Professional learning community	4.74	0.78	4.61	0.76[a]
Teacher efficacy	4.47	0.67	4.33	0.66[a]

[a] $p < 0.01$ (two-tailed test)
[b] $p < 0.05$

scale from 1 to 6. As for the four scale measures of the in-school organizational enabling conditions, charter schools have small but statistically significant higher averages on teacher-reported *professional learning community* and *teacher efficacy*. There are no significant differences on *principal leadership* and *teacher decision making authority*, noted governance structure indicators associated with theoretical aspects of charter schooling.

Findings from the regression analyses are summarized in Table 2.2. Column 1 contains coefficients of charter from the simple model. With

TABLE 2.2
Teachers' Academic Focus on Learning in Charter and Traditional Public Schools

Dependent variables	Academic instructional innovation			Instructional program coherence			Time on task			Focus on achievement		
	(1)	(2)	(3)	(1)	(2)	(3)	(1)	(2)	(3)	(1)	(2)	(3)
Sector												
Charter/traditional public school	0.19	0.15	0.15[a]	0.15	0.05	0.08	0.10	-0.04	-0.02	0.20[a]	-0.10	-0.06
			0.08[b]			0.08[b]			-0.08[b]			0.09[b]
School characteristics												
Total school enrollment		-0.00[a]	0.00		-0.00[c]	-0.00		-0.00[a]	-0.00		-0.00[a]	-0.00
			0.05[b]			0.00[b]			0.00[b]			0.00[b]
Percent fee/reduced-price lunch		0.36	0.34		-0.32	-0.39		0.12	0.05		-0.31	-0.27
			0.18[b]			0.16[b]			0.20[b]			0.22[b]
Percent of black students		-0.52	-0.26		-0.06	0.12		-0.21	0.02		0.16	0.17[b]
			0.14[b]			0.16[b]			0.18[b]			0.16[b]
Percent of Hispanic students		-1.29[c]	-0.27		-0.89[c]	-0.11		-2.01[c]	-1.27[c]		-0.99[a]	-0.49
			0.31[b]			0.20[b]			0.16[b]			0.32[b]
Elementary/nonelementary		0.56	0.07		-0.05	-0.07		-0.03	-0.03		0.13	-0.08
			0.08[b]			0.06[b]			0.08[b]			0.08[b]
Organizational enabling conditions												
Principal leadership			0.14[c]			0.23[c]			0.18[c]			0.08[a]
			0.03[b]			0.03[b]			0.03[b]			0.04[b]
Teacher decision-making			0.14[c]			0.075			0.08[a]			-0.08
			0.03[b]			0.042[b]			0.04[b]			-0.35[b]

TABLE 2.2 (continued)
Teachers' Academic Focus on Learning in Charter and Traditional Public Schools

Dependent variables	Academic instructional innovation	Instructional program coherence	Time on task	Focus on achievement
Professional learning community	0.52^c	0.32^c	0.32^c	0.43^c
	0.04^b	0.04^b	0.04^b	0.05^b
Teacher efficacy	0.25^c	0.23^c	0.17^c	0.13^c
	0.04^b	0.03^b	0.04^b	0.04^b
R^2	.57	.50	.41	.30
	.06	.06	.08	.07
	.01	.014	.004	.05

Note: All estimates are adjusted with clustering at the school level.
[a] $p < 0.05$
[b] Standardized coefficients
[c] $p < 0.01$ (two-tailed test)

clustering at the school level (resulting in larger standard errors), charter status has no statistically significant coefficients on the dependent variables except for *focus on achievement*. Charter school teachers report they are more likely to focus on achievement than their traditional public school counterparts. When analyzing the data without clustering at the school level, we do note, however, that charter status has positive coefficients on all four measures, but the standard errors are smaller and probably imprecise without accounting for common features that teachers share within each school.

As shown in Table 2.2, we find that school and student background characteristics are associated with the level of academic focus (the effect disappears when organizational enabling conditions are added to the model), but account for a small percent of the variance in the levels of teachers' academic focus on learning. Although the percent of black students in the school has a negative relationship to *academic instructional innovation*, the percent of Hispanic students has a consistent negative association with all aspects of teachers' academic focus on learning. Schools with larger percentages of Hispanic students are less likely to indicate that their schools implement innovations focused on academics. They are less likely to report instructional program coherence and less likely to focus on student achievement with high expectations for all students. It may be that limited language proficiency adds a layer of complexity to schooling that precludes a clear focus on academics and a coherent approach.

In the full model, which contains both background characteristics and the estimates for in-school organizational processes, teachers' academic focus has strong associations with in-school processes. The coefficients for school racial–ethnic composition (namely, the percent of Hispanic students) only have a negative relationship with *time on task*. Among the four in-school organizational enabling conditions, *professional learning community* and *teacher efficacy* have statistically significant and positive coefficients on all four measures of teacher academic focus. Schools where teachers feel that diverse opinions are supported, professional collegiality runs through the school, and values and understandings are shared are better able create the conditions where there is a focus on academic learning. The size of the impact of *professional learning community* is the largest among all explanatory variables. Teacher efficacy is another important predictor of levels of academic focus. Those teachers who feel they have the knowledge and ability to impact student learning are most likely to indicate their schools and colleagues are implementing programs pressing toward learning. *Principal leadership* is also associated with *academic instructional innovation, instructional program coherence,* and *time on task,* but not with *focus on achievement*.

It is interesting to note that *teacher decision-making authority* is positively associated—though it is not a strong association—with *academic instructional innovation* and *instructional program coherence,* but not with *time on task* or *focus on achievement*. The governance notion most associated with charter schooling does not have a strong relationship to teachers' academic focus. In fact, associations of *teacher decision-making authority* are stronger with those measures of academic focus directed at the school level (innovation, adoption of programs) than with those directed at the classroom level (*time on task* and *focus on achievement*).

As noted, we also analyzed the data interacting charter status with the four organizational enabling conditions to see if these variables influence teachers' academic focus differently in charter and traditional public schools. All of the interaction coefficients are small and not significant, suggesting that in-school conditions are more important in explaining levels of teacher academic focus, and charter schools are not more likely than traditional public schools to facilitate the in-school enabling conditions.

DISCUSSION

This chapter asks whether charter school teachers indicate higher levels of academic focus on learning than traditional public school teachers (choice qua choice). To what extent is the level of teacher academic focus on learning dependent upon in-school organizational conditions that are associated with effective schools, such as strong instructional leadership? Are charter schools more likely than traditional public schools to implement the in-school organizational conditions that are associated with teachers' academic focus on learning?

We set forth two theoretical foundations that would predict opposite answers to these questions. Market theory suggests that charter schools would evidence stronger teacher academic focus on learning and more in-school conditions associated with effective schools. Institutional theory would predict that there would not be substantial differences between charter and traditional public schools. Institutional theory also suggests that in-school conditions in and of themselves would impact teachers' academic focus on learning because of the strong institutional press and normative culture that the effective school traditions may be asserting on all schools.

Noting that our conclusions pertain only to schools tested by NWEA (and that we do not know the nature of the selection bias for these schools) and recognizing the limitations of our sample and surveys, our investigation suggests that, on average, choice qua choice does not have consistent relationships to teachers' academic focus on learning. Charter school teachers do not indicate higher levels of academic focus on learning. We did find, however, that in-school organizational conditions often attributed to effective schools, such as professional community and principal leadership, are associated with higher levels of academic focus. Furthermore, charter schools were not more likely than regular public schools to exhibit these conditions, even those such as teacher decision-making authority, that are assumed to be associated with flexibility and nonbu-reaucratic forms of choice.

We interpret these findings to suggest that there are significant insti-tutional forces driving all schools to believe that strong leadership and professional cultures and communities are integral aspects of the school organization, and that these aspects can impact the extent to which teach-ers focus on learning. The designation of a school as a charter school does not seem to alter these institutional forces or norms of practice. Charter schooling does not seem to directly challenge what a real school ought to be doing (Cuban & Tyack, 1997). As noted by Hess and Loveless (2005), our findings suggest that in-school processes associated with effective schools seem to be unrelated to school choice and are not dependent on choice-based arrangements.

Our results support previous research about the importance of in-school conditions in maintaining teachers' academic focus on student learning. We would have thought that charter school teachers would have significantly higher levels of efficacy than traditional public school teach-ers. Charter school teachers often self-select to teach in a particular school, and their schools are theoretically freed from constraining rules and reg-ulations. Furthermore, charter schools may be better able to attract and sustain principals who are instructional leaders. However, in all schools in our study, we found a significant effect of teacher efficacy on the level of academic focus on student learning. Research suggests that teacher efficacy can improve with professional development; the most efficacious teachers often gain the most from learning new methods of teaching (see Moran, Hoy, & Hoy, 1998). This line of research suggests that teacher effi-cacy is subject to change and may be an important mediating variable in understanding changes in teaching. "The development of a strong sense of efficacy can pay dividends of higher motivation, greater effort, persis-tence, and resilience across the span of teaching career" (Moran et al., p. 238). Furthermore, as noted in previous research, instructional leadership does support teachers' efforts to focus on academics, but this is no more prevalent in charter schools than in traditional public schools.

Similarly, our results suggest the importance of the teacher professional community and its association with teachers' academic focus on learning; charter schools were not more likely to exhibit this important in-school condition. Research has demonstrated that schools organized as commu-nities, rather than bureaucracies, are more likely to exhibit academic suc-cess (Bryk & Driscoll, 1988; Lee, Smith, & Croninger, 1995; Louis & Miles, 1990). Phillips (1997), for example, found that in schools where teachers are more concerned with affective relations than academic learning, test scores tend to be lower. She cautions that communities in schools must place academic learning at the center.

Given the possible support for the institutional perspective when interpreting our findings, we suggest that it is important to begin to look at charter schools in relation to the current policy context and the institutional environment of schooling. By and large, charter schooling began before the No Child Left Behind (NCLB) legislation. However, we raise the hypothesis that the prevailing accountability mechanisms under NCLB and the normative views of what is involved with helping schools meet adequate yearly progress are creating an institutional environment where choice cannot lead to the types of innovations hoped for by their founders. While it is not directly addressed in this study, we believe the "grammar" of schooling is now even more impervious and unreceptive to the forces of market-based reform efforts.

In the summary chapter in their book about charter schools, Zimmer and colleagues (2003) note that "one of the most significant conclusions of our analysis is there is no single charter school approach and therefore no single charter school effect" (p. 175). Our study suggests that in-school conditions are central for school improvement. There are some traditional public schools that have in-school conditions similar to charter schools and some charter schools that have in-school conditions similar to those in traditional public schools. Choice-based systems do not in and of themselves seem to lead to more of these in-school conditions.

REFERENCES

Allen, J. (2001). Education by charter: The new neighborhood schools. In J. C. Goodman & F. F. Steiger (Eds.), *An education agenda: Let parents choose their children's school* (pp. 56–64). Dallas, TX: National Center for Policy Analysis.

Ashton, P. T., & Webb, R. B. (1986). *Making a difference: Teachers' sense of efficacy and student achievement.* White Plains, NY: Longman.

Betts, J. R. (2005). The economic theory of school choice. In J. R. Betts & T. Loveless (Eds.), *Getting choice right.* Washington, DC: Brookings Institution Press.

Betts, J. R., & Hill, P. T. (2006). Charter school achievement consensus panel. In *Key issues in studying charter schools and achievement: A review and suggestions for national guidelines* (p. 24). Seattle, WA: National Charter School Research Project, Center on Reinventing Public Education.

Betts, J. R., & Loveless, T. (Eds.). (2005). *Getting choice right.* Washington, DC: Brookings Institution Press.

Bruno, V. M., Chester, E. F., Jr., Louann, A. B., & Gregg, V. (1998). How charter schools are different: Lessons and implications from a national study. *Phi Delta Kappa, 79*(7), 488.

Bryk, A., & Driscoll, M. (1988). The school as community: Theoretical foundations, contextual influences, and consequences for students and teachers. Madison, WI: National Center on Effective Secondary Schools, University of Wisconsin.

Bryk, A., Lee, V., & Smith, J. (1990). High school organization and its effects on teachers and students. In W. Clune and J. Witte (Eds.), *Choice and control in American education, Vol. 1: The theory of choice and control in American education* (pp. 135–226). Bristol, PA: Falmer Press.

Budde, R. (1988). *Education by charter: Restructuring school districts: key to long term continuing improvement in American education.* Andover, MA: Regional Laboratory for Educational Improvement of the Northeast & Islands.

Chubb, J., & Moe, T. (1990). *Politics, markets and American schools.* Washington, DC: Brookings Institute.

Cookson, P. W. (1993). *School choice and the creation of community.* Paper presented at a workshop entitled "Theory and practice in school autonomy and choice: Bringing the community and the school back in." Tel Aviv University, Israel.

Cuban, L, & Tyack, D. (1995). *Tinkering toward utopia.* Cambridge, MA: Harvard University Press.

DiMaggio, P. D., & Powell, W. (1983). The iron cage revisited: Institutional isomorphism and collective rationality in organizational fields. *American Sociological Review, 48*(2), 147–160.

Edmonds, R. R. (1979). Effective schools for the urban poor. *Educational Leadership, 37*, 15–27.

Elmore, R. (1996). Getting to scale with good educational practice. *Harvard Education Review, 66*(1), 1–26.

Finn, C. E., & Gau, R. L. (1998). New ways of education. *The Public Interest, 130*, 79–92.

Finn, C. E., Manno, B. V., & Vanourek, G. (2000). *Charter schools in action: Renewing public education.* Princeton, NJ: Princeton University Press.

Fuchs, D. (2005). *Scaling up peer-assisted learning strategies to strengthen reading achievement.* Nashville, TN: Kennedy Center, Vanderbilt University.

Gamoran, A., Nystrand, M., Berends, M., & LePore, P. (1995). An organizational analysis of the effects of ability grouping. *American Educational Research Journal, 32*(4), 687–715.

Garrison, L. F., & Holifield, M. (2005). Are charter schools effective? *Planning and Changing 36*(1&2), 90–103.

Gill, B. P., Timpane, P. M., Ross, K. E., & Brewer, D. J. (2001). *Rhetoric versus reality: What we know and what we need to know about vouchers and charter schools.* Santa Monica, CA: RAND.

Goldring, E. B., & Sullivan, A. S. (1995). Privitization: Integrating private services in public schools. In P. Cookson & B. Schneider (Eds.), *Transforming schools* (pp. 533–556). New York: Garland.

Goodwin, R. K., Kemerer, F. R., & Martinez, V. J. (1998). Comparing public school and private voucher programs in San Antonio. In P. Peterson and B. Hassel (Eds.), *Learning from school choice* (pp. 275–306). Washington, DC: Brookings Institute.

Henig, J. R. (1999). School choice outcomes. In S. Sugarman & F. Kemerer (Eds.), *School choice and social controversy.* Washington, DC: Brookings Institution Press.

Hess, F. M., & Loveless, T. (2005). How school choice affects student achievement. In J. Betts & T. Loveless (Eds.), *Getting choice right: Ensuring equity, and efficiency in education policy* (pp. 85–100). Washington, DC: Brookings Institution Press.

Hoxby, C. M. (2002). Would school choice change the teaching profession? *The Journal of Human Resources, 37*(4), 846–891.

Kirst, M. W. (May, 2006). *Politics of charter schools: Competing national advocacy coalitions meet local politics.* Paper presented at the annual meeting of the American Education Finance Association, Denver, CO.

Laciroeno-Paquet, N., Holyoke, T., Moser, M., & Henig, J. (2002). Creaming versus cropping: Charter school enrollment practices in response to market incentives. *Educational Evaluation and Policy Analysis, 24*(2), 145–158.

Lee, V. E., Dedrick, R. F., & Smith, J. B. (1991). The effect of the social organization of schools on teachers' efficacy and satisfaction. *Sociology of Education 64*(3), 190–208.

Lee, V. E., & Smith, J. B. (1999). Social support and achievement for young adolescents in Chicago: The role of academic press. *American Educational Research Journal, 36*(4) 907–945.

Lee, V. E., Smith, J. B., & Croninger, R. G. (1995). *Another look at high school restructuring. More evidence that it improves student achievement and more insights into why.* Madison, WI: Center on Organization and Restructuring of Schools.

Lee, V., Smith, J. B., Perry, T., & Smylie, M., (1999). *Social support, academic press, and student achievement: A view from the middle grades in Chicago.* Chicago: Consortium on Chicago School Research.

Leonardi, R. C. (1998). *Charter schools in Ohio: The rush to mend them should not end them. Perspective on current issues.* Dayton, OH: Buckeye Institute for Public Policy Solutions.

Levin, H. M. (2006). *Why is educational entrepreneurship so difficult?* Paper presented at the Conference on Educational Entrepreneurship at American Enterprise Institute, Washington, DC.

Lortie, D. (1975). *Schoolteacher.* Chicago: University of Chicago Press.

Louis, K. S., Marks, H. M., & Kruse, S. (1996). Teachers' professional community in restructuring schools. *American Educational Research Journal, 33*(4), 757–798.

Louis, K. S., & Miles, M. B. (1990). *Improving the urban high school: What works and why.* New York: Teachers College Press.

Loveless, T. (2003). *Charter schools: Brown center report on American education.* Washington, DC: Brookings Institution Press.

Lubienski, C. (2003). Innovation in education markets: Theory and evidence on the impact of competition and choice in charter schools. *American Educational Research Journal, 40*(2), 395–443.

McLaughlin, M. W., & Talbert, J. E. (1993). *Contexts that matter for teaching and learning.* Palo Alto, CA: Stanford University, Center for Research on the Context of Secondary School Teaching.

Meyer, J. W., & Rowan, B. (1977). Institutionalized organizations: Formal structure as myth and ceremony. *American Journal of Sociology 83,* 340–363.

Moore-Johnson, S. (1990). *Teachers at work: Achieving success in our schools.* New York: Basic Books.

Moran, M. T., Hoy, A., & Hoy, W. (1998). Teacher efficacy: Its meaning and measure. *Review of Educational Research, 68*(2), 202–248.

National Institute for School Leadership (NISL). Proposal by the Consortium for Policy Research in Education. Assessing the impact of principals' professional development: An evaluation of the National Institute for School Leadership.

Newmann, F. M. (2002). Achieving high-level outcomes for all students: The meaning of staff shared understanding and commitment. In W. D. Hawley (Ed.), *The keys to effective schools: Educational reform as continuous improvement* (pp. 28–42). Thousand Oaks, CA: Corwin Press.

Newmann, F. M., & Associates. (1996). *Authentic achievement: Restructuring school for intellectual quality.* San Francisco, CA: Jossey–Bass.

Newmann, F. M., Ruter, R. A., & Smith, M. S. (1989). Organizational factors that affect school sense of efficacy, community and expectations. *Sociology of Education, 62*(4), 221–238.

Newmann, F. M., Smith, B. A., Allensworth, E., & Bryk, A. S. (2001). Instructional program coherence: What it is and why it should guide school improvement policy. *Educational Evaluation and Policy Analysis, 23*(4), 297–321.

Newmann, F. M., & Wehlage, G. H. (1995). *Successful school restructuring: A report to the public and educators by the Center on Organization and Restructuring of Schools.* Alexandria, VA: Association for Supervision and Curriculum Development; Reston, VA: National Association for Secondary School Principals.

Philips, M. (1997). What makes schools effective? A comparison of the relationships of communitarian climate and academic climate to mathematics achievement and attendance during middle school. *American Educational Research Journal, 34,* 633–662.

Purkey, S. C., & Smith, M. S. (1983). Effective schools: A review. *The Elementary School Journal, 83*(4) 427–452.

Rinehart, J. R., & Lee, J. F. (1991). *American education and the dynamics of choice.* New York: Praeger.

Schneider, M., & Buckley, J. (2002). What do parents want from schools? Evidence from the Internet. *Educational Evaluation and Policy Analysis, 24*(2), 133–144.

Schneider, M., Teske, P., & Marshall, M. (2000). *Choosing schools: Consumer choice and the quality of American schools.* Princeton, NJ: Princeton University Press.

Scott, W. R. (1992). *Organizations: Rational, natural and open systems.* Englewood Cliffs, NJ: Prentice Hall.

Shadish, W. R., Cook, T. D., & Campbell, D. T. (2002). *Experimental and quasi-experimental designs for generalized causal inference.* Boston, MA: Houghton Mifflin Company.

Vanourek, G., Manno, B. V., Finn, C. E., Jr., & Bierlein, L. A. (1998). Charter schools as seen by students, teachers, and parents. In P. Peterson & B. Hassel (Eds.), *Learning from school choice* (pp. 187–212). Washington DC: Brookings Institution Press.

Zimmer, R., Buddin, R., Chau, D., Gill, B., Guarino, C., Hamilton, L., et al. (2003). *Charter school operations and performance: Evidence from California.* Santa Monica, CA: RAND.

3

Teams Versus Bureaucracies
Personnel Policy, Wage Setting, and Teacher Quality in Traditional Public, Charter, and Private Schools[1]

MICHAEL PODGURSKY

INTRODUCTION

Personnel policies in public schools are the subject of considerable policy debate. This debate arises out of concern about the quality of the public school teaching workforce and its effect on student achievement. Research suggests that one of the most important contributions of schools to student achievement gains is the quality of classroom teachers (Goldhaber, 2002; Hanushek & Rivkin, 2004). The No Child Left Behind Act reflects this concern in its requirement that school districts employ only "highly qualified" teachers in order to receive Title I compensatory education funds.

In other industries, human resource policies are seen to play a critical role in employee productivity and business performance. Yet human resource policies in public K–12 schools seem peculiarly out of sync with those in other sectors of our economy, most notably with higher education, and, as we will see, with charter and private K–12 schools.

Several examples illustrate this point. Unlike most other professions, the pay of public school teachers within a district is primarily determined by

[1] The author wishes to acknowledge research support from Smith Richardson Foundation; the research assistance of Samantha Dalton, Keke Liu, and Jae Pil Park; and technical assistance from Dale Ballou. The usual disclaimers apply.

rigid salary schedules that base pay on years of experience and graduate academic degrees or credits, with no differentials by field, effort or quality of performance, or differential working conditions between schools within a district.[1] These rigid pay schemes virtually guarantee shortages by field, since most school districts cannot maintain a pay schedule for all teachers sufficiently attractive to prevent shortages in *any* field. (Could a higher education institution afford to maintain a uniform pay scheme sufficiently high to prevent shortages in finance or accounting?) Moreover, since low socioeconomic status (SES) or high minority enrollment schools tend to have the highest turnover of faculty, these rigid salary schedules virtually guarantee that such schools will have the least experienced teachers.

In the area of contract renewal, most public school teachers earn tenure—automatic contract renewal—after a few years on the job. This makes it very difficult to dismiss senior teachers for anything but the most egregious failures in job performance. In practice, most dismissals of tenured teachers seem to be associated with criminal activity, psychological disorders, or serious moral turpitude—not poor classroom performance (Bridges, 1992).

Recruitment and job assignment are restricted by highly complicated licensing regulations. In medicine, law, dentistry, architecture, nursing, and virtually every other licensed profession, states issue a single license. However, in education, states routinely issue over 100 certificates and endorsements by field. Even excluding vocational and administrative licenses, the number of academic licenses routinely exceeds 50–60. In Missouri, by no means an atypical state, the Department of Elementary and Secondary Education currently issues 89 nonvocational and 171 vocational certificates and endorsements for K–12 teachers.[2]

Finally, teaching is the most highly unionized profession, with roughly 75% of teachers in traditional public schools (i.e., not charter) covered by collective bargaining agreements. In large urban districts, these agreements run roughly 200 pages or more, are highly detailed, and cover not only wage setting, but also staff assignment, recruitment, layoffs, personnel evaluations, dismissals, benefits, and other personnel policies.

In this chapter, we examine differences in personnel policy between traditional public, charter, and private schools and examine how these policies are shaped by the institutional and market framework within which these schools operate. We then explore how these personnel pol-

---

[1] There are some pay differentials, but these are primarily for added responsibility such as coaching and after-school activities.

[2] Even this understates the complexity of the teacher licensing system. These are currently issued certificates and endorsements. However, since states routinely change these licenses and "grandfather" the old codes, the number of valid types of licenses is far greater. In Missouri, the certification file has 781 valid codes. In the face of such complexity, it is hardly surprising that school districts are often forced to resort to the use of emergency or provisionally licensed teachers to staff some classrooms.

icy differences contribute to the academic quality differences observed between the sectors. This chapter builds on earlier research in the area. Ballou (2001) and Ballou and Podgursky (1997, 2001) examined differences in teacher quality and personnel policy in public and private schools using earlier vintages of the Schools and Staffing Survey (SASS) and a small sample of charter and private schools. Both studies find personnel policy differences among private, charter, and traditional public schools. More recently, Caroline Hoxby (2002) augmented the 1994–1995 SASS data with her own survey of charter schools. She found significant differences in the teacher demand between the sectors. Goldhaber, Choi, DeArmond, and Player (2005) developed an analytical model of merit pay adoption to explore why school districts choose to adopt merit pay. This chapter brings some new data and analysis to bear on this topic, particularly for charter schools.

DATA

The primary source of data in this chapter is the 1999–2000 SASS, a representative national survey of schools, districts, principals, and teachers conducted regularly by the National Center for Education Statistics of the U.S. Department of Education. It is a major source of information on public and private K–12 teachers and schools in the United States. Earlier waves of the survey were conducted in 1987–1988, 1990–1991, and 1993–1994. However, the 1999–2000 school year was the first time that SASS included a separate charter school survey. Details on SASS are provided in the appendix at the end of this chapter. In addition, we use state administrative data on schools and teachers in a particular school district—Kansas City, Missouri—that has a particularly high rate of charter school penetration.

INSTITUTIONAL BACKGROUND

The notion that product market conditions spill over into the labor market and influence wages, collective bargaining, and personnel policy has a long history in labor economics (e.g., Lewis, 1963). We take a similar approach. Differences in personnel policies among traditional public, charter, and private schools can be seen as a reaction to the regulatory and market environment within which the schools operate.

The most obvious difference between these sectors has to do with market competition. Charter and private schools are schools of choice and are thus subject to competitive product market pressures. If parents do not choose these schools for their children, the schools will go out of business. For the most part, this is not the case with traditional public schools. While there is some choice—such as magnet schools—within this sector, children typically are assigned to schools within attendance zones. Thus, schools do not need to compete for parent customers.

Of course, there may be political pressures from taxpayers for public schools to adopt cost-efficient personnel policies, but in the political realm these may be offset by the demands of better organized "stakeholder" groups such as teachers, school administrators, and other school employees. In addition, individual taxpayers may be relatively uninformed as to the costs of different management practices.[1] To the extent that public school administrators are insulated from market pressures, we can expect them to adopt more "comfortable" personnel policies that raise their own utility, or that of other education interest groups, rather than increase efficiency. Teacher dismissals and performance-based pay systems require effort on the part of school administrators, increase stress, and usually involve confrontation with teacher unions. A more comfortable path is to acquiesce to teacher union preferences for single salary schedules and other restrictions on managerial authority. We hypothesize that greater competitive pressure in the product market should lead to more market- and performance-based personnel policies.

A second factor explaining the choice of personnel policies is the size of wage-setting units. In private and charter schools, the wage-setting unit is typically the school. In traditional public schools, on the other hand, wage-setting and most personnel policies concerning teachers—the level and structure of teacher pay, benefits, recruiting—are centralized at the district level. Researchers who study personnel policy in business find that the size of an establishment plays an important role in the types of personnel policies that firms use (Brown, 1990; Prendergast, 1999).

Figure 3.1 illustrates the dramatic differences in the size of the wage and personnel units in traditional public and private schools. There are approximately 15,000 public school districts in the United States, but the size distribution of these districts in terms of teacher employment is highly skewed. As a consequence, most teachers are employed in large school districts. One quarter of teachers in traditional public schools are employed in districts with at least 2,100 full time equivalent (FTE) teachers, and half of traditional public school teachers are in districts with at least 561 FTE teachers. Thus, the typical teacher finds herself in a large firm with standardized, bureaucratic wage setting. By contrast, the average charter school—an independent employer—employs just 16 FTE teachers, barely larger than the average private school (15 FTEs).

The size of the employing unit is an important factor in understanding a firm's choice of personnel policies. In small teams, it is much easier for supervisors or fellow workers to monitor job performance. This makes merit or performance-based pay less controversial. On the other hand,

---

[1] Hoxby (2000) has highlighted the role of Tiebout competition among public school districts. Black (1999) finds evidence that school quality is capitalized in housing prices.

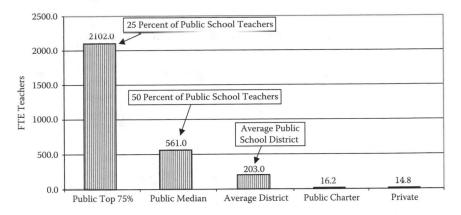

FIGURE 3.1. Size of wage-setting units in traditional public, charter, and private schools: FTE teachers employed. (From U.S. Department of Education, 1999–2000 Schools and Staffing Surveys.)

large school districts have a great deal of trouble implementing merit pay systems for teachers (Hatry, Greiner, & Ashford, 1994). In part, this is because they must come up with evaluation systems that guarantee horizontal "equity" across the many schools in the district bargaining unit— essentially a hopeless endeavor. Private and charter schools are under no requirement that their performance assessments be identical to those of other schools. They need only assure their teachers that they are treated fairly within the school. Teachers unhappy with the pay system at the school can always "vote with their feet" and go to another school with a more compatible pay regime.

Evidence for this "team" perspective is seen in teacher responses to a series of attitudinal questions on job control and work relationships reported in Table 3.1. Charter and private school teachers report greater levels of influence on academic standards and curriculum than did teachers in traditional public schools. More to the point, they report closer and more productive relationships with their principal, greater congruence in values and outlook, and more cooperative relations with colleagues than do teachers in traditional public schools. In short, the small size of charter and private schools combined with a fluid and competitive market allows heterogeneous employers and workers to sort and match in an efficient manner.

In principle, public school districts need not be so bureaucratic. They could adopt more decentralized systems of personnel policy, give school principals more control over teacher recruitment and pay, and adopt more of a team model. However, this brings us to the next important difference between the sectors: collective bargaining. The percent of teachers covered by collective bargaining agreements in charter schools is far lower than that in traditional public schools. (SASS does not bother to elicit this

TABLE 3.1
Teacher Influence and Attitudes in Traditional Public, Charter, and Private Schools

	Traditional public	Charter	Private	Private, nonreligious regular
How much influence do you think teachers have over school policy?				
Setting performance standards for students[a]	3.00 (.010)	3.47[c] (.015)	3.70[c] (.015)	3.89[c] (0.041)
Establishing curriculum[a]	3.18 (.010)	3.70[c] (.017)	3.85[c] (.016)	4.25[c] (0.041)
The school administrator's behavior toward the staff is supportive and encouraging.[b]	.788 (.004)	.802[c] (.004)	.873[c] (.004)	.861[c] (0.021)
Most of my colleagues share my beliefs and values about what the central mission of the school should be.[b]	.847 (.003)	.866[c] (.003)	.922[c] (.003)	.912[c] (.001)
There is a great deal of cooperative effort among the staff.[b]	.783 (.003)	.844[c] (.005)	.890[c] (.005)	.867[c] (.020)

Source: 1999–2000 Schools and Staffing Surveys
[a] Mean value on a scale of 1–5: 1 = no influence; 5 = a great deal of influence
[b] 1–4 Likert scale with 1 = strongly disagree; 4 = strongly agree. Percent reporting agree or strongly agree.
[c] Difference between charter/private and traditional public school significant at 0.01 level of significance.

information from private school respondents since few private schools bargain collectively with their teachers.) Seventy percent of public school districts, employing 73% of teachers, have collective bargaining agreements covering their teachers (Table 3.2). This contrasts with just 14% of charter schools (employing 18% of charter school teachers). The absence of a binding collective bargaining agreement is an important source of personnel flexibility in charter schools. Teacher unions in general have been opposed to more flexible market- or performance-based pay systems. Grievance procedures in collective bargaining agreements also make it more difficult to dismiss poorly performing teachers.

Collective bargaining also creates strong pressure for centralized wage-setting and personnel policies. An important institutional reason for this is that state labor regulators define school districts rather than schools as the "appropriate bargaining unit" for collective bargaining. Given the substantial resource costs in bargaining a contract and the fixed costs of administering it, both labor and management favor centralizing

TABLE 3.2
Percent of Districts, Schools, and Teachers Covered by Collective Bargaining
Agreements

	Public	Charter
Percent of units (public = districts, charter = schools)	69.8 (0.7)	14.4 (0.5)
Percent of teachers	73.4 (0.7)	17.8 (0.7)

Source: 1999–2000 Schools and Staffing Surveys

bargaining at the school district level. Alternately, if a district attempts to implement one set of personnel policies or compensation practices in one set of schools versus another, it is under a great deal of pressure to provide a rational basis for the difference, and leaves itself open to potentially expensive grievances and litigation. Thus, in practice, collective bargaining standardizes personnel policy within the school district, and, in effect, tends to combine all the schools in the district into one large multiplant "firm."

A final environmental factor is teacher licensing. Traditional public schools must hire licensed teachers. Private schools, particularly at the secondary level, routinely hire uncertified teachers. Charter schools fall somewhere in between: Many states permit them to hire uncertified teachers. This permits private and charter schools to recruit from a much larger pool of candidates in filling teaching positions as compared to traditional public schools. Other things being equal, this should raise teacher quality.[1] The percent of teachers holding regular state teacher certification by sector is reported in Table 3.3. Ninety-three percent of teachers in traditional public schools hold regular state licenses. This contrasts with 71% in charter schools and 58% in private schools (slightly lower in nonreligious private schools).[2]

---

[1] This assumes, of course, that school administrators are actually seeking out the best teaching candidates and have good information about teacher quality. Traditional economic rationales for licensing (e.g., Shapiro, 1986) based on asymmetric information do not seem applicable to teaching. Unlike other professions, teachers do not sell their services directly to the public; rather, they are hired by experienced education professionals (principals, superintendents) who are themselves licensed. For further discussion of this point, see Ballou and Podgursky (1999).

[2] In Table 3.3 and subsequent tables, we report results for all private school teachers and for private school teachers in nonreligious regular schools. By "regular," we exclude schools that have a special program emphasis such as special education or education for handicapped students, Montessori, military, etc. Our goal is to identify schools providing educational services similar to those provided by traditional public schools. Because the SASS sample size is so much smaller for these nonreligious regular private schools, the standard errors are considerably higher than for the other groups.

TABLE 3.3
Percent of Teachers Holding Regular State Certification in Traditional Public,
Charter, and Private Schools[a]

	Traditional public	Charter	Private	Private, nonreligious regular
Certified teachers as a percent of teaching workforce	93.0 (0.2)	70.3[b] (0.7)	58.2[b] (0.8)	52.6[b] (2.8)

Source: 1999–2000 Schools and Staffing Surveys
Notes: Standard error in parentheses.
[a] Excludes teachers holding state emergency or temporary state licenses.
[b] Difference between charter/private and traditional public school significant at 0.01 level of significance.

TABLE 3.4
Percent of Teachers Certified in Charter Schools With Certification Waivers

Certification requirement	Not used	Used but not required	Required	Total
Waived	11.5	65.3	23.3	100.0
Not waived	3.8	26.3	69.9	100.0

Source: 1999–2000 Schools and Staffing Surveys

Of course, the lower percent certified in charter and private schools may reflect supply rather than demand factors. One could surmise that charter and private schools wish to hire certified teachers but they do not apply. In the case of charter schools, however, these data suggest otherwise. Administrators in the SASS charter school survey were asked a series of questions about state regulations from which they were waived. ("Does your school's charter include waivers or exemptions from the following state or district policies?") They were also asked about various hiring criteria used by the school (e.g., full standard state certification, graduation from a state-approved teacher education program).

Table 3.4 reports results from a cross-tabulation of these two questions. We split our sample of charter schools into two groups: schools that had the flexibility to hire noncertified teachers and schools that did not. Schools for which the certification requirement was waived were much less likely to use certification as a condition for hiring. Of these schools, 65% used certification as a criterion to consider for hiring, but only 23% actually required it. This suggests that while teacher certification is seen as a valuable attribute by charter school administrators, so are other teacher characteristics. School administrators are willing to "trade off" certification for other desirable attributes.

These tabulations are consistent with open-ended survey questions asked in Ballou and Podgursky (2001). Respondents were asked to comment on "the most important ways that teacher recruitment and hiring differed from traditional public schools in your area." In states where it was permitted, the most common difference noted by charter school respondents was their ability to hire noncertified teachers. One respondent captured the spirit of many with his succinct reply: "Certification is not the gatekeeper."

LEVEL AND STRUCTURE OF COMPENSATION

In the previous section, we hypothesized that a more competitive environment combined with a smaller firm size and greater flexibility would lead to greater differences in compensation policies between traditional public and private or charter schools. At the broadest level, one might compare the use of salary schedules in the three sectors. In Table 3.5 we find that 96% of public school districts (accounting for virtually 100% of

TABLE 3.5
Teacher Salary Schedules and Incentive Pay

	Traditional public (%)	Charter (%)	Private (%)	Private, nonreligious regular (%)
Is there a salary schedule for teachers in this school?	96.3 (0.29)	62.2[a] (0.72)	65.9[a] (1.24)	45.1[a] (5.60)
Does this school currently use pay incentives such as cash bonuses, salary increases, or different steps on the salary schedule to reward:				
NBPTS certification?	8.3 (0.37)	11.0[a] (0.43)	9.6 (0.88)	14.8 (5.5)
Excellence in teaching?	5.5 (0.35)	35.7[a] (0.65)	21.5[a] (0.93)	42.9[a] (5.5)
Completion of in-service professional development?	26.4 (0.70)	20.5[a] (0.56)	18.7[a] (0.88)	26.0 (5.67)
Recruit or retain teachers in fields of shortage?	10.4 (0.464)	14.9[a] (0.54)	7.9[a] (0.61)	15.0[a] (3.40)

Source: 1999–2000 Schools and Staffing Surveys
Note: Standard error in parentheses.
[a] Difference between charter/private and traditional public school significant at 0.01 level of significance.

teachers) report that the district has a salary schedule for teachers. In contrast, only 62% of charter and 66% of private schools report using a salary schedule to set teacher pay.

What other factors, then, determine pay in charter and private schools? In SASS, school administrators were asked a series of questions about incentive pay: "Does the district (school) use any pay incentives such as cash bonuses, salary increases, or different steps on the salary schedule to [reward x]?" Responses to these questions are reported in rows 2–6 of the table. The question that most closely corresponds to traditional merit pay is "excellence." In that case, only 6% of traditional public school administrators responded in the affirmative. The rates for charter (36%) and private (22%) schools were much higher. Charter and nonreligious private schools were also more likely to pay bonuses to recruit or retain teachers in shortage fields.

While private and charter schools seem less inclined to use salary schedules and somewhat more inclined to use incentive pay, on the face of it most seem to have pay systems similar to those in public schools. However, this overlooks a very important source of pay flexibility in private and charter schools. In the latter, pay is set at the school level, whereas in traditional public schools, the pay is set district wide. This means that dozens or, in larger school districts, hundreds of schools are locked into a single salary schedule. For example, the New York City school district has 1,206 schools, LA Unified has 660, Chicago has 602, and Miami–Dade County has 356. In each of these cases all teachers in the district are covered by a single district-wide salary schedule.

Unfortunately, the sampling design in SASS limits our ability to analyze the dispersion of teacher pay within metropolitan labor markets or within districts. For a better appreciation of these sources of pay variation, we examine data for charter and traditional public schools in the Kansas City area. (Similar private school data are not available.) Missouri's charter school law is unusual in that it only permits charter schools in the two largest school districts: St. Louis and Kansas City. The Kansas City (KC) case is interesting because the penetration rate of charters is very high.[1] In fall 2002, there were 17 charter schools in operation with a total enrollment of roughly 6,700 students, or 19% of the total public school enrollment. This high penetration rate makes it reasonable to talk about a charter school sector in this local labor market.

Table 3.6 presents data on public school teacher pay in the KC charter sector and the surrounding labor market for public school teachers. Our dependent variable is regular-term teacher pay for full-time teach-

---

[1] A recent study by Ziebarth (2006) estimated the 2005–2006 Kansas City penetration rate at 20%, giving it a tie for fourth place in U.S. metro areas, behind New Orleans, Dayton, Ohio, Washington, DC, and tied with Pontiac, Michigan, and Youngtown, Ohio.

TABLE 3.6

Variation in Teacher Pay: Kansas City Area, Regular Term, Full-Time Teachers, 2002–2003

	Charter schools	All Jackson County (12 school districts)	Kansas City, MO, school district
Average salary	$34,918	$41,466	$41,748
Average public school teaching experience	8.0 years	13.3 years	14.1 years
Residual variation in pay[a] root MSE	$6,703	$4,716	$5,534
R^2	.292	.762	.699
N teachers	314	7,018	2,278
ANOVA			
Variation between schools			
All teachers	33.9%	5.1%	6.7%
Public experience 10 years or less	45.5%	22.4%	11.5%
N schools	17	118	72

Source: Missouri Department of Elementary and Secondary Education, Core Data Files.

[a] Root MSE and R^2 from following regression: RTPAY = b0 + b1 E + b2 E2 + b3 E3 + b4 MA+, where RTPAY is regular-term teacher pay, E is years of public school teaching experience, and MA+ is a dummy variable indicating whether the teacher had an MA degree or higher.

ers.[1] We present data on the KC school district and all school districts in the county. Average pay in the charter schools ($34,918) is lower, but this reflects in part the lower average level of teacher seniority. Our interest, however, is in the dispersion of teacher pay. The third and fourth rows of the table report the R^2 and mean squared error (MSE) from a regression of regular-term teacher pay on a cubic in experience and an indicator variable for whether the teacher holds an MA degree. These statistics clearly indicate that education and experience explain much less of the dispersion in teacher pay in the charter sector. However, the lower R^2 may be due to the fact that there is less variation in experience (and fewer MAs) in the sector. More striking is the higher MSE. In spite of the lower average pay in the charter sector, the MSE is significantly higher. Thus, pay is considerably more variable in the charter school sector, in ways not explained by teacher experience or graduate degrees.

---

[1] All pay and school data are from administrative data files maintained by the Missouri Department of Elementary and Secondary Education.

How much of this dispersion is within versus between schools? The bottom rows in the table provide a simple ANOVA decomposition of pay in the charter and traditional sectors. In the traditional public schools, interschool variation accounts for only 5–7% of the total variation in pay. By contrast, in the charter sector, interschool variation accounts for 34% of total variation. If we restrict this comparison to teachers with relatively low seniority (less than 10 years), the charter–noncharter differences narrow, but the same pattern holds. Interschool differences in average pay account for 46% of total variation in charters, as compared to just 22% in the KC district and only 12% in the county.

While we should be cautious about generalizing to other teacher labor markets, these comparisons suggest that there is a larger unexplained dispersion of teacher pay in the charter school sector. In fact, Ballou (2001) reports similar findings in comparisons of teacher pay in public and private schools. Thus, even if teachers within a charter school are paid entirely off rigid salary schedules, these data suggest that there is considerable variation in pay between schools, which may permit pay at the school level to adjust to market conditions. One market factor, for example, may be the level of the school. For example, Podgursky (2001) reports that in the 1993–1994 school year, starting teacher pay in private elementary schools was 12% lower than in private secondary schools. For teachers with an MA and 10 years of experience, the gap was 17%.

DISMISSALS FOR PERFORMANCE

Rigid salary schedules might not be as costly if teacher experience and graduate education were strong predictors of teacher productivity. Surveys of the education production find little support for a positive effect of teacher MA degrees, and teacher experience has little effect beyond the first few years (Hanushek & Rivkin, 2004; Rivkin, Hanushek, & Kain, 2005). Nonetheless, in principle, a seniority-based wage structure might be efficient if less effective teachers are weeded out over time. However, personnel policies in traditional public schools are not likely to produce such an effect. Teachers in traditional public school districts receive automatic contract renewal or tenure after 3–5 years on the job. After a school grants tenure, it is difficult to dismiss a teacher for poor job performance. Moreover it is not at all clear that public school districts take full advantage of the opportunity to weed out poorly performing probationary teachers. Interestingly, although there has been much discussion of this problem of poor monitoring of probationary teachers, there has been little systematic data collection. The only empirical study of which we are aware is Bridges (1992), who surveyed 141 midsize school districts in California. He found annual dismissal rates for probationary teachers of roughly 1%—hardly consistent with rigorous screening.

TABLE 3.7
Teachers Dismissed Annually for Performance

	Traditional public	Charter	Private	Private, nonreligious regular
Number with less than 3 years experience	0.831 (0.016)	0.533[a] (0.014)	0.208[a] (0.012)	.249[a] (0.043)
Number with 4 or more years experience	0.293 (0.046)	0.318 (0.014)	0.228 (0.023)	.224 (0.077)
Dismissed as a percent of the teaching workforce[b]	1.1% (0.2)	7.5%[a] (0.2)	3.7%[a] (0.3)	2.3%[a] (0.4)

Source: 1999–2000 Schools and Staffing Surveys
Note: Standard error in parentheses.
[a] Difference between charter/private and traditional public school significant at 0.01, 0.05 levels.
[b] For charter and private, percent of total teaching workforce; for traditional public, percent of FTE teacher employment in the district.

Fortunately, for the first time, the 1999–2000 SASS has included items on teacher dismissals. School or district administrators were asked about the number of teachers dismissed for poor performance over the previous year. Respondents were asked about total dismissals of teachers with 3 or fewer years' experience (typically untenured) and more than 3 years (usually tenured). These totals are reported in Table 3.7. The typical public school district dismissed just 0.9 low-experience teachers and only 0.3 high-experience teachers. The average charter school dismissed 0.5 low-experience and 0.3 high-experience teachers. The total dismissals for private schools were lower for both groups (0.2). As we saw in Figure 3.1, the teaching workforce in public school districts is far larger than for charter or private schools. Thus, the dismissal rate for traditional public school districts (i.e., dismissals as a percent of the teaching workforce) is far lower than for charter or private schools. The annual dismissal rate for all teachers in traditional public schools is just 1.1% of the teaching workforce.[1] For charter schools, the dismissal rate is 7.5% and for private schools it is 3.7%.

Of course, at the time of this survey, the vast majority of charter schools had been in existence just 1 or 2 years. One might expect higher dismissal

---

[1] Unfortunately, the SASS school survey did not ask school administrators the number of teachers with 3 or fewer or more than 3 years of seniority. Thus, we cannot compute dismissal rates for the two groups separately.

rates as part of the "shakeout" of staff involved in opening a new school. After all, in such schools virtually all the teachers are probationary. Multivariate analysis of the charter school dismissal rate finds that it tends to decline sharply with the age of the charter school and approaches the rate of private schools after several years of operation.

TEACHER QUALITY MEASURES

Ideally, one would like the personnel policies described earlier to be linked to direct measures of teacher performance as measured by student learning. Unfortunately, such data are generally not available.[1] Instead, we must make do with indirect measures of teacher quality. In our case, we will use measures of teacher academic quality. There is some evidence in the education production function literature that broad-based measures of teacher academic skill such as ACT or SAT scores, or proxies like college selectivity, are associated with greater teacher effectiveness (Ballou & Podgursky, 1997; National Research Council, 2002). In addition, education policymakers have shown a strong desire to recruit teachers with more rigorous academic backgrounds. In this spirit, we consider several measures of the broad general skills and academic training of teachers.

Table 3.8 reports estimates of linear probability models for these teacher quality measures. We estimate these models on samples of teachers from the 1999–2000 SASS. For each teacher quality measure, we estimate four models. The first has no covariates and simply amounts to a t-test comparing mean quality in charter and private schools with traditional public schools. For example, in row 1 we find the probability that a charter school teacher had an academic major was 0.095 (9.5%) higher than a teacher in a traditional public school. A similar finding holds for private schools. Adding covariates and state effects lowers the charter effect somewhat, to 6.9%, but has little effect on the private school advantage. As in the previous tables, in the next two rows we disaggregate the private school estimates to secular, regular emphasis versus all other private schools. The difference between the traditional public and secular private schools on this academic wage variable is quite substantial (15.6%).

The remaining rows in the table consider three other teacher quality measures: math or science major, and two measures of college selectivity (Barron's top 2 and top 3). In nearly all cases, private schools (particu-

---

[1] Interestingly, the limited evaluation literature on performance-based compensation for teachers finds generally positive effects on student achievement. For a survey of this literature, see Podgursky and Springer (2007). The evaluation literature on charter schools and student achievement is slender as well, with mixed findings. However, there is clear evidence that the performance of charter schools improves as they mature (Bifulco & Ladd, 2006; Sass, 2006).

TABLE 3.8
Measures of Teacher Academic Quality

Teacher characteristic	Public	Charter	Private, all	Private, nonreligious regular	Private, other	Covariates and state effects (51)[a]	N
Academic major	—	.095[b] (10.38)	.075[b] (12.42)	—	—	No	52,031
	—	.069[c] (7.20)	.072[c] (11.27)	—	—	Yes	51,762
	—	.095[b] (10.39)	—	.236[b] (14.09)	.054[b] (8.57)	No	52,031
	—	.069[b] (7.17)	—	.156[b] (9.53)	.061[b] (9.12)	Yes	51,762
Math or science major	—	.000 (1.00)	.022[c] (3.69)	—	—	No	52,031
	—	−.015 (1.47)	.008 (1.21)	—	—	Yes	51,762
	—	.000 (1.00)	—	.044[b] (3.14)	.018[b] (2.74)	No	52,031
	—	−.015 (1.47)	—	.025[d] (1.73)	.004 (.65)	Yes	51,762
Undergraduate college selectivity (top 3)	—	.162[b] (20.44)	.042[b] (8.01)	—	—	No	52,031
	—	.146[b] (16.91)	.027[b] (4.74)	—	—	Yes	51,762
	—	.162[c] (20.48)	—	.238[b] (16.33)	.017[b] (3.09)	No	52,031

TABLE 3.8 (continued)
Measures of Teacher Academic Quality

Teacher characteristic	Public	Charter	Private, all	Private, nonreligious, regular	Private, other	Covariates and state effects (51)[a]	N
	—	.145[b] (16.85)	—	.201[c] (13.76)	.004 (.71)	Yes	51,762
Undergraduate college selectivity (top 2)	—	.159[b] (20.94)	.002 (.40)	—	—	No	52,031
	—	.131[b] (15.95)	-.012[d] (2.26)	—	—	Yes	51,762
	—	.159[b] (20.96)	—	.122[b] (8.77)	-.013[b] (2.53)	No	52,031
	—	.131[b] (15.90)	—	.096[b] (6.88)	-.026[b] (4.66)	Yes	51,762

Source: 1999–2000 Schools and Staffing Surveys
Note: T-statistics in parentheses.
[a] Covariates include rural, suburban, central city indicators, secondary/combined indicator, percent minority students in the school, and 51 state/DC effects.
[b] Significant at 0.01%.
[c] Significant at 0.05.
[d] Significant at 0.10.

TABLE 3.9
Academic Measures of Teacher Quality: Kansas City, Missouri, and Jackson
County School Districts, 2002–2003

	Barron's selectivity level	
	Top 2	Top 3
Kansas City charter schools	2.1%	31.3%
Kansas City district schools	1.1%[a]	28.3%[a]
Rest of Jackson County	.6%[a]	30.4%[a]

Source: Missouri Department of Elementary and Secondary Education, Core Data and
    Teacher Certification Administrative Data files
[a] Difference between Kansas City charters and other cells significant at 1%.

larly secular, regular emphasis) and charter schools are significantly more
likely to have teachers of higher academic quality.

Table 3.9 provides a robustness check for these findings. Here we return
to our Kansas City area public schools. Unfortunately, state administrative data do not readily permit identification of a teacher's undergraduate
major. However, it is possible to code the selectivity of the teacher's undergraduate college. The results of this exercise are reported in Table 3.9.
Consistent with our finding with SASS, charter schools in the Kansas
City teacher labor market, in spite of their somewhat lower pay, seem to
be attracting teachers of higher academic quality, as measured by college
selectivity. The advantage is largest when comparing the charters to traditional public schools in the Kansas City district. However, it is interesting
to note that the charter advantage even holds when the sample is broad-
ened to suburban schools in the rest of Jackson County.

CONCLUSION

This chapter examines reasons that personnel policy and wage setting differ among traditional public, private, and charter schools and the
effects of these policies on academic measures of teacher quality. Survey
and administrative data suggest that regulatory freedom, small wage-setting units, and a competitive market environment make pay and personnel practices more market and performance based in private and charter
schools than in traditional public schools. These practices, in turn, permit
charter and private schools to recruit teachers with better academic credentials as compared to traditional public schools.

One criticism of charter schools has been that they are not particularly
innovative and, in terms of classroom practice, tend to resemble traditional public schools (e.g., American Federation of Teachers, 2002; Wells,
1998). Whether this is a correct assessment of pedagogy and curriculum,
we cannot say. However, in the area of teacher personnel policy, available

evidence suggests that there are major differences between traditional public schools and charter schools. These findings reinforce those found in our earlier survey research (Podgursky & Ballou, 2001) and in Hoxby (2002). Charter schools seem to be using the regulatory flexibility they have been granted in this area to forge vastly different policies. Our analysis finds that, in many respects, personnel policy in charter schools more closely resembles that in private schools than in traditional public schools.

REFERENCES

American Federation of Teachers. (July 2002). *Do charter schools measure up? The charter school experiment after 10 years.* Washington, DC.

Ballou, D. (2001). Pay for performance in public and private schools. *Economics of Education Review, 20,* 51–61.

Ballou, D., & Podgursky, M. (1997). *Teacher pay and teacher quality.* Kalamazoo, MI: W. E. Upjohn Institute for Employment Research.

Bifulco, R., & Ladd, H. F. (2006). The impacts of charter schools on student achievement: Evidence from North Carolina. *Education Finance and Policy, 1,* 50–90.

Black, S. (1999). Do better schools matter? Parental valuation of elementary education. *Quarterly Journal of Economics, 114,* 577–599.

Bridges, E. (1992). *The incompetent teacher: The challenge and the response.* Philadelphia, PA: Flamer Press.

Brown, C. (1990). Firm's choice of methods of pay. *Industrial and Labor Relations Review, 43,* 165S–182S.

Goldhaber, D. 2002. The mystery of good teaching. *Education Next, 2,* 50–55. http://www.educationnext.org/20021/50.html.

Goldhaber, D., Choi, H., DeArmond, M., & Player, D. (2005). *Why do so few public school districts use merit pay?* University of Washington.

Hanushek, E., & Rivkin, S. (2004). How to improve the supply of high quality teachers. *Brookings Papers on Education Policy: 2004* (pp. 7–44). Washington, DC: The Brookings Institution.

Hatry, H. P., Greiner, J. M., & Ashford, B. G. (1994). *Issues and case studies in teacher incentive pay.* Washington, DC: Urban Institute.

Hoxby, C. (2000). Does competition among public schools benefit students and taxpayers? *American Economic Review, 90,* 1209–1238.

Hoxby, C. (2002). Would school choice change the teaching profession? *Journal of Human Resources, 37,* 892–912.

Lazear, E. (2003). Teacher incentives. *Swedish Economic Policy Review, 10,* 197–213.

Lewis, H. G. (1963). *Unionism and relative wages in the United States: An empirical inquiry.* Chicago: University of Chicago Press.

National Research Council. (2002). *Testing teacher candidates: The role of licensure tests in improving teacher quality.* Washington, DC: National Academy Press.

Podgursky, M. (2001). Regulation versus markets: The case for greater flexibility in the market for public school teachers. In H. Walberg & M. Wang (Eds.), *Tomorrow's teachers* (pp. 117–148). Richmond, CA: McCutchan Publishing.

Podgursky, M., & Ballou, D. (2001). *Personnel policy in charter schools.* Washington DC: Fordham Foundation. www.edexcellence.net.

Podgursky, M., & Springer, M. (2007). Teacher performance pay: A review. *Journal of Policy Analysis and Management, 26* (4), forthcoming.

Prendergast, C. (1999). The provision of incentives in firms. *Journal of Economic Literature, 37,* 7–63.

Rivkin, S. G., Hanushek, E. A., & Kain, J. F. (2005). Teachers, schools, and academic achievement. *Econometrica, 73,* 417–458.

Sass, T. R. (2005). Charter schools and student achievement in Florida. *Education Finance and Policy, 1,* 91–122.

Shapiro, C. (1986). Investment, moral hazard, and occupational licensing. *Review of Economic Studies, 53,* 843–862.

Wells, A. S. (1998). *Beyond the rhetoric of charter school reform: A study of ten California school districts.* Los Angeles, CA: University of California at Los Angeles.

Ziebarth, T. (2006). Top 10 charter communities by market share. Washington, DC: National Alliance for Public Charter Schools (September). http://www.publiccharters.org/content/publication/detail/1420/.

APPENDIX

DATA

The 1999–2000 SASS is a representative national survey of schools, districts, principals, and teachers conducted regularly by the U.S. Department of Education's National Center for Education Statistics. It is a major source of information on public and private K–12 teachers and schools in the United States. Earlier waves of the survey were conducted in 1987–1988, 1990–1991, and 1993–1994. However, the 1999–2000 school year was the first time that SASS included a separate charter school survey.

The following are descriptive statistics on the 1999–2000 SASS:

- Traditional public schools:
  4,690 districts; 8,432 schools; 8,524 principals; 42,086 teachers
- Public charter schools:
  870 schools; 891 principals; 2,847 teachers
- Private schools:
  2,611 schools; 2,734 principals; 7,098 teachers

Section 2

Charter School Finance, Governance, and Law

PAUL E. PETERSON

Together, the following three chapters illustrate the serious political challenges still facing the charter school movement. Charter schools constitute an alternative to traditional, district-operated public schools; they operate outside the sphere of influence of school boards responsible for public schooling within a territorially defined area. Also, they compete for parents who, for the first time, have the option of sending their children to independently operated public schools. Not surprisingly, then, school boards, their employees, and organizations that represent those employees, as well as other political allies, have resisted the appearance of schooling alternatives to the traditional district school.

SHEREE SPEAKMAN, "BACK TO THE FUTURE"

Much of that opposition materialized even as the legislation establishing charter schools was being written. As is shown by Sheree T. Speakman and her colleagues in their Fordham report, from which Speakman's chapter, "Back to the Future," is largely drawn, charter schools receive less funding from public sources than traditional district schools do. Also, they appear to receive less funding than state statutes seem to require.

It has been pointed out that the Fordham data are inconsistent with those provided on charter school finance by the U.S. Department of Education in its Common Core of Data file. The Speakman chapter would be strengthened by a frank discussion of the limits of the U.S. Department of Education data-gathering system. Resting as it does on what it learns from local school districts, the system simply cannot be taken as authoritative. That situation is quite unfortunate, since the U.S. Department of Education has been a repository of key educational statistics since 1870. The time has come for that department to upgrade its information-gathering systems so that it can provide timely information to the American public on the state of its schools.

PAUL HILL AND ROBIN LAKE, "CHARTER SCHOOL GOVERNANCE"

In their chapter, Hill and Lake discuss a second burden that has been placed upon many charter schools: the requirement that they, too, report to a local school board for their school. This happens despite the fact that most charters are also responsible to an external chartering agency that has the capacity to withdraw the school's charter. Hill and Lake see little reason to have dual governing structures, which saddle school leaders with multiple responsibilities to negotiate with competing political elites. It is precisely this kind of political mediation that has so often frustrated effective education in traditional district schools, as John Chubb and Terry Moe have shown in their study of public and private schools. Hill and Lake give many good reasons for freeing charter schools from those political obligations.

Hill and Lake might have gone further by also recommending that those who hold charters be allowed to establish multiple schools under their charters. Although some states currently give this flexibility to charter schools and their authorizers, this practice has yet to become widespread. Still, it is only through the replication and multiplication of good charter schools that quality education is likely to expand.

KENNETH K. WONG AND FRANCIS SHEN, "CHARTER LAW AND CHARTER OPERATION: RE-EXAMINING THE CHARTER SCHOOL MARKETPLACE"

In their chapter, Wong and Shen focus on the personnel policies of charter schools, showing how much they can vary from one state to another. Some states allow for a good deal of movement of teachers between charter and district public schools, while others do not. Some states restrict the hiring flexibility of charter schools, while others are more permissive. It would be interesting to see what Wong and Shen would find were they to construct an index of "strong" charter personnel policies—that is, policies that are likely to produce a strong teaching force within the charter sector. What are the political factors that facilitate strong legislation giving charters the flexibility they need?

The question is all the more worth exploring now that other studies are showing that effective teachers can raise student achievement by substantial amounts, but traditional credentialing practices do little, if anything, to identify which practices are most effective. Charters are expected to have the flexibility that would enable them to create a strong teaching force, but many state provisions and practices impede that development. What are the factors that affect the political outcomes? The Wong–Shen research, as it progresses, should be able to illuminate this critical question.

4

Back to the Future
Sustaining an Equitable Public–Private Model of School Funding[1]

SHEREE T. SPEAKMAN

INTRODUCTION

This chapter summarizes the primary outcomes of a report issued in August 2005, *Charter School Funding: Inequity's Next Frontier*, by the Thomas B. Fordham Institute, Progress Analytics Institute, and Public Impact (Fordham Report). The report uses a national sample of data from 16 states, the District of Columbia, and 27 cities to examine annual funding differences between charter schools and traditional public schools. It concludes that, compared to traditional public schools, charter schools are significantly underfunded.

After documenting the state- and city-specific annual revenue shortfalls, this chapter goes on to discuss state funding policies that sustain these disparities, including statutory and legal considerations. When charter school laws were created in 40 states and the District of Columbia, many state legislatures funded charters as dependent on their host public school district. The effect has been that most charter schools today are

[1] The author wishes to thank Chester Finn and Eric Osberg from the Thomas B. Fordham Institute, and Bryan Hassell from Public Impact for working and writing in close partnership to steward "Charter School Funding: Inequity's Next Frontier" to completion. The heavy lifting of the state analysis, reporting, and reliability were completed by the extraordinary efforts of Larry D. Maloney, Aspire Consulting, and Michelle Goddard Terrell and Meagan Batdorff of Public Impact.

treated as secondary to traditional public schools in resource distribution and service support.

Additionally, they endure the criticism of the public sector. Charter schools are often accused of inhabiting the best of both worlds—benefiting from private, independent management while receiving public funding. In the popular press, their performance is frequently questioned for falling short. In fact, the reverse is true. They tend to suffer both the pressures of being private and independent, and the problems created by poor funding from public sources. Reliable studies show that, as learning institutions, they are holding their own when compared to traditional public schools.

This chapter makes the case that, if public charter schools are expected to perform at the same level as traditional public schools, they should be granted the freedoms of private leadership and educational entrepreneurship, and the public benefits of full and adequate funding and facilities for all children. The chapter concludes with company, industry, and national efforts to improve productivity and thus learning outcomes in public schools around the world.[1]

In this context, the chapter reaches four major conclusions. First, charter funding disparities are a matter of course and not of exception. Second, equity and adequacy provisions and fiscal support (including a range of court decisions like *Serrano* in California, *Rodriguez* in Texas, and the *Campaign for Fiscal Equity* in New York) would apply, if tested legally, to charter school entities. This would guarantee them parity with the local and state funds traditional public schools receive since charter schools are similar in legal structure and in accountabilities. Third, each independently founded and organized charter school must be consistently defined in state statutes as a local education authority (LEA)—an independent unit district with one school, having the rights and resources provided to traditional public schools. Finally, the real issue for charter and district schools is both parity *and* productivity because one without the other puts learning at risk.

If we fail to address these issues, charters will continue to be small, underfunded, poorly housed recipients of inadequately prepared students who are transferring out of the local public schools but cannot afford a private school or a move to the suburbs, where other, perhaps better school choices await them. If we give these issues proper attention, however, we may find—judging by early yet substantive research on educational providers and school outcomes in other countries—that combining private, independent governance of public schools with public funding may be

---

[1] Further, the references present a wide body of information on school finance, with references for Professor Bruce Cooper of Fordham University. Dr. Cooper really initiated and has sustained a body of work on school site accounting since 1990 that has informed the study and analysis of school-site finance for the field. The author is deeply indebted to his generosity with knowledge and time these past 12 years.

the single best governance and operating solution to improved student learning outcomes.

FAIRY TALE NO MORE: FUNDING CHARTERS FOR THE REAL WORLD

Each nation has a wonderful storytelling tradition, with a unique variety of fairy tales that horrify, delight, and provide moral lessons to young and old alike. In America, funding for charter schools reads like one of our fairy tales. In 1991, at the beginning of the movement, committed teachers and families were enticed into school leadership by the false promise of public funding without regulatory strings in exchange for improving the school model and learning outcomes of traditional public schools, particularly urban public schools. Many years later, the truth about charter schools' success and hardship and the associated impact of unequal funding reads like the scariest part of the tale. It is time to write the denouement, with ideas that can improve the ability of charter schools to enhance learning for children.

Evidence abounds about the need for new thinking when it comes to charter school funding. The Fordham Report revealed, after its detailed examination of 2002–2003 federal, state, local, and facility revenues data, that charter schools were underfunded by a weighted student average of $1,801 when compared to similarly weighted state per-pupil funding for districts. A complementary analysis of charter and district funding in 27 urban cities produced an even greater disparity: a charter weighted funding shortfall of $2,256, or 23.5%.

The expenditure data used were a state-by-state and city-by-city disaggregation of the federal, state, local, and other funding streams distributed annually to traditional pubic and charter schools. The study used school enrollment at the state and city levels to weight the funding disparities. In 2002–2003, only one state, Minnesota, and one city, Albuquerque, New Mexico, had charter schools that received higher per-pupil dollars than their comparable district schools. The results were eye-opening and representative: These states enrolled 582,133 of the nation's 1 million charter school students counted in the 2002–2003 school year.

The body of the report offers a national summary of the trends and implications for charter schools and recommends specific efforts by which state and local policymakers can remedy or significantly diminish the identifiable funding shortfalls. Further, for policymakers and local charter advocates, the report presents a detailed analysis and discussion of financial and policy information for each state and the District of Columbia.

The tables and figures in this chapter should be read as a supplement to the report itself. This analysis does not revisit the secondary issues or conclusions in the report, or comment on any findings in the individual state reports. Instead, it connects the reality of a double-digit funding shortfall to legal, policy, and productivity issues that could sharply

improve the access, quality, and breadth of learning for children in charter schools.

State Comparisons

Data-gathering for the states took on the characteristics of a game of
tug-of-war. Researchers for the study would meet, set the data standards,
and refine and redefine the methodology to standardize the vagaries of the
data already gathered. Then, the team would begin again, calling states
to request additional data, question specifics, or ask why the traditional
public and charter school revenue and demographic data for 2002–2003
had not been posted as of the spring of 2005. Many of the individuals
contacted in the state departments of education were forthcoming. However, in one-on-one discussions, it became apparent that charter data are
treated like the Cinderella of the school finance world at both state and
federal levels.

Researchers examined many data sets of traditional public and charter
school demographics and finance for comparability, depth, and reliability.
After evaluating the available options, including data from the National
Center for Education Statistics' Common Core of Data, school finance data
from the U.S. Census Bureau, and data collected and collated by individual state agencies, the researchers selected state agencies as the source
of financial, demographic, and capital information. The team decided
to focus on revenues received rather than expenditures made so that it
could evaluate how federal and state policy funds traditional public and
charter schools. Even when using revenues, 5 states of the 16—California,
Georgia, Ohio, South Carolina, and Wisconsin—did not publicly report
or respond to repeated requests for revenue information. Their statewide
calculations were extrapolated from large data sets of school spending
and demographics.[1]

Funding disparities for charter schools were pervasive in every state
studied, with only two exceptions. Other than these, as Table 4.1 shows,
the charter school per-pupil funding gap ranged from 4.8 to 39.5% lower
than for students in comparable traditional public schools.

Tables 4.1 and 4.2 both reflect a ranking of results. Disparities were
divided using descriptions of "severe," "large," "moderate," and "approach-
ing parity." All of the "severe" percentage disparities identified exceeded
23 percentage points. The highest state charter funding percentage shortfall was 39.5%, or $3,453 per student, in South Carolina. Reporting these
figures at the school rather than per-pupil level would have shown South
Carolina with an aggregate dollar shortfall of $863,250 for a charter school
with 250 students.

---

[1] Detailed text and endnotes on these reporting and data analysis issues are available in the chapter on each state included in the study.

TABLE 4.1
State Disparities Between Charter and Traditional Public School Funding,
2002–2003

Gap	State	District PPR ($)	Charter PPR ($)	Variance ($)	% Variance
Approaching parity	Minnesota	10,056	10,302	245	2.4
	New Mexico	9,020	8,589	(430)	–4.8
Moderate	North Carolina	7,465	7,051	(414)	–5.5
	Florida	7,831	6,936	(896)	–11.4
	Michigan	9,199	8,031	(1,169)	–12.7
	Texas	8,456	7,300	(1,155)	–13.7
Large	Colorado	10,270	8,363	(1,908)	–18.6
	Arizona	8,503	6,771	(1,732)	–20.4
	New York	13,291	10,548	(2,743)	–20.6
	Washington, D.C.	16,117	12,565	(3,552)	–22.0
	Ilinois	8,801	6,779	(2,023)	–23.0
Severe	Missouri	12,640	9,003	(3,638)	–28.8
	Wisconsin (est.)[a]	10,283	7,250	(3,034)	–29.5
	Georgia (est.)[a]	7,406	5,125	(2,281)	–30.8
	Ohio (est.)[a]	8,193	5,629	(2,564)	–31.3
	California (est.)[a]	7,058	4,835	(2,223)	–31.5
	South Carolina (est.)[a]	8,743	5,289	(3,453)	–39.5
State average[b]		8,504	6,704	(1,801)	–21.7

[a] In five states, we were unable to obtain statewide data on charter and/or district revenues. In those states, we used data from large districts as a proxy.
[b] Weighted by charter enrollment.

For all states and the District of Columbia, the $1,801 funding short-fall would have reduced by $450,250 the annual revenues every charter school received with a student enrollment of 250. While the primary reasons for the shortfalls are examined, in total and within each state, student demographic differences are not the cause. The available data on free or reduced-price lunch, percentage of students eligible for Title I, and the percentage of students by grade level were examined to draw this conclusion. Charter schools in this study overall could not be accused of enrolling students who might cost less to educate than district schools.

Each state differs as to how its respective legal, policy, and political circumstances affect the funding of its K–12 schools. The differences are the result of a negotiated set of discussions and documents codified in state statutes. These statutes detail comprehensive information on which schools, programs, and specific students are allowed to be funded and which revenue streams can fund them. School funding is about both eligibility and funding source at the same time. Contemplating changes to existing laws is a nontrivial exercise, in terms of both effort expended and political capital used.

As part of the Fordham Report, Larry Maloney of Aspire Consulting contributed his evaluation of the fiscal components of the New York State Education Code, cross-referenced to the finance elements defined in the *New York State Aid Handbook* for FY2003 (Maloney, 2005). Maloney's work was designed to determine which of the New York Education Code components received funding in the 2002–2003 school year. An additional consideration was whether the New York state code required funding for each line-item program to be provided to districts, services support centers, charter schools, nonpublic schools, or any combination of these four entities.

Maloney's (2005) review shows a mind-boggling array of both funded and unfunded revenue streams. It reveals charters' limited access to revenue and program funds. In New York, these discrepancies seem to be a simple case of statutory neglect, with the state purposefully failing to update statutes to allow the charter segment of public schools to have equitable access. A close inspection of the statute describing eligibility for each of these revenue streams shows that the overwhelming majority is available only to traditional public schools within districts. Few of these same annual revenue dollars specified in the New York State Education Code are made available to charter schools. The annual priority of lawmakers committed to charter equity should be that of aligning equal access to revenue and program funds for charter and traditional public schools.

City Comparisons

After completing the state level work, researchers focused primarily on large cities. This perspective was useful not only to compare state-specific funding disparities, but also to determine the location of inequity from city to city. Table 4.2 shows that the average per-pupil charter funding shortfall in large cities—$2,256, or 23.5%—was larger than the disparity identified in the state analysis. More remarkably, many of the individual cities experienced higher absolute percentage disparities than existed statewide. The highest shortfall was 40.4%, or $3,369 per student, in San Diego, California. There, the annual charter school shortfall for the same size student body would have been $842,250. Valid comparisons of the gaps between statewide and district figures meant that charter schools were worse off, in percentage terms, in 12 of the 16 districts.

This extreme funding problem in urban schools is a double whammy as urban charter school start-ups are the most difficult owing to the expense differentials that plague these areas. The facilities are difficult to find and

TABLE 4.2
City Disparities Between Charter and Traditional Public School Funding,
2002–2003

Gap	District	District PPR ($)	Charter PPR ($)	Variance ($)	% Variance
Approaching parity	Albuquerque, NM	7,745	8,511	766	9.9
	St. Paul, MN	11,876	10,800	(1,076)	–9.1
Moderate	Denver, CO	9,954	8,755	(1,199)	–12.0
	New York City, NY	12,505	10,881	(1,624)	–13.0
	Dallas, TX	8,300	7,125	(1,174)	–14.2
Large	Detroit, MI	9,899	8,395	(1,504)	–15.2
	Minneapolis, MN	13,701	11,575	(2,127)	–15.5
	Houston, TX	7,724	6,382	(1,341)	–17.4
	Broward Co., FL	7,669	6,273	(1,396)	–18.2
	Miami–Dade, FL	7,971	6,465	(1,506)	–18.9
	Fulton Co., GA	11,748	9,325	(2,423)	–20.6
	Washington, D.C.	16,117	12,565	(3,552)	–22.0
	Buffalo, NY	13,197	10,211	(2,986)	–22.6
	Chicago, IL	8,907	6,847	(2,060)	–23.1
Severe	Maricopa Co., AZ	8,743	6,389	(2,354)	–26.9
	Colorado Springs, CO	8,401	6,100	(2,301)	–27.4
	St. Louis, MO	12,531	9,035	(3,495)	–27.9
	Cleveland, OH	10,732	7,704	(3,028)	–28.2
	Los Angeles, CA	7,960	5,653	(2,307)	–29.0
	Milwaukee, WI	11,267	7,944	(3,323)	–29.5
	Wake Co., NC	9,237	6,510	(2,727)	–29.5
	Kansas City, MO	12,795	8,990	(3,806)	–29.7
	Albany, NY	15,226	10,235	(4,991)	–32.8
	Dayton, OH	11,498	7,614	(3,884)	–33.8
	Atlanta, GA	12,766	7,949	(4,818)	–37.7
	Greenville, SC	8,477	5,126	(3,351)	–39.5
	San Diego, CA	8,333	4,964	(3,369)	–40.4
District average[a]		9,604	7,348	(2,256)	–23.5

[a] Weighted by charter enrollment.

costly to bring to a high standard by opening day. Much of the available
space is shared with other institutions and tends to be inadequate for anything but the short term. On an operating basis, research has shown that

small schools are more expensive to operate than larger ones. To compensate, charter school operators soldier on in real estate or philanthropic circles—or both—making the best on behalf of their kids. But the short-term efforts of hero-like leaders are not a sustainable substitute for equity.

FUNDING INEQUITIES: WHY THEY HAPPEN

The methodology section of the Fordham Report discusses in general how the federal, local, state, and facilities funds were used to calculate funding gaps between charter and district schools, state to state. Even though aggregate shortfalls were reported in each state and city except Minnesota and Albuquerque, respectively, the reasons for state shortfalls were not the same. Using federal, state, local, and facility funding, there were significant differences among states in the categories of funding included or not in the state's methodology for funding charter schools. Further, individual states differed significantly in the definition of line-item funds made available to charter schools. Extensive discussion with state education department or revenue officials was required to decipher annual charter funding, making it almost certain that most charter leaders without a lot of administrative support would not be able to understand how to obtain their annual full funding allotments

The Policy–Practice Divide

Table 4.3 presents funding norms in the following ways for federal, state, local, and facility dollars:

- Row 1 in each section asks, "Did charter schools have access to funds *as codified in state statute?*"
- Row 2 asks, "Did charter schools have access to funds *in practice?*"

This comparison, from row to row of the data, shows a clear visual pattern from theoretical access to dollars in statute to little access to dollars in practice. Almost all states have funding statutes that protect access to charter funding. However, most states dilute the various funding mechanisms in myriad ways documented in each state report. Thus, as the table shows, between statute and practice, charter funding erodes.

A secondary test of the revenue data and funding parity was conducted by calculating the percentage of charter school enrollment in each state. This calculation was used to determine if charters were getting their proportionate share of each of the four funding streams. This result (see row 3) showed that charter schools in 2002–2003 were not getting close to their fair share in most states. No state offered local or facility dollars in proportion

TABLE 4.3
Charter Schools' Access to Federal, State, Local, and Facilities Funding by State, 2002–2003

	Findings	AZ	CA	CO	DC	FL	GA	IL	MI	MN	MO	NC	NM	NY	OH	SC	TX	WI
										States								
Federal Funding	Charters have access to federal funds according to state statutes (yes = Y; no = N)[a]	Y	Y	Y	Y	Y	Y	Y	Y	Y	Y	Y	Y	Y	Y	Y	Y	N
	Charters have full access to federal funds in practice (yes = Y; partial = P; not available = N/A)	Y	P	Y	Y	P	P	P	Y	Y	P	P	Y	P	P	P	Y	N/A
	Percentage of federal revenue equals percentage of total enrollment for charter schools (yes = Y; no = N; not available = N/A)	N	N/A	N	N	N	N/A	N	Y	Y	N	N	Y	Y	N/A	N/A	Y	N/A
State Funding	Charters have access to state funds according to state statutes (yes = Y)	Y	Y	Y	Y	Y	Y	Y	Y	Y	Y	Y	Y	Y	Y	Y	Y	Y
	Charters have full access to state funds in practice (yes = Y; partial = P)	Y	P	Y	Y	Y	P	P	P	Y	Y	P	Y	P	Y	P	P	P
	Percentage of state revenue equals percentage of total enrollment for charter schools (yes = Y; no = N; not available = N/A)	Y	N/A	Y	N	Y	N/A	N	Y	Y	Y	Y	Y	N	N/A	N/A	Y	N/A
Local Funding	Charters have access to local funds according to state statutes (yes = Y; no = N; not available = N/A)	N	Y	Y	N/A	Y	Y	Y	N	Y	Y	Y	N	N	N	Y	N	N
	Charters have full access to local funds in practice (partial = P; no = n; not available = N/A)	N	P	P	N/A	P	P	P	P	P	P	P	N	P	N	P	N	N/A

TABLE 4.3 (continued)

Charter Schools' Access to Federal, State, Local, and Facilities Funding by State, 2002–2003

	Findings	States																
		AZ	CA	CO	DC	FL	GA	IL	MI	MN	MO	NC	NM	NY	OH	SC	TX	WI
	Percentage of local revenue equals percentage of total enrollment for charter schools (yes = Y; no = N; not available = N/A)	N	N/A	N	N/A	N	N/A	N	N	N	N	N	N	N	N/A	N/A	N	N/A
Facilities Funding	Charters have access to facilities funds according to state statutes (yes = Y; no = N)	Y	Y	Y	Y	Y	Y	N	N	Y	N	N	N	N	N	N	N	N
	Charters have full access to facilities funds in practice (partial = P; no = N)	N	N	P	P	P	P	N	N	P	N	N	N	N	N	N	N	N
	Percentage of facilities revenue equals percentage of total enrollment for charter schools (no = N; not available = N/A)	N	N/A	N	N	N	N/A	N	N	N	N	N	N	N	N/A	N/A	N	N
	Funding is fair and equitable?	No	No	No	No	No	No	No	No	No	No	No	No	No	No	No	No	No

a For this finding, "N" could indicate that the statute is silent or that it denies access.

to enrollment and many states did not provide even state or federal dollars in proportion to enrollment. Only Colorado, the District of Columbia, Florida, Georgia, and Minnesota provided at least partial access to all four revenue sources.

After considerable discussion of the 2002–2003 data and debate, moving from state statute to school revenues received, the study concluded that in no state, including the District of Columbia, was funding fair or equitable. The research team took its time sorting out this reality. Rarely were researchers told that the statutory access did not translate into revenues received. But the results were re-examined closely once the team understood that what was said in phone interviews did not match what was experienced in the schools.

The Problem of Local Funding

Table 4.3 is summarized in Table 4.4, which shows the degree to which each of the 16 states and the District of Columbia offer charters access to federal, state, local, and facilities revenues. No state provided full access to either local or facilities funds as shown under the column heading "full access."

These two funding streams are closely linked because, in most of these states, local revenues and borrowing authority are aligned to local taxing jurisdictions. Taxing jurisdictions are the authorities that can issue long-term bonds to raise capital for new facilities and extensive building improvements. Thus, if a city or state has restricted a charter's access to local revenues, charters likely will be doubly affected.

When it comes to funding shortfalls, the study concludes that "lack of access to local funding is the primary driver of funding disparities between district and charter schools" (Maloney, 2005, p. 13). This is illustrated in Table 4.5. The study identifies two reasons for the disparities. First, states that attempt to replace local funding restrictions on charters with state-funded dollars often fall short. Certain states intentionally exempt charter schools from local funding, with the stated intention to fund them through state-distributed dollars. But in a surprising number

TABLE 4.4
Number of States Providing Access to Specific Revenue Categories

Type of funding	Full access	Partial access	No access	Not applicable
Federal	7	9	0	1
State	9	8	0	0
Local	0	11	4	2
Facilities	0	5	12	0

TABLE 4.5
Proportion of Nonfederal Funds for Public Education Derived From Local Sources
by State, 2002–2003

State	Local share of funding (%)
New Mexico	15.2
Minnesota	21.5
North Carolina	29.5
Michigan	31.4
Arizona	45.4
New York	51.0
Florida	51.2
Colorado	53.9
Texas	54.6
Missouri	61.1
Illinois	63.9

Source: National Center for Education Statistics
Note: Table excludes states for which we were not able to obtain statewide data on charter
         school revenues.

of cases, a dollar shorted at the local level was not exchanged for a dollar provided at the state level, making the outcomes inequitable even with the best of intentions.

Second, states that do not create the legal designation of LEA for independent charter schools set up a dynamic whereby district offices control how many dollars flow to charters; in many cases, these same districts are allowed to skim dollars from the charter per-pupil support in exchange for services to be rendered. Anecdotally, charters report restrictions on services or slow response times for services requested from district providers. Most frequently, charter leaders say that per-unit charges for district services are much higher than those of independent service providers.

The research team further studied the proportionate share of total state education funding that local taxing authorities support for district schools. Certain states attempt to replace—with supplemental state revenues—local funding that is denied in all or in part to charters. Table 4.5 lists the 11 states for which statewide funding data on traditional public and charter schools were available. Five of the states have relatively low percentages of local dollars supporting public education, led by New Mexico, where local dollars support only 15.2% of the total state funding. At the other end of the spectrum, Illinois communities contribute 63.9% to total education funding.

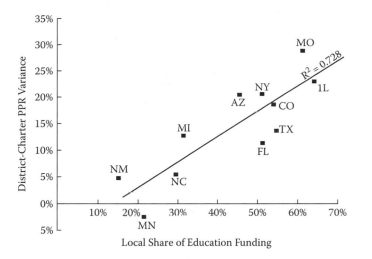

FIGURE 4.1. Relationship between local funding and charter funding shortfalls.

These data and the dollar funding data were evidence for the observation that "the more reliant a state is on local funding for education, the larger a revenue gap its charter schools are apt to encounter" (Maloney, 2005, p. 13). Figure 4.1 is a correlation analysis using each state's local percentage share of education funding and the dollar value of the per-pupil charter funding variance. The "R-squared" of the model was 0.73, a strong correlation. Our analysis made clear a pattern that suggests that model policy for charter funding needs to take into account the existing low, average, or high state contributions to school funding.

Table 4.6 shows the percentage of total dollars for traditional public schools and charter schools funded using state revenues. Twelve of the states and the District of Columbia had data sets that allowed researchers to calculate the percentages. On average, traditional public schools received 50.4% of funding from state sources and charter schools received 69.9%.[1]

In every state reported, charter schools received a higher percentage of dollars from state funds than did their comparable district schools. So, the evidence suggests that local and facility funds make up the bulk of these funding shortfalls. But the evidence also shows that states fail to compensate fully for these disparities even though they are the primary funders for charter schools.

---

[1] Illinois' stated percentage of 6.4 is not valid in comparison to the other state charter school results because most Illinois state revenue distributed is counted as "local" because it is channeled through corresponding districts.

TABLE 4.6
State Revenue as a Percentage of Total Revenue: Traditional Versus Charter
Schools, 2002–2003

State	District schools (%)	Charter schools (%)
Georgia (estimated)	N/A	N/A
South Carolina (estimated)	44.1	N/A
Ohio (estimated)	44.9	N/A
Wisconsin (estimated)	53.0	N/A
California (estimated)	58.5	N/A
Illinois	30.0	6.4
New York	46.0	50.2
North Carolina	60.3	63.2
Colorado	36.1	71.5
Florida	45.3	75.9
Texas	37.9	79.0
New Mexico	67.4	79.1
Arizona	44.3	80.2
Minnesota	72.7	80.6
Washington, D.C.	67.1	81.2
Missouri	34.4	82.4
Michigan	63.7	89.4
State average	**50.4**	**69.9**

FUNDING INEQUITIES: WHY THEY MATTER

Equal Tasks, Equal Funding

It would be easy to create excuses as to why charter schools should not have and do not need the same dollars as their traditional public school counterparts. In fact, a long list of reasons is in use every day. However, relative to student obligations, regulations, school compliance, and accountability, charter schools are tasked equally with traditional public schools in every way.

When policy analysts and researchers evaluate the accountability requirements placed upon traditional public and charter schools alike, clearly all schools are influenced by state regulations and No Child Left Behind (NCLB) at both the expense and performance levels. Since the available state and federal funding sources are demographic and/or programmatic, it follows that all charter schools enrolling children that meet the demographic or programmatic qualifiers should be made equal at the revenue end as well. Conversely, if states persist in charter funding inequity, certain obligations should be diminished to bring charters to equity in alternative ways.

The Cost of Education

Little agreement exists in America about how much money schools need to meet student learning outcomes, whether the learning standard is set at basic skills or mastery targets. The foundation aid level in most states is taken as the "amount required" to provide an adequate education. But without proof to the contrary, the foundation level of education funding is a political statement of the dollars that happen to be available as opposed to what the dollars need to be. Without equitable agreement on the annual funding amount required to educate each student in a state, the differences in funding received by public versus charter schools will continue. However, persistent funding differences between district and charter schools will allow data on funding and relative student testing outcomes to inform the debate on the efficiency of the public versus charter schools. In this regard, charter schools with comparable performance outcomes can therefore be judged as more efficient given the reduced funding received.

Table 4.7 summarizes in ascending order the traditional public and charter per-pupil revenues from the study. Apart from the calculation of variance already examined, the dollar value of funds received in absolute terms is remarkable for its range: from $4,835 per pupil estimated in California to $12,565 in Washington, DC. This demonstrates that in some locations like California, Georgia, and South Carolina, charter funding is equal to traditional public school funding. So, while charter schools in these states suffer major disparities, not all are underfunded. Charter schools in seven of the states studied received more than $8,000 per pupil for the 2002–2003 school year (Maloney, 2005, p. 19, Table 14). These states included Michigan at $8,031, Colorado at $8,363, New Mexico at $8,589, Missouri at $9,003, Minnesota at $10,302, New York at $10,548, and Washington, DC, at $12,565.

Student educational spending continues to grow annually across the nation, regardless of the rhetoric that surrounds the political landscape of school funding. As ThinkEquity Partners reports:

> Per-pupil funding (not including property expenditures) has grown, on an inflation-adjusted basis, from $6,996 per student per year in 1990 to $7,780 in 2000, an average annualized rate of 1.2 percent. The National Center for Education Statistics (NCES) projects that per-pupil funding will continue to grow at an inflation-adjusted annualized rate of 1.2 percent, through 2010. This would create an annual per pupil expenditure of $8,878 in 2010 (in constant 2002 dollars) (2005, p. 19).

TABLE 4.7
Traditional Public–Charter Schools Funding Gap, 2002–2003[a]

State	District PPR ($)	Charter PPR ($)	Variance ($)	% Variance
California (est.)	7,058	4,835	(2,223)	−31.5
Georgia (est.)	7,406	5,125	(2,281)	−30.8
South Carolina (est.)	8,743	5,289	(3,453)	−39.5
Ohio (est.)	8,193	5,629	(2,564)	−31.3
Arizona	8,503	6,771	(1,732)	−20.4
Illinois	8,801	6,779	(2,023)	−23.0
Florida	7,831	6,936	(896)	−11.4
North Carolina	7,465	7,051	(414)	−5.5
Wisconsin (est.)	10,283	7,250	(3,034)	−29.5
Texas	8,456	7,300	(1,155)	−13.7
Michigan	9,199	8,031	(1,169)	−12.7
Colorado	10,270	8,363	(1,908)	−18.6
New Mexico	9,020	8,589	(430)	−4.8
Missouri	12,640	9,003	(3,638)	−28.8
Minnesota	10,056	10,302	245	2.4
New York	13,291	10,548	(2,743)	−20.6
Washington, D.C.	16,117	12,565	(3,552)	−22.0

Note: In California, Georgia, Ohio, South Carolina, and Wisconsin, we were unable to obtain statewide data on both charter and district revenues. In those states, we used reliable data sets from large districts as a proxy. Using the district data on per-pupil spending in traditional and charter schools, we extrapolated these results to statewide average PPR. Full details on this procedure appear in the methodology section and the state chapters.

[a] States ranked by charter per-pupil revenue.

Comparable to the 2002–2003 year for the Fordham Report, NCES reported for the nation as a whole that the current expenditures per student (using membership) in school year 2002–2003 was $8,044. Using the 27 cities and associated district spending, the Fordham Report showed an average traditional public per-pupil revenue of $9,604 and average charter per-pupil revenue of $7,438.[1] This difference in reported spending—$9,604 versus $8,044—is primarily due to methodology; the Fordham Report used

---

[1] Fordham Report, p. 2. For this point of comparison, the district and charter per pupil revenue figures from Table 4.2 are used for comparability since the study noted that statewide data for charter and/or district revenues in five states were unavailable and derived from large district data, as noted in the methodology section of the study.

revenues versus expenditures and skewed the dollar reported levels of revenues by selecting only large cities. These large city districts (including their associated charter schools) have a higher average level of receipts (and expenditures) than would the average of all districts in the United States.

Policy Changes for Charter Funding Equity

Charter school growth is certain to continue in many states in the years ahead. If policymakers are intent on equalizing access to all funds and closing dollar discrepancies between district and charter schools, there are easy remedies for study and implementation.

Table 4.8 reports LEA status, which is both a descriptor and a legal designation in almost all states. Only four jurisdictions—the District of Columbia, Michigan, Minnesota, and Ohio—consistently treated charter schools as equal to traditional public schools. When a school is not designated as an LEA, its revenues are funneled to an LEA—typically a district office but sometimes a county office of education. These agencies, while allowed certain withholdings, then pass through the funding to charter

TABLE 4.8
LEA Status of Charter Schools by State

State	Are charter schools treated as LEAs?
Arizona	P
California	P
Colorado	P
District of Columbia	Y
Florida	N
Georgia	N
Illinois	N
Michigan	Y
Minnesota	Y
Missouri	N
New Mexico	N
New York	P
North Carolina	P
Ohio	Y
South Carolina	N
Texas	P
Wisconsin	P

Notes: Y = yes; P = partial; N = no.

schools for school operations. When money is tracked through multiple agencies, many states are allowed to retain some dollars for administrative handling charges. Given the significant shortfall charter schools already bear, demanding administrative fees is like adding insult to injury.

Data presented in Tables 4.4–4.7 serve as examples to policymakers intent on reducing charter funding disparities. A first step is to review state statute and funding guidelines to ensure that charters are defined to allow access to and receipt of dollars equal to traditional public schools with comparable student demographics. Second, a statutory definition that gives charter schools LEA status must be codified. Third, states must adjust their funding formulae to make the state replace dollar-for-dollar charter funding lost because of local funding restrictions and overhead.

As a last policy measure, open enrollment laws help support the most effective charter laws. Charter laws and school choice provisions in many states are embedded in open enrollment laws, allowing children to enroll in charters from multiple attendance zones, or from other communities or counties. There has been a steady increase in students attending schools of choice, as seen in Figure 4.2 (Fordham Report, p. 15). The percentage of children whose parents enrolled them in chosen public schools increased between 1993 and 2003. The percentage of students in grades 1–12 attending a chosen public school increased from 11 to 15% between 1993 and 2003, while the percentage attending assigned public schools decreased from 80 to 74% .

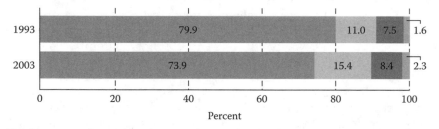

■ Public, assigned   ■ Public, chosen   ■ Private, church-related   ■ Private, not church-related

Type of school	1993	2003	Percentage point difference	Percent change
Public, assigned	79.9	73.9	−6.0	−7.5
Public, chosen	11.0	15.4	4.4	40.0
Private, church-related	7.5	8.4	0.9	12.0
Private, not church-related	1.6	2.3	0.8	50.0

FIGURE 4.2 Differences in parental choice. Percentage of student distribution grades 1–12 by school type 1992–1993 and 2002–2003. (From "The Condition of Education in 2006 in Brief," U.S. Department of Education National Center for Education Statitistcs. 2006.)

State policymakers who need examples of effective policy for open enrollment can study the evolution of Minnesota's law, the first charter law in the nation (Schroeder, 2004). Authorized in 1988, the law established an interdistrict open enrollment program allowing students to choose schools and programs run outside traditional district control. Currently, about 21.5% of the state's public school students are enrolled in these schools and programs (Schroeder, p. 23). While this law had its weaknesses, its greatest benefit was the freedom it gave schools—from districts and from state laws and regulations. "Each school was to be treated as an independent local education agency (LEA), hiring its own teachers and having total control of its funds, which were to flow directly from the state" (Schroeder, p. 26).

Policy changes are the insurance supporting fair funding for charter schools, in proportion and access. Statutory updates of the education funding provision to include charter schools, LEA status for charters, expanding access to each type of funding available in the state to charters, and open enrollment laws are critical elements of laws that seek to remedy charter funding inequities.

SCHOOL PRODUCTIVITY: WHY IT IS IMPORTANT

Discussions about funding parities for charter schools are best accompanied by an equal emphasis on tracking the efficient and effective use of resources. When charter school achievement is indistinguishable from that of district schools, charters appear to use resources far more effectively, since they produce a comparable level of student outcomes for less cost. This chapter began with a review of charter funding disparities and made policy recommendations for fixing perceived inequities. School productivity (doing more with less) is an important next step in the discussion. With the accelerating availability of more robust revenue and expenditure data, the practice of indexing school funding to student outcomes can now begin in a more valid way.

Productivity is the critical debate remaining in this country. Even today, the subject of educational productivity is supported by a modest level of valid research, for which there is little professional consensus. *The Scientific Basis of Educational Productivity*, by Rena Subotnik and Herbert Walberg (August 2006), is the right study for its time. The knowledge, understanding, and more than ample cross-references to other related works provide the roadmap from which a committed stakeholder in education can make important policy decisions to support improved learning.

Beginning the Productivity Discussion

In February 2004, the State of Virginia Department of Education hosted NCES's 17th Annual MIS Conference. The audience comprised nearly 500 professionals from the 50 state departments of education, as well as staff and leadership from NCES, the conference's annual sponsor. NCLB was in full swing, adequate yearly progress was the topic of scorn, and subgroup discussions were shrouded in data-driven despair.

During her speech, "From Data to Knowledge—Know IT, Use IT," the keynote speaker quoted a *New York Times* article by Dr. Hal R. Varian, dean of the School of Information Management and Systems at UC Berkeley, who has written extensively on the role of technology in industry and productivity improvements:

> Recently two Brookings Institution economists, Jack E. Triplett and Barry P. Bosworth, have been investigating productivity growth in the services industry and have reached a surprising conclusion: most of the post-1996 growth in productivity has come in services ... They found that from 1995 to 2001, labor productivity in services grew at a 2.6 percent rate, outpacing the 2.3 percent rate for goods-producing sectors. Furthermore, this phenomenon was widespread: 24 out of the 29 service industries they studied exhibited growth in labor productivity after 1995, and 17 experienced accelerated growth. Interestingly enough, the service industries where overall productivity did not grow were hotels, health, education, and entertainment. These are all examples where customers tend to perceive that more labor is associated with higher quality, as Mr. Baumol had originally suggested (Varian, 2004).

With this quote as background, the speaker asked the conference audience of 500, "How many of you believe that the discussion has begun about how best to improve productivity in American education?" Eight people raised their hands.

In a theoretical world, the effort directed toward school- and classroom-based productivity ought to precede the request for additional money since money will buy the time, resources, or institutional facilities that will serve students. But backing into the question, we must know what we need to ask and where to invest resources for better outcomes. Economists Triplett and Bosworth have developed an important framework and body of evidence for ongoing application.

The Challenge of Measuring Education Output

Triplett and Bosworth coauthored *Productivity in the U.S. Services Sector—New Sources of Economic Growth* in 2004. Over the course of 5 years, they ran 15 workshops for specific industry classifications at the Brookings Institution, studying productivity outcomes, multifactor productivity, the role of information technology (IT) in services productivity (and not), and data metrics and quality.

The work involved many participants, but chief among them were representatives from the Bureau of Economic Analysis, U.S. Department of Commerce, and the Bureau of Labor Statistics within the U.S. Department of Labor. These agencies were critical to the workshops, scope of the study and the book itself, because Triplett and Bosworth used many of their statistics to raise questions and draw conclusions.

In the end, the research centered on 29 services sector industries, using the original two-digit standard industrial classification (SIC) system (which has since been updated). Education was one of the services sector industries studied, although using the SIC system meant that elementary and secondary education were classified together with higher education.

The book is remarkable for its breadth and depth, including its detailed focus on whether and how information technology contributed to accelerated productivity in each sector studied. The work supporting the book was initiated at an important time because, for nearly all of the twentieth century, the expanding industrial or capital goods sectors had driven U.S. economic growth. A primary reason for the study was the hypothesis that the "services-producing industries have emerged as the dominant engines of U.S. economic growth" (Triplett & Bosworth, 2004, p. 1).

Triplett and Bosworth devote a chapter to education, providing statistics for both elementary and secondary education on the one hand, and higher education on the other. They comment that their own research and feedback of participants in the April 2000 education workshop point to the insufficiency of education data and the lack of agreement on how to define outcomes and quality:

> Educational productivity failed to distinguish itself between 1995 and 2002. Specifically, education and five other categories of the 29 services industries studied had negative growth in output per worker. Education's negative growth was calculated at −0.95 percent (SIC Code 82). The other five were construction at −1.12 percent (SIC Code[s] 15–17); local and interurban passenger transit at −0.61 percent (SIC Code 41); insurance carriers at −1.66 percent (SIC Code 63); hotels and other lodging places at −0.57 percent (SIC Code 70); and amusement and recreation services at −0.41 percent (SIC Code 79).[1]

The authors expressed concern about the calculations for education owing to problems with the validity of the available data. While some of the imprecision was the result of a decision to use SIC classification segments, the combination of higher education and elementary and secondary education allowed the productivity measure of lifetime earnings to be used as an output measure. However, even with these flaws, a rea-

---

[1] Triplett and Bosworth, 2004, Appendix A, Table A-1: Sources of Change in Output per Worker, 1987–2001, Least Squares Trend Growth, p. 342.

sonable observer of elementary and secondary education, to say nothing of its researchers and economists, would agree that K–12 education does not profess productivity on many measures whatsoever. It is not that we cannot observe or document many of the metrics in the industry. It boils down to a battle of wills between stakeholder ideology and the perceived immeasurable lifetime value of student learning.

Close examination of the production function factors Triplett and Bosworth researched will show how IT investments drove productivity in the service industries studied. Elementary and secondary education make substandard investments in technology. We can gauge the validity of this comment using vendor-generated industry statistics, the IT investment metrics for education presented in Triplett and Bosworth's book, or both. The sheer scale of education makes it imperative that we address its negative productivity growth using information technology for instructional and noninstructional purposes in a more sophisticated manner than our traditional school systems do today. While the research and solutions are outside the scope of this chapter, information technology investment is the single best opportunity to improve the outputs resulting from student learning.

So, with this background, how do we best examine contributors to the problem of negative productivity in our schools: using the time contributed by a child in a lifetime of learning, the time contributed by adults to student learning, and the resource allocation practices of private schools, who might have a lower administrative burden and increased standards of performance? A few more facts provide a definition and understanding.

The Matter of Time on Task

In an editorial, Chester E. Finn, Jr. (2006), recalled a surprising and alarming calculation he had made some 15 years ago.

> An American child with perfect attendance at a conventional public school from (full day) kindergarten through high school would, upon reaching his/her 18th birthday, have spent just 9 percent of his/her hours on earth under the school's roof—and 91 percent elsewhere. That ratio still amazes me but you can calculate it for yourself. The numerator consists of 13 (years of school) × 180 (days per year) × 6 (hours per day). The denominator consists of 18 (years alive) × 365 (days per year) × 24 (hours per day). I didn't even take account of Leap Year. To be sure, the 91 percent includes sleeping time, but even when you make that adjustment you find that non-school time exceeds school time by a multiple of four or five. "What," I asked in 1991, "is the leverage of the 9 percent, especially in situations where the other 91 percent works at cross-purposes? How much should we expect schools to accomplish?"

In other words, what do we do with less modest student time on task and reduced adult output while challenged to increase student outcomes and understanding?

The Example of New York City Public Schools

Shortly after taking office in 1994, Mayor Rudy Giuliani asked the firm of Coopers & Lybrand L.L.P. to complete a comprehensive study of the city's 1993–1994 Board of Education budget and spending. The budget totaled $8.05 billion for the 1,016,728 students enrolled. Heading the work for the mayor was Herman Badillo, special counsel for fiscal oversight of education, a long-time Giuliani colleague and four-time U.S. congressman.

Since the political forces were highly visible in this "debate" about spending, many of the work's complexities were lost. But its primary value is seen in the presentation of resource allocation patterns indexed into teacher time as defined by the 1993–1994 New York City (NYC) labor contract. Table 4.9 disaggregates the spending data from the top down, effectively from administration to schools and from dollars to percentages. The work analyzes how money gets allocated across a district office and system of schools.

The analysis of the budget starts in frame 1, showing the per-pupil dollars associated with 100% of spending in the 1993–1994 budget year. The model of analysis was set up to disaggregate all data into one of three

TABLE 4.9
Systemic Cost Structure by Frame—New York Public Schools, 1993–1994 Budget

		Percent	Per pupil ($)	Dollars (in billions)
Frame 1: aggregation	Systemic	100.0	7,918	8.050
Frame 2: structural	School site	81.4	6,442	6.660
Frame 3: functional	Instructional	47.8	3,787	3.850
Frame 4: by type	High schools	39.5	3,126	0.951
Frame 5: program	Regular/special	29.2	2,308	2.176
Frame 6: contractual teacher time	6/8 Time	21.9		1.763
	5/8 Time	18.2		1.465

Source: Cooper, B. and Speakman, S. T. (1996). In H. J. Walberg (Ed.), *Advances in educational productivity* (Vol. 6, pp. 1–14). Greenwich, CT: JAI Press, Inc.

categories—by function, by program, and by level—defined to mean dollars under central office or school control. Thus, schools in the 1993–1994 budget year received 81.4% or $6,442 of all dollars available to the system. Of that, direct classroom instruction—primarily teacher salary and benefit costs—received $3,787, or 47.8%.

Frame 6 presents the dollar and percent calculations that deconstruct the time-on-task effects of the teachers' contract on costs. For teachers instructing six eighths of a day, as do the elementary and a portion of the middle-school teachers, the percent of elementary teacher costs actually dedicated to instruction is 21.9%, or $1,734 per pupil out of the system average of $7,918 per pupil (Randall, Cooper, Speakman, & Rosenfield, 1998). High school (and some middle school) teachers are contracted to teach for five eighths of the day and thus their equivalent percentage of the total budget is 18.2%.

Many people say that the magic of education takes place in the interactions between adult and child. We see that the time and dollars of that magic are confined to the 9% of time children spend in school through their 18th birthday. Their elementary teacher, a child's springboard to learning, is instructing six eighths of a day at a dollar equivalent of 21.9% of total spending in the 1993–1994 school year, using NYC as our basis of reference. Table 4.9 shows us that, contractually, this is not enough time or money for magic.

This section on the complexity of school productivity began with the issue of resource allocation and then referenced work by Triplett and Bosworth on the growth, positive or negative, in service industries using multifactor productivity analysis and information technology investments as inputs. It cited Finn's analysis of the time a child spends in school and finished with the relatively small proportion of contractual dollars invested in the classroom, using as an example the salary and benefits of NYC teachers in 1993–1994. All of this analysis shows that none of these issues examined on its individual merits appears to be the magic bullet that can improve the productivity of American schools. Conversely, all of these factors combined make it appear that U.S. education uses a model of time and expenditures that is unworkable if we want the next generation of American children to have a crack at mastery learning.

Productivity and Foreign Student Outcomes

In October 2005, Harvard University's John F. Kennedy School of Government held a conference entitled Mobilizing the Private Sector for Public Education. Many papers were presented on education issues affecting countries around the world. Specific examples were provided, notably in Latin America and India, of efforts to educate children in partnership with private industry and faith-based enterprises. One of the papers presented was "Public–Private Partnerships in Schooling: Cross Country

Evidence on their Effectiveness in Providing Cognitive Skills" by Ludger WÖβmann of the University of Munich.

WÖβmann's research was conducted using outcomes generated in the administration of Organization for Economic Cooperation and Development's Program for International Student Assessment (PISA) and Trends in International Mathematics and Science Study (TIMMSS) as the baseline. His goal was to determine the effectiveness of the education offered through both independent and government-sponsored school providers. His findings show the outcome differences between publicly operated and publicly funded schools. That is, publicly operated schools are negatively associated with student performance in math, reading, and science; conversely, publicly funded schools are positively associated with student performance in those subjects. This indicates that the most effective school systems are those that receive financing from the state and operation oversight from the private sector.

This raises many questions, of course, about which WÖβmann (2005) writes that "aspects of efficiency, equity and noncognitive skills have been left for future research." At the conference, much debate about WÖβmann's findings ensued. Some comments were directed at the nature of and differences in the PISA and TIMMS tests themselves. The remainder of the comments fit into a wide number of categories. But the central theme was that, from every alternative combination of independent and government schools and private or public funding, privately governed schools use public money most successfully to produce higher cognitive outcomes.

CONCLUSION

WÖβmann's (2005) research gives us a welcome clue that the 15-year U.S. charter governance experiment itself could be the backbone of the most successful outcomes-driven solution yet. Independently governed but publicly financed schools might be the best solution *at scale* to deliver improvements in cognitive skills for students that the traditional system has failed.

Understanding school finance norms for charter schools is preparation for the next push to expand high-quality charter schools. We have now valid student outcomes data for charter schools and a good baseline of school finance data for charter school revenues and disparities. With successful policy amendments and careful accountabilities, committed policymakers could scale up and improve fiscal equity for charters, while holding fast on accountability requirements. By focusing more efforts on bringing independent charter schools up to parity in public funding, we might draw more high-quality start-up schools into urban cities and start to sustain the more productive learning outcomes America covets for its children. Specific changes can be made to improve equity of funding access for charter schools, including line-item funding earmarks for charters, policy enhancements for LEA designation for charters, and state supplementary funding for local dollars lost.

Many more opportunities exist to improve productivity within our current system of schools, including increased investment in information technology that might substitute human capital for information technology; supplementary instructional resources delivered at scale for less; more teacher and/or student time embedded in the traditional system; and more high-quality curriculum, pedagogical strategies, and organizational structures copied from nontraditional educational systems and providers. We can implement these productivity improvements today, setting aside for the moment the political will it takes to change something that serves as a paycheck for a visible percentage of the U.S. working population.

REFERENCES

Cooper, B., & Speakman, S. (1996). Introduction: Twenty-five years later, Serrano goes to school. In H. J. Walberg (Ed.), *Advances in educational productivity* (Vol. 6, pp. 1–14). Greenwich, CT: JAI Press, Inc.

Finn, C. E. (August 2006). March of the pessimists: From Checker's desk. In The Thomas B. Fordham Foundation's *The Education Gadfly*, August 17, 2006, Vol. 6, No. 31, available at http://www.edexcellence.net/foundation/gadfly/issue.cfm?id=253#2962.

Maloney, L. (2005). *State education code and the New York State funding formula. Analysis for the Thomas B. Fordham Institute weighted per pupil funding formula meeting.* Unpublished.

National Center for Education Statistics. (2005). *Revenues and expenditures for public elementary and secondary education: School year 2002–03.*

Randall, E., Cooper, B., Speakman, S., & Rosenfield, D. (1998). In W. Hartman & W. L. Boyd (Eds.), *The new politics of information in education. Resource allocations and productivity in education: Theory and practice* (pp. 57–81). Westport, CT: Greenwood Publishing Group.

Roza, M., & Hill, P. (2004). How within-district spending inequities help some schools to fail. In D. Ravitch (Ed.), Brookings papers on education policy (pp. 201–218). Washington, DC: The Brookings Institution.

Schroeder, J. (2004). *Ripples of innovation: Charter schooling in Minnesota, the nation's first charter school state* (pp. 23–31). Washington, DC: The Progressive Policy Institute.

Speakman, S., Hassel, B., & Finn, C. (2005). *Charter school funding: Inequity's next frontier.* Washington, DC: Thomas B. Fordham Institute.

ThinkEquity Partners Institutional Research (2005). New rules, new schools, new market. In ThinkEquity Partners LLC: Industry Outlook 2005, K–12 market growth drivers, p. 19.

Triplett, J., & Bosworth B. (2004). *Productivity in the U.S. services sector—New sources of economic growth.* Washington, DC: Brookings Institution Press.

Varian, H. (2004). Economic scene; information technology may have been what cured low service-sector productivity." *The New York Times,* February 12, 2004.

WÖβmann, L. (2005). *Public–private partnerships in schooling: Cross-country evidence on their effectiveness in providing cognitive skills.* Prepared for the conference "Mobilizing the Private Sector for Public Education." Cosponsored by the World Bank. Kennedy School of Government, Ifo Institute for Economic Research at the University of Munich.

5

Charter School Governance

PAUL T. HILL AND ROBIN J. LAKE

INTRODUCTION

The debate over whether charter schools offer different or more effective instruction will go on for some time, but there is no question that chartering is an innovation in public school governance. This is the case both for charter schools' external governance—their relationships with government agencies that determine whether they may admit students and receive public funds—and for their internal governance, which must be involved in making decisions about school policies and programs. Most people are aware of charter schools' external governance arrangements. Unlike district-run public schools, they are not subject to detailed direction from district-wide central offices and school boards, and can hire staff, use time and money, and deliver instruction in ways that (at least in theory) fit the needs of their staff, parents, and students. Charter schools need designated public authorities to authorize their existence and transfer public funds for student tuition. But they are not subject to frequent changes in policy and can expect that, barring management disasters or terrible student performance, they can operate for set periods (3–5 years) with relatively little interference.

This external governance arrangement is the one stressed by school reformers who thought district and board oversight created inefficiencies and stifled innovation. They hoped to give charter schools greater freedom of action but wanted to make sure bad charter schools were closed or forced, through threat of closure, to change.

The rationale for charter schools' internal governance arrangements is much less clear. In all but a handful of states (Arizona, Colorado, Michigan, Virginia, and Wisconsin), charter schools must operate as nonprofit entities (Green & Mead, 2006). Though state laws do not mandate that nonprofit boards be constructed in a certain way, nonprofit boards in general must be broadly representative of the public interest. All nonprofit boards of charter schools also hire and fire staff, and in some cases boards have fired the principals who founded the school and assembled the board in the first place. Though some boards have played constructive roles in the lives of their schools, many have become sources of instability and disruption.

As we will discuss later, charter school law drafters probably did not require these internal governance arrangements in order to make charter schools better providers of instruction. Framers of the laws understood that governance arrangements can prevent some bad outcomes, like abuse or neglect of some group, but they cannot create organizational effectiveness. However, as it has turned out, the prescribed internal governance effects often work against school effectiveness while doing little to prevent abuses or protect stakeholders.

Some early supporters hoped charter schools would operate like private firms in a competitive market for students. But the internal governance arrangements prescribed by state law limited school heads' freedom of action and created a good deal of internal friction by demanding too much of board members and hamstringing school managers. The requirement that every charter school be governed by a nonprofit board has created internal stresses that take time, amplify conflicts that might otherwise be minor, and destabilize school leadership and program offerings.

In ways we will detail, charter schools' internal governance arrangements take away the freedom of actions that their external governance arrangements are supposed to promote. In this chapter we will argue that nobody had sufficiently thought through charter schools' external and internal governance arrangements before they were enacted into law, and that the key parties have still not learned to play their roles well. In the conclusion we will suggest ways that external governance—essentially, oversight by public authorities that approve and monitor charter schools—can be improved; in addition, we will address how internal governance can be simplified and strengthened so that it can become a contributor to, not a detractor from, sustained school quality.

WHAT IS GOVERNANCE AND WHY IS IT SO IMPORTANT?

Governance is the set of processes, customs, policies, laws, and institutions by which an organization is controlled. It defines the relationships among the many players who have stakes in an organization's activities and outcomes. Formal governance arrangements therefore ensure representation of key stakeholders. Governance and leadership are different. The essence of leadership is influencing the behavior of others; governance constrains leadership.

Governance is not relevant when only one person's interests are at stake or a leader needs no one's support but her own in order to take action. We do not talk about governance of sole proprietorships, in which decision making is not structured to constrain the owner or chief executive.

Governance becomes relevant when different and possibly opposed interests are at stake, or where a leader can act effectively only if others provide resources or cooperation. Even then, formal governance arrangements are not always evident: A skillful leader can maintain support through consultation and carefully balanced action. But, when gifted leadership is not available or cannot be assumed always to exist, specific arrangements for sharing power, reaching compromises, and voting are needed.

It is clear enough why state legislatures created specific external governance arrangements (i.e., sponsors or authorizers) for charter schools. Taxpayers, teachers, parents, students, and school neighbors all have different interests related to the operation of a charter school. By designating a public agency to authorize and oversee charter schools—school boards and, depending on the state, special state boards, state institutions of higher education, or major nonprofits—legislatures ensured that someone would be available to hear complaints and balance claims. Whether the exact arrangements work as intended is an empirical question, but it is clear why they exist.

The warrant for specified internal governance arrangements is less clear. As schools that must attract families and maintain functioning teacher forces, charter schools already have strong incentives to take account of the needs of those constituencies. These marketplace incentives might not be enough to ensure that a school does not exclude disadvantaged children or create nuisances in their neighborhoods, but the interests affected have a great deal of access to external authorizers.

EXTERNAL GOVERNANCE REQUIREMENTS: NECESSARY BUT UNDERDEVELOPED

Government agencies have always had a role in chartering as the parties that determined whether a group could run a school and had the power to close a school down for failure to keep the terms of its charter. But no one thought carefully about how these agencies would operate.

The emphasis was on what schools might do with their assumed new freedoms, not on how the government agency would act to define and in some ways limit those freedoms. From the perspective of groups who wanted to run and promote charter schools, the governmental role was not their problem and they preferred not to think about it. They assumed that the less government the better, especially since the vast majority of agencies designated to authorize charters were local school boards, exactly the entities that pro-charter people most distrusted and wanted to avoid.

On the other side, school board members generally opposed chartering. They had little interest in authorizing schools that would operate independently and take away money formerly controlled by the school district, yet whose performance deficiencies and parent-teacher blow-ups might still fall back into the school board's lap. School boards generally saw charter schools as something inflicted upon them by state legislators who were not their allies in the first place. Few had any interest in figuring out how to do chartering in ways that maximized the likelihood that charter schools would succeed.

A case in point is the elected Washington, DC, Public School Board, which early this year concluded that charter oversight is just too hard, and asked to be relieved of all responsibility for approving charter school applications and monitoring performance. The DC board frankly admitted that it did not know how to tell the difference between a good charter school proposal and a bad one, or how to monitor performance of existing charters. The board preferred to run a hierarchical structure of jobs and entitlements where hard judgments about performance simply did not need to be made.

Other school boards have been more politic but have taken essentially the same position. Less than one in ten of the school districts with the authority to charter schools has ever done so, and with the exception of a few districts that have embraced chartering (e.g., Los Angeles, New York, Philadelphia, Oakland, California, New Orleans, Milwaukee, Wisconsin, District of Columbia, and Chicago), the average district that has been willing to charter any schools has limited itself to one or two.

Why is chartering so hard for government? The answer is that it establishes a completely different relationship between a government agency and a school, and requires government to develop entirely new capacities. Until chartering came along, all public schools were run by school districts that owned all the buildings; hired all the employees, made all the decisions about leadership, instructional methods, and materials; and listened (or did not listen) to families' aspirations and complaints.

Chartering is a whole new approach to providing public education, analogous to Japanese manufacturers' method of producing cars by relying on a group of highly qualified independent suppliers. Government organizations other than school boards have learned to work through third parties, but it is a tough and demanding task.

One thing that is clear from the experience of private firms and government agencies that get critical work done via contracts with third parties is the need for substantial capacity within the authorizer organization.[1] Organizations using third parties to do essential work must know exactly what results they need, be able to tell the difference between a provider capable of delivering results and one that is not, be able to identify problems in provider performance early enough to intervene before bad results are inevitable, work constantly to build or identify other suppliers to keep current ones under competitive pressure, and replace providers in cases of low performance. Working through third parties requires clar-

---

[1] For a more complete development of the arguments made in this section, see Destler (2006).

ity and diligent oversight, not abdication. Agencies and firms that accomplish critical work via contracts with independent parties need to know a great deal about the work their partners are to do, and they must know how to monitor progress and identify needs for improvement, all without creating confusion about who is responsible for what.

External governance of charter schools has not been thought through thoroughly, and few authorizers have invested more than a trivial amount in building staff expertise and oversight tools. Most school districts assign charter oversight to one or two individuals or to units that are already pressed to fulfill other responsibilities. A few school districts that have embraced chartering as one of the ways they provide schools—notably Chicago and Milwaukee—have created capable oversight units. Several non-school-district agencies for which chartering is their whole mission (e.g., Central Michigan University and the Indianapolis mayor's office) have built substantial capacities. However, many authorizers still have little or no capacity. In Ohio, the recent addition of dozens of inexperienced nonprofits to the list of potential charter school authorizers has definitely lowered the average.

Authorizers that take chartering seriously are learning through trial and error, but they still have much less experience than other governmental and public and private sector entities. These include other public sector organizations that obtain key capacities through contracting (e.g., the U.S. Armed Services and the English public school system, which now provides the vast majority of its high schools via charter-like independent provider arrangements) and private companies that use third parties for many functions that traditional manufacturers performed internally. Based on case studies of oversight agencies in the United States and abroad, a study under way at the national Charter School Research Project has already distilled several potential lessons for charter authorizers:

- *Contracting and oversight require very different capacities than management of vertically integrated organizations.* The people overseeing important activities like schools must be knowledgeable about how they work and must have access to rich data. This means that contracting agencies like school authorizers must have expert staff that are numerous enough to remain knowledgeable about all the providers they oversee. This also means these agencies need good data, including leading indicators like staff turnover that can foretell performance problems before they occur. All of this requires investments in people and data that very few charter authorizers have made.
- *The best time to clarify expectations and screen out weak providers is before they are hired.* Firms and agencies that get good performance from their contractors know what performance is reasonable to expect and discourage applicants that cannot or do not want to deliver on expectations. The reason for fine initial screens is straightforward: If a

product or service is vital to the success of the authorizing organization, it cannot be entrusted to just anybody. When agencies and firms take a looser approach to source selection, hiring any provider whose proposal and capacities are remotely plausible, the result is often a disappointing performance and loss of the authorizer's legitimacy.

- *Arms-length relationships with providers are likely to have disappointing results.* Authorizers need to communicate a lot about performance expectations, and must know the provider organizations well. They must not be afraid to point out problems or threaten consequences, or to insist that changes be made when failure is imminent. Private firms in particular are comfortable helping a struggling provider but then replacing it if performance does not improve or if a better provider becomes available.

- *Contract termination decisions are not made lightly or before alternatives are in hand.* When good suppliers are scarce, authorizers must make trade-offs; they need to reward performance and abandon failed efforts, but they also need to make sure the job (in public education, providing schooling for all students) is done.

- *Authorizers must avoid being forced to choose between a bad provider and none at all.* Authorizers need to offer favorable enough terms so that capable organizations will be willing to provide the service. A government or business that establishes an uninviting or hostile environment, one that subjects providers to harsh treatment, regulatory roadblocks, and political interference, will drive away good potential partners and might not be able to find enough good organizations to do the work needed. For private firms and government agencies that depend on independent providers, the stakes are high. If any part of the authorizing and oversight process is mishandled, the company might lose money, an agency might fail to attain its mission, and service recipients might be hurt. In such high-stakes situations, authorizers need to make more than a reasonable effort to get good outcomes. The people responsible for authorizing must figure out how to do it better—and make an unshakeable case for more money, better staff, better data, or whatever else they lack—or put someone else in charge of the function.

These lessons constitute a revolution in thinking for school districts. At the same time that school boards like DC's are trying to lay down the burden of charter authorization, many others are recognizing that they must abandon traditional compliance-based modes of school oversight and focus on school performance.[1] Some, such as Chicago, Philadelphia,

---

[1] Destler discusses the special problems that school districts encounter as they charter and operate schools directly. These are particularly vexing unless, as they and Finn and Hill propose, school districts adopt common performance standards and accountability options for all schools no matter who runs them.

Denver, New York, Oakland, and the state agency responsible for most schools in New Orleans, are openly characterizing themselves as portfolio managers, running some schools directly and chartering others. No Child Left Behind is likely to drive more districts toward what British Prime Minister Tony Blair calls contingent provision, working with schools and school providers as long as they benefit children and no longer.

What might good performance oversight of charter schools look like? Finn and Hill (2006) acknowledge that there are inevitably some compliance-focused elements of oversight. They argue that the most important functions are quality- and promotion-focused oversight.

The contractual compliance functions are necessary but manifestly insufficient. A compliance-focused authorizer could overlook many opportunities to charter good schools while also allowing weak but obedient schools to obtain and keep charters. There are, moreover, examples of authorizers that take the compliance functions seriously but also promote quality schools. Central Michigan University not only demands that all charter schools file every report required by the state, but also gives schools the report formats and basic data they need to complete those documents. Taking compliance seriously does not prevent Central Michigan from promoting school quality and working proactively to find and promote promising charter providers.

Some might claim that the quality and the promotional functions are in direct conflict with the compliance function—that an authorizer cannot be both a source of assistance and a judge. Yet the Chicago school district and the DC charter board offer proof that authorizing can be both ambitious and quality focused. Both encourage promising applications via public information sessions and workshops, and both suggest ways whereby interesting applicants can gain capacities missing from their original proposals. Chicago even encourages competent charter operators to take on additional challenges, including opening more campuses. However, Chicago has also shown its willingness to close bad charter schools and withdraw a charter before a school opens if the school's finances or academic program seem near collapse. The independent DC chartering authority has been tougher on the schools it approves than the District's board of education, which has apparently granted charters to political cronies and allowed abusive situations to continue.

Constructive external governance of charter schools is complex, and it costs money. The fact that many state laws provide no funding for charter school authorizers shows how little thought was put into the external governance function.

There is now serious work under way on how to rationalize and strengthen external governance, motivated in no small part by charter school operators who have learned that an inattentive authorizer can turn unpredictable and punitive. The National Association of Charter School Authorizers (NACSA) has developed a set of "principles and standards for quality charter school authorizing" (see http://www.charterauthorizers.

org/files/nacsa/BECSA/Quality.pdf) and is working to assemble examples of thoughtful problem solving. Via conferences and publications, NACSA is also trying to convince school district leaders and other sponsors that good charter authorizing is not rocket science and that it can pay off.[1] The National Charter School Research Project is also assembling ideas from other sectors that might suggest what capacities authorizers need, how they can be developed, and what they will cost.

The conclusion of this chapter will make additional suggestions about policy changes that can strengthen the external governance of charter schools.

INTERNAL GOVERNANCE REQUIREMENTS: BURDENSOME AND UNNECESSARY

The introduction points out that it is not clear why legislatures chose to specify charter schools' internal governance arrangements. Legislatures needed to make sure there was a legal person qualified to be the second party in a contract in which an authorizer was the first party. However, a variety of legal persons would have served, including individuals, partnerships, private companies, for-profit corporations, and cooperatives, as well as nonprofit corporations. Moreover, it was not necessary for legislatures to require that a nonprofit corporation hold only one charter, as is the case in many states.

In some states legislatures simply imitated other states' charter laws. There might not have been much discussion about whether to restrict charters to nonprofits. However, in states where charter laws were intentionally drafted, legislatures had reasons for limiting charters to nonprofit boards. Three explanations are possible: (1) Some legislators who opposed charter legislation but could not block it inserted the requirement to impose costs on charter schools and reduce their chances of success; (2) the requirement was a necessary concession to gain support from moderate legislators who distrusted profit motive and feared that charter proposals were vouchers in disguise; or (3) legislators were actually trying to build community-based representation within charter schools themselves because of communitarian ideas or because they wanted to

---

[1] A sampling of recent NACSA publications includes: "Principles and Standards for Quality Charter School Authorizing," "A Reference Guide to Special Education Law for Charter School Authorizers," "Charter School Accountability Action Guide," "Charter School Accountability: A Guide to Issues and Options for Charter Authorizers," "Charter Schools and the Education of Students With Disabilities," "Charting a Clear Course: A Resource Guide for Building Successful Partnerships Between Charter Schools & School Management Organizations," "Guidelines for Ensuring the Quality of a National Design-Based Assistance Provider," and "Measuring Up: How Chicago's Charter Schools Make Their Missions Count."

buttress the external governance arrangements, which they were not sure would work as intended.[1]

The three explanations might each have a share of the truth. The first, that the nonprofit board requirement was inserted by opponents in order to burden charter schools, is consistent with charter schools' experience. However, it might also be a self-inflicted wound by charter proponents, some of whom started with romantic views about what community groups could accomplish. The nonprofit boards and "one school, one board" provisions in most states required creation of many new boards, often in communities where few adults have the expertise or the free time necessary for board membership. The sheer number of people required to fill charter boards is larger than the number of people who have direct experience in maintaining board-management relationships in productive institutions. (This is probably true of other community nonprofit organizations as well.) Charter boards must therefore include people who do not understand the limitations of board members or the need for clear delegation to management. As we shall see, these requirements have indeed handicapped charter schools and caused some to fail.

The second explanation is obvious enough from the statements of state legislators, some of whom claimed that for-profits would divert funds away from instruction and thereby cheat children and others who feared that for-profits would bring in private investment capital and could therefore compete unfairly with regular public schools and charters run by for-profits. Contradictory though these rationales are, they combined to create strong voting blocs against for-profit participation.

In many states, however, for-profits have exploited a loophole by becoming contractors to nonprofit boards—essentially working as management companies hired by a community board that holds a charter. Heads of for-profit organizations claim that this two-step agreement is inefficient and subjects them to arbitrary constraints and the vicissitudes of life with an inexperienced board.[2] But there is little evidence that for-profits have provided inferior services in the schools they run,[3] or have used their access to

---

[1] Dean Millot has suggested a fourth possibility: that legislatures wanted to make sure someone would be responsible for a charter even if the original founders died or stopped working. That motive could explain legislatures' reluctance to allow individuals to hold charters, but not their rejection of other organizational forms, such as for-profit corporations, that provide continuity.

[2] For a comprehensive review of the difficulties encountered by for-profit providers that entered contracts with nonprofit school boards, see Wilson (2006, especially pp. 183–191). See also the comments by for-profit school operators in Rainey and Harvey (2006).

[3] Some nonprofits apparently do use money in novel ways. See Hannaway and Sharkey (2004).

investment capital to run other schools out of business.[1,2] As it has worked out, the nonprofit board requirement neither excludes for-profits nor protects any of the harms expected to result from for-profit management. But it does create disadvantages for charter schools operated by for-profits.

The third explanation looks ingenious. It imitates the higher education practice of delegating the state's responsibility for overseeing private institutions to boards of regents including alumni and other distinguished citizens.[3] These boards arguably could stand in for government oversight because they represent the best elements of the community plus people who care deeply about the children served. Board members will be deeply engaged with the school and can therefore make richer judgments about school performance than can district or state bureaucrats who only look at test scores.

However, what made sense for the small number of well established private higher education institutions did not work so well for large numbers of new public schools in the same community. In retrospect, the differences between higher education and K–12 boards should have been obvious. They include the following:

- Service on college and university boards is prestigious and can attract people with significant talent, experience, and money to give. Charter school boards are much more obscure and cannot reliably attract the most experienced people.
- Existing colleges and universities have long traditions valued by faculty and alumni. Charter schools were new and largely undefined, so nonprofit boards were forced to grapple with basic mission and values questions that, for higher education institutions, were answered by history and tradition.
- Battling factions within a higher education institution are normally held in check by alumni, the president, and major donors. Charter boards, however, were new and had no revered traditions or distinguished former leaders, and thus could more readily dissolve into factional feuding.

Whatever the motive for the nonprofit boards' requirement, anyone familiar with the literature on nonprofit boards could have predicted the results.[4] Board members are difficult to recruit and have trouble finding

---

[1] Strong critics of for-profit management accuse firms of making many decisions for financial advantage but conclude that they do not offer more effective or attractive services. See Molnar (2001).

[2] Edison schools official John Chubb (2006) has shown, however, that access to investment capital has made for-profit schools more likely to replicate promising models and expand the numbers of students served.

[3] On the history of this idea in higher education, see Zumeta (2004).

[4] See, for example, Ryan, Chait, and Taylor (2003).

time to do all that the role implies. Few have experience as board members or understand the distinction between the roles of boards and management. Charter boards make it more difficult (though not impossible) for managers to take extreme unilateral actions, but they do not cause charter schools to be effective, equitable, inefficient, or stable.

Some charter schools have reached accommodations between board and management and have slowly developed board expertise. However, many other charter boards have suffered from unstable memberships and had trouble establishing boundaries between board and management.[1] Board melt-downs have destabilized many charter schools, and leadership and staff turnover due in part to conflicts with the board has been a major reason for charter school failure. Boards with little financial or legal expertise have allowed improper funding and spending.

Since nonprofit board members are often people with only short-term interests in the school, they have a powerful incentive to spend all their money on salaries and current services, and little incentive to generate surpluses that can be reinvested in technology or process improvements. Boards heavy with current parents can be a particular problem due to their greater interest in their own children than in the school as a whole, and because rapid turnover caused by graduation leads to frequent changes in board direction (National Study of Charter Schools Second Year Report, 1998, pp. 99–100).

As Stephen Wilson has shown, boards that contract with independent organizations to operate schools often hire the principal and key staff (Wilson, 2006). This can lead the staff to have mixed loyalties—to the board that hired them and to the management company that provides the school's instructional methods and is responsible for performance—that they often resolve in favor of the board. Without a loyal staff, Wilson claims, for-profit organizations cannot deliver the instructional program they were hired to provide, and ultimately cannot fulfill the contract under which they were hired.[2]

The most vivid reports about board problems emerged early in the life of the charter school movement. But in early 2006 a report on increasing the number of high-quality charter schools again cited nonprofit boards as a major problem, saying:

> Some nonprofit boards are agenda driven and wind up trying to micromanage the schools ... Many have weak governing boards; they have little capacity to oversee the school ... Most, even the nonprofits established by

[1] According to an early national survey of charter schools, 27% of new charter schools and 17% of existing ones were disrupted by internal conflicts that could be related to governance. See National Study of Charter Schools Second Year Report (1998, p. 4).

[2] Katrina Bulkley reports that independent school contractors in Philadelphia are similarly handicapped by principals' mixed loyalties. See Bulkley, Mundell, and Riffer (2004) and Bulkley, Useem, Gold, and Christman (2005).

profit-making vendors, have trouble distinguishing between the oversight function of a board and running the school. (Rainey & Harvey, 2006, p. 10)

Charter school heads interviewed for the study said that inexperienced board members are still a big problem: "It's hard to work with people who've never managed anything more than a home budget" (Rainey & Harvey, 2006, p. 11). School heads also noted that board capacities often do not change even if the school's needs evolve: "The qualities that make for a good start-up board aren't necessarily the qualities the board needs as the school grows."

For a governance mechanism that nominally represents stakeholders and could in theory have protected charter schools from instabilities caused by leadership turnover, charter school boards have not worked particularly well. Activist parents with extreme points of view tend to be over-represented on boards (as they are in PTA and other boards in public education). Because charter schools are new, they cannot benefit from the historical perspective and commitment to the institution that alumni board members of private schools often provide.

Now teacher unions are trying to take advantage of the governance vacuum many charter boards leave, by trying to unionize teachers. They argue plausibly that collective bargaining asserts teacher interests more powerfully than governing board membership can.[1]

If nonprofit boards do not provide useful forums for setting strategy and working out differences, what purpose do they serve? Some schools have assembled boards that include experts in legal, finance, personnel, real estate, and public relations issues. These resemble the boards of private companies, and are often able to help rather than impede management. However, such expert boards are rare, and there is nothing in the state laws compelling school-level boards to require them.

Some school managers can get help from their boards. Some boards can help tide schools over during staff transitions. But these desirable results are far from normal. It is hard to argue that the internal governance arrangements imposed by law help or protect anyone.

As we will suggest in the conclusion, it makes sense to permit schools to create such boards, but not to require them. It is necessary for a charter school to be a legal entity that can enter a contract with its authorizer, manage funds, and employ staff. However, in other sectors, this legal entity can take many forms—a sole proprietorship, partnership, affiliate of another organization, or a board-governed corporation. Each of those organizational forms has its own governance issues, but none is likely to be as destructive for charter schools as is the typical nonprofit board.

We fear that the internal governance arrangements imposed on charter schools have prevented what they were supposed to cause—that is,

---

[1] For a review of teacher unions' relationships with charter schools see Hill, Rainey, and Rotherham (2006).

institutional stability and mission continuity. Charter school leadership—entrepreneurial initiative, planning ahead, unification of budgetary and service strategies, on the spot problem solving, and coordination of diverse professionals—is extremely demanding. Scholars are just starting to ask what it takes to lead a charter school and how enough people with the requisite skills and motivation can be found for the thousands of new charter schools likely to open in the next few years.[1] It is clear that people trained to run traditional public schools lack many of the skills and attitudes necessary to lead charter schools effectively (Portin, DeArmond, et al., 2002). Compared to working further on how to mandate a better form of charter school governance, it makes more sense to focus on leadership requirements and supply issues, including clarifying how to rehabilitate existing public school leaders and what training and experience people from social services and business need to lead charter schools.

CONCLUSION

It is hard to see what purpose is served by requiring that every charter school have its own dedicated nonprofit board. Under the best circumstances, nonprofit boards can stabilize schools and free up school leaders to focus on instruction by supporting them on business and marketing. However, the best circumstances are rare; nonprofit boards are more likely to destabilize schools and burden school heads.

Legislatures might also have hoped that nonprofit boards would serve as proxies for public oversight, representing key constituencies within and outside schools and helping the schools avoid problems and scandals. Boards have met those expectations in some cases, but they have also become sources of problems that legislatures hoped they would help schools avoid, such as mismanagement of funds, school instability, and failure to keep promises to parents and students. Nonprofit boards do not help make charter schools more accountable to the public. As we will argue later, the only way to accomplish that aim is to strengthen the external governance arrangements by which designated government agencies approve and oversee charter schools.

Though it is appropriate for state law to allow nonprofit boards to hold charters, there is no reason for states to mandate them in every case. If other entities could hold charters—sole proprietors, partnerships, for-profit corporations, and organizations that run multiple charter schools—many schools could be run more efficiently. As Chubb (2006) has suggested, for-profits in particular could help make the charter sector more competitive, and could attract private investment that could fuel innovation.

---

[1] In *Learning on the Job*, Wilson (2006) shows how hard it is to find and keep competent charter school principals.

Despite the fact that school districts can and do contract with for-profit school management companies in most states, allowing for-profits to hold charters directly remains a controversial idea; it is unlikely that the legal requirements for nonprofit governance will disappear anytime soon. Even if they did, for-profit boards are susceptible to some of the same problems as nonprofits. For these reasons, those who care about the quality of charter schools must pay more attention to strengthening existing and future charter boards. The situation could be improved if

- More states allowed one nonprofit board to run multiple campuses in one state or city (this would reduce the number of qualified board members needed and might make serving on a charter board more attractive to strong civic leaders).
- Charter authorizers did a better job assessing the governance plans in charter applications.
- State associations and technical assistance groups helped recruit strong board members, provided high-level consultants to work with dysfunctional boards, and assigned mentors to new charter board members.

If internal governance cannot substitute for weak external governance, how then should legislatures strengthen the institutions that are supposed to authorize and oversee charter schools? We think four lines of actions are necessary.

- Invest in authorizer capacity.
- Provide reliable public funding for authorizers.
- Encourage competition among authorizers.
- Establish performance accountability for authorizers.

Invest in Authorizer Capacity

Foundation-funded charter school associations and research projects are trying to help authorizers understand the decisions they must make and access information that can support those decisions. This process will continue for some time, though ongoing work by NACSA and the National Charter School Research Center is producing results. Soon a professional consensus will emerge about the skills and information sources an authorizer needs. It is also increasingly clear that effective authorizer organizations cannot be hidden deep in school district bureaucracies, or assigned tasks unrelated to authorizing. If school districts want charter authorizing done well, they must invest in chartering offices and give them direct access to the superintendent and school board.

Provide Public Funding

Capable authorizers need money. They certainly need experienced and well-paid leaders who both understand schools and know the difference between operating a school directly and overseeing an independently run school on the basis of a contract. They also need enough staff to conduct thorough reviews of new school applications, stay in close contact with existing charter schools, intervene in schools that are experiencing trouble, run open and responsible charter termination processes, and maintain portfolios of school providers who might replace a failed school provider. These functions entail significant salary, equipment, and facilities costs; government agencies that cannot or will not pay them will not get competent authorizing. As Finn and Hill (2006) have suggested:

> [S]tates need to fund charter authorizers as they do school districts, providing a fixed minimum amount for an authorizer that oversees even one school (e.g., the equivalent of one senior staff member and a clerk plus a small facilities allowance) with additional amounts for every school overseen. NACSA will develop models for authorizer operations that can be the basis for funding. None of these is likely to cost less than $150 thousand for the smallest authorizer and $20,000 for each additional school overseen. This seems a hefty sum, but consider that under these assumptions, the New York City public schools central office would have a budget of about $22 million—a far cry from the hundreds of millions its activities cost today.

Encourage Competition Among Authorizers

Given school districts' reluctance to support charter schools and (with some important exceptions) their reluctance to build capable authorizers, it makes sense for state legislatures to give them some positive incentives in the form of competition. States could create multiple authorizers to operate in the same school district (as in Milwaukee and, under federal legislation, the District of Columbia). Alternatively, states could make statewide alternative authorizers like state colleges and universities—many of which also compete on the margins with school districts—more effective competitors simply by removing the caps on the numbers of schools they may authorize. Then, an alternative authorizer could compete with a district and in time might oversee more schools than the district. Districts, too, would face a need to become good authorizers or risk going of out business altogether.

Lifting caps can allow special-purpose authorizers to become larger and more capable. This measure alone will not create responsible authorizing. It could allow authorizers to develop large enough portfolios of schools, and to receive enough income from state fees, to make serious investments in oversight capacity.

Establish Accountability for Authorizers

Whether school districts and other authorizers fulfill their responsibilities matters to families, children, people who work in charter schools, and people who want alternatives to their existing public schools. It should also matter to the authorizers themselves. States could create standards for authorizers, including requirements for fair assessment of proposals, diligent oversight, effective intervention into struggling schools, and aggressive action to give families alternatives to low-performing schools, whether district run or charter. States could disband or create competitors for any authorizer that proves unwilling to charter any schools, or that neglects its oversight responsibilities. This could be done if all authorizers, including local school boards, were placed under revocable, results-based accountability contracts (and public transparency).[1] In effect, authorizers will also work under performance-contingent charters.

These suggestions will not solve all the problems of charter schools, but they will reduce the burdens of internal governance that charter schools must bear and focus external governance on one issue only: school performance.

REFERENCES

Bulkley, K., Mundell, L., & Riffer, M. (2004). *Contracting out schools: The first year of the Philadelphia diverse provider model.* Philadelphia, PA: Research for Action.

Bulkley, K., Useem, E., Gold, E., & Christman, J. (2005). *Blurring the boundaries: Nonsystem actors and the central role of the Philadelphia schools.* Presented at the 2005 Convention of the American Educational Research Association.

Chubb, J. (2006). Should charter schools be a cottage industry? In P. T. Hill (Ed.), *Charter schools against the odds.* Stanford, CA: Education Next Press.

Destler, K. (2006). Charter authorizing: It's a dirty job, but somebody's got to do it. In R. J. Lake & P. T. Hill (Eds.), *Hopes, fears, and reality.* Seattle, WA: National Charter School Research Project.

Finn, C. E., & Hill, P. T. (2006). Charter authorizers. In P. T. Hill (Ed.), *Charter schools against the odds.* Stanford, CA: Education Next Press.

Green, P. C., & Mead, J. F. (2006). *Charter schools and the law: Establishing new relationships.* Norwood, MA: Christopher–Gordon Publishers.

Hannaway, J., & Sharkey, N. (2004). Does profit status make a difference: Resource allocation in EMO-run and traditional public schools. *Journal of Education Finance 30*(1), 27–49.

Hill, P., Rainey, L., & Rotherham, A. (2006). *The future of charter schools and teachers' unions: Proceedings of a symposium.* Seattle, WA: National Charter School Research Project & the Progressive Policy Institute.

Lake, R. J. (2006). *Holding charter school authorizers accountable.* Seattle, WA: National Charter School Research Project.

---

[1] The first paper to address oversight and performance incentives for authorizers was recently published. See Lake (2006).

Molnar, A. (2001). Calculating the benefits and costs of for-profit public education. *Education Policy Analysis Archives, 9*(15).

National Study of Charter Schools Second Year Report (1998). U.S. Department of Education Office of Educational Research and Improvement.

Portin, B., DeArmond, M., et al. (2002). *Making sense of leading schools: A study of the school principalship.* Seattle, WA: Center on Reinventing Public Education, University of Washington.

Rainey, L., & Harvey, J. (2006). *High-quality charter schools at scale in big cities.* Seattle, WA: National Charter School Research Project.

Ryan, W. P., Chait, R. P., & Taylor, B. E. (2003). Problem boards or board problem? *The Nonprofit Quarterly, 10*(2).

Wilson, S. F. (2006). *Learning on the job: When business takes on public schools.* Cambridge, MA: Harvard University Press.

Zumeta, W. (2004). Accountability and the private sector: State and federal perspectives. In J. Burke (Ed.), *Achieving accountability in higher education: Balancing public, academic, and market demands.* Los Angeles, CA: Jossey–Bass.

6

Charter Law and Charter Operation
Re-examining the Charter School Marketplace[1]

KENNETH K. WONG AND FRANCIS X. SHEN

INTRODUCTION

Charter school laws are often characterized as either enabling or constraining the creation and operation of charter schools. In making these characterizations, researchers have primarily compared variation across, rather than within, states. The Center for Education Reform (CER), for instance, has ranked states relative to each other by grading their laws and then labeling each state as "weak" or "strong." In this chapter, we build on this and other works that have sought to identify the elements in the state policy environment that facilitate or hinder charter schools.

This chapter provides a new outlook on the charter school policy environment, however, by examining more closely the layers of legal provisions in states' charter laws. Consistent with the first wave of charter school literature, which found charter school politics to be complicated and often working at cross-purposes, we provide evidence of legislative and regulatory "layering" (Wong, 1999). That is, since charter law involves administrative and legislative rule-making, we see layering in terms of legislative provisions and interpretations working at cross-purposes. The politics of layering is created by multiple institutions, each operating with

---

[1] The authors acknowledge Caroline Watral of Vanderbilt University for her research assistance on charter legislation and the policy database.

its own political logics, political allies, and policy functions. The implication is that policy layering tends to undermine an "ideal marketplace" for charter schools. Thus, charter schools are the creation of competing political influences and multiple (or seemingly fragmented) institutional decisions.

The chapter examines two key questions. First, what are the political and policy conditions that facilitate a system that supports charter reform and growth? Second, what are the likely consequences of this political and legal variation on charter school operation and enrollment? Drawing on a newly created charter legislation and policy database, we use a political science state politics framework to perform preliminary empirical analysis on both of these questions. Our results suggest that state-level political and economic variables do not easily explain the formation of charter school policy.

This chapter is organized into four sections. First, we review the existing literature on charter law and charter outcomes, finding the need for a revised and updated charter law database. Second, we describe our work in coding legislative provisions to fill this empirical need. We discuss both our broad strategy and our first steps in coding provisions related to the traditional and reform goals of teachers' unions. Third, we show how this database can be employed in traditional state political empirical analysis. We find that a state's union bargaining rights are significantly related to the provisions likely to be of material concern for teachers, but not to provisions less central to material benefits. Finally, we synthesize our findings and propose a future research agenda for studying charter school laws and their influence on charter school creation and operation. We argue that evaluation of the charter school market should recognize the internal workings of state laws.

LITERATURE ON CHARTER SCHOOL LAWS AND CHARTER OUTCOMES

In the first wave of charter school research, as states were still forming their charter laws, much attention was given to the legislation's political foundations. Bryan Hassel's (1999) detailed study made it clear that legislative compromise was central to the formation of charter school law. From caps on the number of charter schools to limitations on those whom charters could contract with, Hassel found that the state political environment significantly affected the type of law the legislature passed. Compromise in the statehouse led to charter laws that would sometimes work at cross-purposes. Research conducted by Amy Stuart Wells in the 1990s confirmed this picture of charter school politics as confused and contested (Wells, Grutzik, Carnochan, Slayton, & Vasudeva, 1999).

At the same time, a series of studies and reports sought to map out the details of emerging charter school legislation. Much of this early research identified complexity and variation across states in charter legislation.[1] It also found variation within a single state's charter law between permissive provisions and restrictive regulations.[2]

Subsequent to this early work, several groups have maintained updated information about charter school legal provisions. The Education Commission of the States (ECS) provides an online charter school law resource allowing users to compare charter school provisions across states.[3] The U.S. Charter Schools Website also provides state-by-state profiles of charter school laws.[4] In addition, recent studies have identified charter legal provisions relevant to specific policy questions. Wohlstetter, Malloy, Smith, and Hentschke (2004), for instance, looked at provisions related to cross-sector alliances.

Beyond efforts simply to catalog charter law provisions, independent studies have attempted to rank the laws. After its founding in 1993, the CER began grading state charter school laws, and then labeling each state accordingly. Those with As or Bs have "strong to medium-strength" laws. Those with Cs or lower have "weak laws."[5] To be sure, the CER is not the only group to employ a grading strategy. Others have done so using different criteria (Wohlstetter et al., 2004). The American Federation of Teachers (1996) and also Palmer and Gau (2003) have produced independent charter school grading studies that rank charter school laws in terms of their authorization provisions.[6]

Current Scholarship Focused on Charter School Outcomes

The old line of research on charter legislation has gradually given way to studies that focus on the outcomes of charter schools. This is important

---

[1] For example, see Molnar (1996), Vanourek (1997), U.S. General Accounting Office (1995), and U.S. Department of Education (1998).

[2] See, for example, Mauhs-Pugh (1995).

[3] The Education Commission of the States (ECS) is a nonpartisan, nonprofit organization. See: http://www.ecs.org/ecsmain.asp?page=/html/statesTerritories/state_map.htm.

[4] The site was originally funded by the U.S. Department of Education, but is now independent. See: http://www.uscharterschools.org/pub/uscs_docs/sp/index.htm.

[5] As of July 2006, CER categorizes the states in this way: charter school states that have strong to medium strength laws (grades A–B): Arizona, California, Colorado, Delaware, Florida, Georgia, Indiana, Massachusetts, Michigan, Minnesota, Missouri, New Jersey, New Mexico, New York, North Carolina, Ohio, Oklahoma, Oregon, Pennsylvania, Washington, DC, Wisconsin. Charter school states that have weak laws (grades C–F): Alaska, Arkansas, Connecticut, Hawaii, Idaho, Illinois, Iowa, Kansas, Louisiana, Maryland, Mississippi, Nevada, New Hampshire, Rhode Island, South Carolina, Tennessee, Texas, Utah, Virginia, Wyoming.

[6] American Federation of Teachers. (1996). Charter school laws: Do they measure up? Palmer, L.B., and Gau, R. (2003). Charter school authorizing: Are states making the grade? Thomas B. Fordham Institute.

because it means that, absent a redirection of research, the literature on charter school legislation is likely to be even more heavily influenced by legal summaries such as the CER's. We believe that several trends in this literature make continued analysis of legal frameworks important.

First, a consensus seems to be building that charter school evaluation is not about whether charter schools are working, but rather about what makes some charters work and others falter. Buddin and Zimmer (2005) echo many when they conclude that "it may be very difficult to develop universal conclusions about charter schools nationally as charter school performance varies from state to state, charter type to charter type, and even charter school to charter school." Hassel's (2005) synthesis of findings supports this conclusion, and even pro-charter school advocate Chester Finn acknowledges that charter schools are "astoundingly diverse. Some are the highest-performing schools in town. Others are total messes." In trying to explain divergent results, charter school legislation may be an important factor to consider. This may be particularly true in explaining variation *within* states along urban/rural, economic, or racial dimensions.

Analysis of charter school legislation is all the more important given that—and here we identify another trend in the current literature—the evidence is mixed on whether charter school performance is raising student achievement. State legislatures still do not know what to make of all the research. In a *State Legislatures* 2005 brief entitled "No Answers to Charter School Questions," policymakers were warned:

> With so many studies revealing different results, it may be too soon to compare charter schools to traditional ones. Since charter laws vary widely across the country, specific state studies that use new methodologies and the age old test of time may be the best hope for reliable data.[1]

For questions of charters and student achievement, analysis of charter school legislation may help provide answers.

Recognizing the Political Economy of the Charter School Market

Researchers with an eye to state politics have sought to introduce a new brand of charter law scholarship that goes beyond the CER's weak law–strong law approach. Witte, Shober, and Manna (2003) argue that although the CER framework was "useful to earlier research," it "provides a limited description and judgment of the values underlying these laws." So they examine charter law provisions and develop five dimensions to

---

[1] *State Legislatures* is a magazine that "informs legislators, staff, lobbyists and the interested public about state actions and innovations in public policy issues before they reach the mainstream." Accessed June 2005 in http://www.ncsl. org/programs/pubs/slmag/SLoverview.htm.

focus on: application and authorization, local oversight, fiscal support, employees, and accountability. Witte et al. improve upon the CER methodology by more explicitly grounding their analysis in prior literature, and in performing statistical analysis to identify clustered provisions. In doing so, they find that state laws include some internal checks and balances: More flexibility in running charter schools is positively correlated with increased accountability requirements.

Another line of research has sought to determine the political factors behind the formation and makeup of charter school legislation. Using a state politics framework, Henig, Holyoke, Moser, Brown, and Lacireno-Paquet (2002); Wong and Shen (2002, 2004); and Shen (2003) have all empirically investigated the link between charter law adoption and state political climate. Wong and Shen (2002) use event history analysis to examine the factors that explain why certain states adopted charter school laws before others. Shen (2003) uses the same approach, but tries to avoid some methodological pitfalls by introducing Bayesian model averaging to the study. Henig et al. (2002) also examine state-level political dynamics, but place their focus on how charter school policies have changed over time. In light of the difficulty of explaining overall strength or adoption of entire charter school laws, Wong and Shen (2004) make an effort to look at the component provisions of charter school laws (Yearbook of the American Education Finance Association, 2004). Taken together, the findings suggest that Republican Party strength is positively associated with charter law strength, but that there is also tremendous variation within charter legislation. Politics intersects charter school laws, but not uniformly across all provisions.

CREATING AN UPDATED CHARTER LEGISLATION AND POLICY DATABASE

The legal provision analysis that abounded in the first wave of charter school research has tailed off since 2000. To provide researchers and policymakers with an accurate picture of current charter legislation, we have begun a project to code important charter provisions. In selecting which provisions to focus on, we use Jennings et al. (1998) as a starting point. Their careful analysis of legislation in the 33 states that had charter laws in 1998 includes seven categories for provisions: charter development, school status, fiscal, students, staffing and labor relations, instruction, and accountability. We lay out four slightly broader categories to examine:

- authorizing process (e.g., single or multiple venues of gaining authorization such as university as authorizer), application procedures, caps on enrollment or number of schools
- personnel policy flexibility (e.g., constraints on labor negotiation)
- operation

- accountability, standards, and expectations (e.g., whether charters are subject to the same No Child Left Behind testing and reporting requirements or whether they are given more flexibility with time frame and types of assessments)

We are coding provisions in each of the 40 states with charter laws, as well as the District of Columbia.[1] At present, however, we report only findings related to personnel policy and teachers' unions. In each case we follow three principles. First, we perform cross-state analysis of legislation and build, from the microfoundations of the law, its individual provisions. Second, we use methods of legal statutory interpretation to carefully evaluate statutory silence in charter laws. Third, we recognize the complexity of charter school legislation and its interplay with state and federal law.

The data source for the state legislation analyzed here is the Lexis–Nexis database of state codes. For each question on charter school personnel policy, we identify the specific legal authority that addresses the question.[2] We then code 0–1 based on our careful interpretation of the state code, including relevant authorities such as opinions of the state attorney general.

Initial Focus on Personnel Policy

As a first step in our study, we examine the dimensions of legislation that will likely be subject to political bargaining due to the interests of teachers' unions. Both the National Education Association (NEA) and the AFT have made explicit statements about what they want to see in charter school laws. At its 2005 Representative Assembly, the NEA approved an updated version of its charter school resolution (National Education Association, 2005). This outlined a statement of principles, including:

(a) Local school boards should be the only entity that can grant or renew charter applications ... (b) charter schools must meet the same requirements as mainstream public schools with regard to licensure/certification and other requirements of teachers and education employees ... (c) teachers and education support professionals should be considered public employees ... (d) teachers and education support professionals should have the same constitutional and statutory rights as other public employees ... (e) charter schools should be subject to the same public sector labor relations laws as mainstream public schools and charter school employees should have the same collective bargaining rights under law and local practice as their counterparts in mainstream public schools ... (i) charter schools should

---

[1] For more details on the coding procedure, see Shen (2006).
[2] A complete table of provisions, coding, and legal citations is available from the authors. Space limitations prevented inclusion of the table with the text.

meet the needs of at-risk students and those students requiring special education services ... (j) employment in a charter school should be voluntary ... and (k) charter schools should not disproportionately divert resources from mainstream public schools.

The AFT, in its 1996 report evaluating charter school laws, identified five similar essential criteria for charter school success (American Federation of Teachers, 1999).

Teachers' unions can be understood to have both limited economic interests in protecting jobs and wages and more broadly based policy interests in promoting high-quality teaching and learning in public schools. These two interest strands have been labeled "old" or "traditional" unionism versus "new" or "reform" unionism (Hardy, 2005; Keller, 2002; Urbanski, 2001). Reform unionism is generally more favorable to charter schools, stressing the need for high-quality teachers, accountability, and assessment. This sentiment can be seen in the unions' calls for legal provisions that maintain high standards. On the other hand, traditional unionism aims to promote job security, high wages, and benefits,[1] economic interests that remain prevalent despite the rise of new unionism.[2] Terry Moe, who is skeptical of new unionism, contends that the primary goal of unions is still to protect jobs, wages, and benefits (Moe, 2001a; Moe & Chubb, 1990).

Most relevant to our study is the role that teachers' unions play in the state-level political process.[3] Moe (2001b) has argued that the unions' "massive memberships and awesome resources give them unrivaled power in the politics of education, allowing them to affect which policies are imposed on the schools by government—and to block reforms they don't like." Whether or not their power is unrivaled, it is widely acknowledged that unions have the potential for significant influence in the statehouse. As Hess and West (2006) point out, both major teachers' unions have made strategic donations to protect their economic interests (p. 36).

Because of their influence in state policymaking, as well as their interest in shaping charter school policy, teachers' unions provide a useful starting point for analyzing charter legislation. In this study, we consider provisions linked to both traditional and reform unionism. Under the *traditional unionism* umbrella, we place the following provisions:

- Must the local district provide a leave of absence to teachers going to charter schools?
- If a charter teacher returns to the school district immediately after a leave of absence, is employment in the district guaranteed?

---

[1] For example, see Baugh and Stone (1982), Eberts and Stone (1984, 1986), and Saltzman (1988).

[2] Hess and West (2006) show that collective bargaining arrangements, a hallmark of traditional union activity, remain central to the unions' agendas.

[3] Teachers' unions have also been shown to have significant influence at the local level, primarily through school board elections. See, for example, Moe (2005).

- If a teacher goes to a charter school and returns, does tenure remain secure?
- Are all charter school teachers automatically covered by the district's or state's retirement plan?
- Are all charter school teachers automatically covered by the district's health care plan?
- Is the default arrangement for all charter schools to be subject to the district's pre-existing collective bargaining agreement?
- For a charter conversion to occur, must a majority of teachers approve?
- Can charters automatically hire and fire teachers without district oversight?

Related to *reform unionism* interests, we identify the following provisions:

- Does the charter statute articulate a preference for charter schools to serve at-risk students?
- Must the charter school application go through the local school district (i.e., no alternative routes)?
- For a charter conversion to occur, must a majority of parents approve?
- Do at least some charter schools automatically have more relaxed certification requirements?

To be sure, the traditional-reform distinction is not set in stone. We use it here as an analytical tool to consider differences in the relative interest unions may have when lobbying the state for these provisions. Each provision, however, is likely to be shaped by political compromise, interest group contention, and legislative debates.

Next to these individual provisions, we sum up sets of provisions (traditional and reform) to create indices. When we run correlations between these and the overall CER grade, we find an inverse relationship between the grade and our index of traditional union goals. Further, we find no significant relationship between the CER's grade and the index of reform union goals. This suggests, in keeping with the literature just reviewed, that the CER's interests lie opposed to those of the AFT and NEA.

It is true that there is much variation within states on these union dimensions. Consistent with the characterization of charter laws as uniformly weak or strong, we find little correlation between the individual provisions. Of the 66 bivariate relationships we examined, only 13 reach at least a $p < .1$ level of statistical significance.

We believe the lack of many significant relationships suggests that unions focus their attention on certain clusters of provisions, not legislation in total. For instance, there are positive correlations between protection of health, retirement, and tenure. There are also positive correlations between requiring local school districts to approve charters, adherence to existing district collective bargaining agreements, and preventing charters from hiring and firing teachers without district oversight. These indicate that union strength may be able to push through some provisions in tandem. However, these clusters of influence do not seem to extend to all the provisions. This finding on the unions' lack of complete influence implies that they play a more targeted political role than the more universalistic role Terry Moe's research suggests.

EMPIRICAL ASSESSMENT: APPLYING A TRADITIONAL STATE POLITICS FRAMEWORK

State politics research has traditionally sought to explain legislative outcomes with state-level political, economic, and social factors. We adopt a state politics framework that attempts to model these factors as they may influence state education policy. The question we seek to answer is this: What political, economic, and demographic factors are likely to explain the adoption of the labor-related charter school provisions? Our approach here is to consider multiple measures of our key explanatory variable (union strength), and to ground our set of additional control variables in existing literature. Summary statistics for the independent variables are presented in Table 6.1.

Factors Influencing State Education Policy

Union strength. Measuring the strength of teachers' unions in each state has been a persistent challenge for researchers. As summarized by Castelo (2005), early measures have looked at the pervasiveness of collective bargaining agreements.[1] In addition to the statewide percentage of teachers covered by a collective bargaining agreement, Steelman, Powell, and Carini (2000) introduced the percentage of school district employees represented by bargaining units. The problem with this approach—looking at collective bargaining agreements to make inferences about union strength—is that it does not examine the factors that led to the collective bargaining agreement in the first place. Hoxby (1996) has described the identification problem.

The measure we use in this study comes from Valletta and Freeman's (1988) Public Sector Collective Bargaining Law Data Set.[2] Measured over the period 1955–1985, the data set is an attempt to code public sector union strength numerically across the 50 states. Freeman and Valletta examine

---

[1] Castelo notes that Eberts and Stone (1987) used the presence of collective bargaining to infer strong unionization.

[2] The data set is publicly available at http://www.nber.org/publaw/, and the details of the study and coding scheme are available in a technical appendix: http://www.nber.org/publaw/publaw.pdf.

TABLE 6.1
Summary of Variables Used in Analysis

Provision	No	Yes
Can the charter school choose its own grades to serve?	2	39
Is a lottery required if there is oversubscription?	9	32
Must charter schools take the same standardized tests as students in noncharter public schools?	1	40
Can an existing public school be converted into a charter school?	0	41
Can a teacher be assigned to a charter school without his or her consent?	40	1
Does the statute contain explicit nonsectarian or nonreligious language?	3	38
Is there a preference for serving at-risk students?	23	18
Must the charter school application go through the local school district (i.e., no alternative routes)?	10	31
In order for a charter conversion to occur, must a majority of teachers approve?	16	25
In order for a charter conversion to occur, must a majority of parents approve?	21	20
Must local district provide a leave of absence to teachers going to charter schools?	12	22
Is tenure automatically secured when a teacher goes to a charter school and returns?	6	35
Are all charter school teachers automatically covered by the district's or state's retirement plan?	8	33
Are all charter school teachers automatically covered by the district's health care plan?	24	17
If a charter teacher returns to the school district immediately after the leave of absence, is he or she guaranteed employment in the district?	13	26
Is the default arrangement for all charter schools to be subject to the district's pre-existing collective bargaining agreement?	22	13
Do at least some charter schools automatically have more relaxed certification requirements?	20	21
Can charters automatically hire and fire teachers without district oversight?	7	34

Explanatory variables	Obs	Mean	Std. dev.	Min	Max
Percent of state's students residing in largest urban district	40	0.11	0.08	0.03	0.38
Union strength–union bargaining rights	40	3.73	1.95	0	6
Beginning teacher salaries ($000)	40	28.39	1.95	24.52	34.40

TABLE 6.1 (continued)
Summary of Variables Used in Analysis

Explanatory variables	Obs	Mean	Std. dev.	Min	Max
Public school enrollment (000,000)	40	1.02	1.04	0.10	5.25
Percent non-white in state population	40	0.24	0.14	0.03	0.69
Democratic party strength (Ranney index)	40	0.53	0.17	0.18	0.83
Percent enrolled in private schools	40	0.10	0.04	0.02	0.19
Percent of education revenue from state sources	40	0.49	0.14	0.08	0.90

Note: Summary statistics of the explanatory variables are for the 40 states with charter school laws, excluding Washington, DC.

state laws in five primary areas: contract negotiation, union recognition, union security, impasse procedures, and strike policy.[1] The authors track public sector union strength for five groups: state employees, local police, local firefighters, teachers (noncollege), and other local employees. In our study, we utilize the most recent year of data (1984) available across all states for the group of noncollege teachers. We focus on the measure most relevant to our study: the right to collective bargaining.[2] This is measured on a 0–6 scale, with higher numbers representing broader rights.[3]

Big city influence. Major urban school systems have heavily influenced state education policy, especially policies surrounding school choice. Big city school districts face unique challenges that may make charter schools an attractive option. In Indianapolis, for instance, Mayor Bart Peterson successfully gained chartering authority under the 2001 Indiana charter school law. Since its enactment, Mayor Peterson has chartered 13 schools and frequently voiced his support for increasing choice options. In nearby Chicago, Mayor Daley has also made charter schools a prominent part of his new Renaissance 2010 plan.

To serve as a proxy for big city influence, we include in our models a measure of the percentage of the state's public school students in the largest school district. We expect that the greater this ratio is, the more likely a state will be to adopt a provision that promotes charter school growth.

---

[1] The authors develop 14 specific variables to capture these aspects of union strength.

[2] The other variables concern whether the bargaining includes compensation; union recognition; agency shop; dues check off; union shop; right to work law; mediation availability; fact-finding availability; arbitration availability; scope of arbitration; type of arbitration; and strike policy.

[3] The variable is measured as: 0 = no provision; 1 = collective bargaining prohibited; 2 = employer authorized, but not required to bargain with union; 3 = right to present proposals; 4 = right to meet and confer; 5 = implied duty to bargain; 6 = explicit duty to bargain.

Democratic Party strength. Where charter schools and political parties intersect, Democrats are often characterized as more anti-charter than their Republican counterparts. Empirical analysis backs up this story (Henig et al., 2002; Wong & Shen, 2002). The political story is complicated, however. Since the first charter school law was passed in Minnesota in 1992, support for charter schools has come from both Democrats and Republicans (Pipho, 1993). The New Democrat movement in the 1990s included many proponents of charter schools (From, 1998[1]). Therefore, though the Democratic Party's influence on the charter school movement may be muted by internal traditional/new Democrat conflicts, it is still important to control for party strength in the state. To do so, we utilize a Ranney party control index as described in Bibby and Holbrook (1999).[2] As calculated, it is a proxy for the degree to which the Democratic Party holds control (in the previous 4 years) of the governor's seat, the state House of Representatives, and the state Senate.

Starting teacher salaries. The level of state resources available for public education can affect the adoption of charter school legislation in several ways. First, if larger salaries attract higher quality teachers to the traditional public schools, the pressure for reform through charters may be lessened. In other words, lower public school starting salaries create a greater potential threat from charter schools because the public–charter pay differential is presumably lower. Higher starting salaries may also reflect stronger teachers' unions in the state. For all of these reasons, we expect that higher starting teacher salaries should be associated with charter provisions that tend to restrict the charter market. The starting salary data we use are available from Taylor and Fowler (2006) and are unique because they have been corrected for geographic cost variations.

Race politics. A wide body of literature has noted the importance of race-based politics in the charter school debate. On the one hand, concerns have been raised that charter schools perpetuate or even worsen racial stratification (see Frankenberg & Lee, 2002). On the other hand, some have argued that charter schools can improve educational opportunities for

---

[1] Al From, director of the Democratic Leadership Council, is on record as saying, "I'm a big proponent of charter schools. I'd like to see charter school districts, where all public schools are run under contract or charter, with high standards and performance accountability, but with choice for parents and without bureaucratic restraints; though they're less resistant than they were, the teachers' unions support charter schools only reluctantly."

[2] The 4-year Ranney index was calculated by averaging four percentages: "the average percentage of the popular vote won by Democratic gubernatorial candidates; the average percentage of seats held by Democrats in the state senate, in all legislative sessions; the average percentage of seats held by Democrats in the state house of representatives, in all sessions; and the percentage of all gubernatorial, senate, and house terms that were controlled by the Democrats" (Bibby & Holbrook, 1999, p. 93).

minorities.[1] In the context of labor market charter school provisions, the most salient argument may be Henig's (2004), which maintains that for the African-American community, urban school systems are important not only for educational purposes but also for the jobs they provide to the minority community. In the present analysis, we include the percentage of non-white residents in the state.[2] To the extent that the Henig argument holds, we would expect a higher percentage of non-white residents to be correlated with provisions that offer greater job security.

Private school market share. Charter schools are designed to straddle the public–private school divide because they contain elements of both (Mead, 2003). Existing private schools may see charter schools as competition for students and parents. Thus, we would expect a greater private school market share to be associated with labor market provisions that raise the costs of teacher transfers to the charter sector. We measure private school market share by estimating the percentage of students in a state enrolled in private schools.[3]

Size of the state school system. School system sizes vary widely across the 50 states. It is likely that politics in large states are fundamentally different from those in smaller states because of the differences in the number of constituent interests being developed. In particular, the presence of large urban districts may drive state policy to provide more flexible charter school opportunities to meet scale-up demand. To control for these size-related influences, we include a measure of the state school system size by calculating the number of students enrolled in the year of charter law enactment.

Revenue from the state. Finally, we include a measure of the percentage of educational revenue that comes from the state (as opposed to local and federal sources). This is determined using data from the U.S. Department of Education's National Center for Education Statistics (NCES), which provide the annual amount of each state's revenue from state, local, federal, and other sources. In the context of charter schools, more state revenue suggests more state control in guiding educational policy. This may be

---

[1] See the collection of essays in Rofes and Stulbert (2004).

[2] We utilize the same method for assigning either 1990 or 2000 census figures. See Pipho (1993).

[3] Using data from the Department of Education's Private School Universe Survey, combined with data from the Common Core of Data on student enrollment, we calculated the percentage of students who attend private schools. The measure was created by dividing the total number of elementary and secondary private school enrollment by the total number of elementary and secondary students in the state (public and private). Because the private school survey is administered every other year, we calculated this measure for every odd year from 1991 through 2001. In our empirical analysis we then used the measure in the year of enactment (for odd years), or just prior to enactment (for even years). For Maryland, with enactment in 2003, we used the 2001 measure for private school market share.

particularly important in regard to the question of whether local districts have veto power of charter school authorization.

Dependent Variables

Our first set of dependent variables includes eleven of the twelve 0–1 provisions. We present summary statistics for these variables in Table 6.1. We do not perform regression analysis on the question of whether or not the district's collective bargaining agreement is automatically binding on the charter schools. The reason is that in six of the states, there is no collective bargaining for public school teachers at baseline.[1] Thus, in these states, the question was not applicable. With these states reduced, the N for the analysis drops to 34. More importantly, a significant bias is introduced because there is selection on the independent variable of interest. All of the dropped observations are weak union states.

A similar issue arises in the context of our leave of absence provision. In cases where charter school teachers are considered the same as public school teachers, there is no need for a leave of absence. To address this issue, we consider multiple models. In the first, we drop observations where the two leave-of-absence questions are not applicable. The N for these models is 33. In a second alternative model, we code the dropped states as 1, under the assumption that in considering charter teachers the same as public school teachers, districts are essentially offering an indefinite leave. The results from the two models turn out to be substantively similar.

Because these are dichotomous outcomes, we employ logistic regression. Our state-level measures of union strength and Democratic Party strength are not available for Washington, DC, so it is not included in our analysis and our N is 40. Putting these variables together in one equation, our final model for the first round of analysis is:

$$PROVISION_i = \beta_0 + b_1UNION_i + \beta_2PCT\_NON\_WHITE_i + \beta_3START\_SALARY_i \\ + \beta_3PCT\_BIG\_CITY_i + \beta_4PRIVATE\_SCHOOL_i \\ + \beta_5DEMOCRAT_i + \beta_6ENROLL_i + \beta_7STATE\_REV_i + e_i \quad (6.1)$$

where

$PROVISION_i$ is a dichotomous variable indicating whether or not a state adopted one of the twelve charter law provisions we analyze
$UNION$ is the measure of public sector union bargaining rights in the state
PCT_NON_WHITE is the percentage of state population that is not white, non-Hispanic

---

[1] The six states are Georgia, Missouri, Mississippi, North Carolina, South Carolina, and Virginia.

PCT_BIG CITY is the percentage of state students who reside in the state's
          largest city
PRIVATE_SCHOOL is the percentage of students who attend private schools
DEMOCRAT is the 4-year lagged Ranney party index of Democratic
          party strength
ENROLL is total public school enrollment
START_SALARY is the cost-adjusted starting teacher salary in the state
STATE_REVENUE is the percentage of education revenue from the state

RESULTS

Our results call into question the ability of state-level variables to predict the adoption of individual charter law provisions. The results of the
first set of regressions are presented in Tables 6.2, 6.3, and 6.4. Because the
analysis employs logit regression, the results in these tables are in odds-
ratios. These can be interpreted as the increase in odds of the provision
being adopted, given a one unit change in the independent variable.

Indices Sensitive Only to Enrollment and Big City Influence

The results of our models predicting the union and CER aggregate indices (Table 6.2) suggest that they are sensitive only to the percentage of students located in a state's largest urban city and to overall state size. Larger
school systems are inversely related to the indices of both traditional and
reform goals and positively correlated with the CER's overall grade. This
finding suggests that large states may be more likely to seek new choice
options and less likely to be restrained by union interests. It may be that in
larger states, union power tends to be countered by pro-charter forces and
organized interests. Larger states are also likely to face more accountability challenges, thereby producing broader public support for alternative
reform strategies, including charter schools. In contrast, there is a positive
correlation between our proxy for big city influence and support for traditional union goals. This makes sense in light of the entrenched teachers'
union interests in many major U.S. cities.

It is striking that none of the other control variables are significant predictors of the charter law indices. This suggests either limitations with the
model (e.g., omitted variables) or the inability of the indices to capture the
nuances of the charter law adequately.

TABLE 6.2

Analysis of Union Goals Indexes and Comparison to CER Overall Score Measure

	Index of traditional union goals	Modified index of traditional union goals	Index of reform union goals	CER overall score
Percent of state's students residing in largest urban district	9.147[a]	4.431	4.306	−16.389
	(4.97)	(−3.977)	(−4.492)	(−20.571)
Union strength	−0.049	−0.105	−0.206	0.109
	(−0.181)	(−0.154)	(−0.204)	(−0.888)
Beginning teacher salaries ($000)	0.098	−0.027	0.104	0.319
	(−0.215)	(−0.167)	(−0.186)	(−0.899)
Public school enrollment (000,000)	−1.32[b]	−0.743[b]	0.239	4.338[c]
	(0.521)	(0.316)	(−0.357)	(1.479)
Percent non-white in state population	7.289	2.427	2.814	−17.351
	(−5.193)	(−3.327)	(−3.584)	(−16.549)
Democratic Party strength	−1.958	−2.029	−1.835	−10.497
	(−3.776)	(−2.288)	(−2.76)	(−11.172)
Percent enrolled in private schools	4.636	5.856	18.128	57.202
	(−11.787)	(−7.841)	(−11.612)	(−35.929)
Percent of education revenue from state	−7.078	−2.233	−2.715	15.753
	(−6.259)	(−3.74)	(−3.155)	(−11.834)
Constant				12.72
				(−23.322)
Observations	29	40	40	40
R2	0.18	0.06	0.1	0.22

Notes: Odds ratios reported for ordered logit models; coefficients reported for CER model; robust standard errors in parentheses. The modified traditional union goals index includes states in which charter school teachers are considered public school employees. See text for discussion. Index models estimated using the ologit command in Stata. OLS regression employed for the CER overall score model. All models use robust standard errors. Pseudo R^2 reported for logit models.
[a] Two-tailed significance for $p < 0.1$.
[b] Two-tailed significance for $p < 0.05$.
[c] Two-tailed significance for $p < 0.01$.

Mixed Union Influence

The results of our individual provision analysis suggest that once additional factors are controlled for, union influence may not be as strong as hypothesized. We find our measure of union strength to be significant on only two of the traditional union interest provisions; it is not significant in relationship to the reform unionism interest provisions. Unions' mixed influence suggests that political compromises are at work. Politicians may be willing to grant union demands on certain bottom-line issues, but in return policymakers prevail on other operation issues.

States with stronger union bargaining rights are more likely not to require leaves of absence for charter school teachers and less likely to secure tenure when a teacher moves from a public to a charter school. On the one hand, this would seem to cut against the unions' interest in considering charter school teachers as part of the local school district. But on the other hand, to strengthen their position relative to charter schools, unions have an interest in raising the costs of charter transfer. When tenure securities are removed and district employment statutes are at risk, the costs of teaching at a charter school increase.

The lack of significant union strength on automatic participation in the district's retirement plan can likely be traced to the independent interest of state legislatures in providing retirement plans for all public employees. In other words, a strong union is not necessary for protection of retirement benefits because the state is already cognizant of this need.

While the measurement of union strength is a significant predictor for two of the traditional union interest provisions, it does not fare as well in predicting those more closely related to reform unionism. These null findings support the contention that political interests are likely to target their influence on the provisions most closely related to their economic interests. Whether a charter school must give preference to at-risk students, for instance, is likely to be of less concern to teachers' unions since it does not directly affect pay, benefits, or tenure.

Race

Our findings with regard to race provide strong support for Henig's (2004) argument that, for minority constituencies (primarily African Americans), charter schools threaten an important source of jobs. We find that states with greater percentages of non-white residents are more likely to be guaranteed employment in the school district after return from a charter school leave of absence and more likely to have charter school teachers automatically covered by health care (Table 6.3). These findings are consistent with recent statements from Bob Lydia, president of the NAACP's Dallas branch. In response to President Bush's July 2006 address to the NAACP, Lydia said, "Charter schools are a sore spot with

TABLE 6.3
Results From Logit Regression Models for Charter School Provisions

	Must local district provide a leave of absence to teachers going to charter schools?		If a charter teacher returns to the school district immediately after the leave of absence, is he or she guaranteed employment in the district?		Is tenure automatically secured when a teacher goes to a charter school and returns?	Are all charter school teachers automatically covered by the district or state's retirement plan?	Are all charter school teachers automatically covered by the district's health care plan?
	A	B	A	B			
Percent of state's students residing in largest urban district	1.173	2.839	−2.387	2.443	61.114[a]	13.958[b]	−13.024[c]
	(−5.071)	(−5.047)	(−9.244)	(−7.962)	(16.844)	(7.084)	(7.774)
Union strength	−0.468[c]	−0.508[c]	−0.104	−0.197	−1.603[a]	0.08	0.499[c]
	(0.241)	(0.273)	(−0.239)	(−0.229)	(0.496)	(−0.324)	(0.258)[c]
Beginning teacher salaries ($000)	0.173	0.23	−0.222	−0.12	−0.219	−0.218	0.379
	(−0.242)	(−0.244)	(−0.357)	(−0.292)	(−0.348)	(−0.288)	(−0.242)
Public school enrollment (000,000)	−0.459	−0.595	−2.248[a]	−2.167[a]	−2.6[c]	−0.947[b]	−1.339[b]
	(−0.419)	(−0.434)	(0.787)	(0.694)	(1.538)	(0.462)	(0.606)
Percent non-white in state population	1.314	0.47	25.119[a]	19.403[a]	−6.446	3.204	10.612[a]
	(−4.5)	(−4.084)	(9.419)	(6.172)	(−5.653)	(−4.162)	(3.995)
Democratic party strength	−2.159	−1.141	−4.504	−2.263	−5.914	−0.733	−1.336

Percent enrolled in private schools	23.515[b] (10.868)	18.353[c] (9.71)	75.219[a] (27.413)	58.719[b] (23.602)	−5.646 (−19.796)	−34.886[c] (17.857)	−28.984[c] (14.981)
Percent of education revenue from state sources	−4.871 (−5.561)	−5.271 (−5.577)	3.297 (−3.775)	3.098 (−3.789)	−11.597 (−12.007)	−0.046 (−8.751)	−1.781 (−3.186)
Constant	−1.106 (−6.794)	−1.924 (−6.762)	−1.357 (−9.472)	−2.472 (−7.059)	25.071b (10.892)	10.891 (−8.178)	−8.613 (−6.608)
Adjusted R2	0.22	0.22	0.42	0.36	0.66	0.28	0.29
N	33	40	33	40	40	40	40

Notes: Model-B for the leave of absence models includes states in which charter school teachers are considered public school employees. See text for discussion. Models estimated using the logit command in Stata. All models use robust standard errors. Standard errors reported in parentheses.

[a] Two-tailed significance for $p < 0.01$.
[b] Two-tailed significance for $p < 0.05$.
[c] Two-tailed significance for $p < 0.1$.

us" (Douglas, 2006). He pointed out that money is moved out of the traditional public education system.

Private School Market and Size of School System

We find that states with larger public school systems are more likely to loosen the constraints of their labor-related provisions in charter school laws. Those with larger student enrollment are less likely to require districts to provide retirement benefits, health care, or jobs upon a teacher's return from a charter school. They also give charters more autonomy to hire and fire without district oversight.

Why are larger states less stringent on these provisions, which would seem to encourage teachers to experiment with teaching in charters? The question deserves further investigation, but one preliminary explanation is that the administrative costs related to these services are greater in larger school systems. Consider, for example, the administrative costs in requiring that charter school employees be covered in the local school district's health care plan. In a small system, where probably only a small number of people fit this category, it seems economically feasible to track all personnel. As system size increases, however, the cost of tracking every charter school employee increases.

The private school market share variable is a significant predictor of labor provisions, but the relationship is not consistent across provisions. Our competition hypothesis—that private schools would have an interest in preventing charter operation—gains support from findings that states with more private school students are less likely to require districts to give leaves of absence. They are also less likely to require districts to cover charter school retirement and health care plans (Table 6.3). At the same time, however, these states are more likely to ensure jobs upon return from charter teaching and to require both teacher and parent approval of charter conversions (Tables 6.3 and 6.4). These mixed findings suggest that the relationship between private and charter schools is about more than just competition. It may be that our measure of private school enrollment is also picking up a state's positive predisposition toward school choice. If this is the case, then a more favorable private school climate might lead to more favorable charter provisions. More work is necessary to tease out these competing effects.

NEW MODEL FOR UNDERSTANDING CHARTER LAW AND CHARTER OUTCOMES

From a policy perspective, the most pressing questions for charter schools are (1) whether the reform can be scaled up, and (2) whether the charter movement is sustainable, moving from its experimental

TABLE 6.4
Results From Logit Regression Models for Charter School Provisions

	Must the charter school application go through the local school district (i.e., no alternative routes)?	In order for a charter conversion to occur, must a majority of teachers approve?	In order for a charter conversion to occur, must a majority of parents approve?	Is there a preference for serving at-risk students?	Do at least some charter schools automatically have more relaxed certification requirements?	Can charters automatically hire and fire teachers without district oversight?
Percent of state's students residing in largest urban district	57.931[a] (19.783)	3.51 (-5.061)	1.209 (-5.749)	4.357 (-4.622)	-7.539 (-5.066)	-1.167 (-7.508)
Union strength	-0.289 (-0.324)	-0.173 (-0.24)	-0.217 (-0.221)	-0.11 (-0.211)	-0.019 (-0.219)	0.074 (-0.222)
Beginning teacher salaries ($000)	0.148 (-0.278)	-0.078 (-0.227)	0.065 (-0.231)	-0.017 (-0.234)	0.217 (-0.222)	-0.068 (-0.271)
Public school enrollment (000,000)	-0.566 (-0.627)	0.155 (-0.372)	-0.558 (-0.36)	0.379 (-0.35)	0.651 (-0.472)	1.569[b] (0.694)
Percent non-white in state population	6.444 (-6.64)	-0.875 (-3.789)	5.189 (-4.123)	-1.178 (-3.608)	3.705 (-3.493)	-4.772 (-4.038)
Democratic Party strength	-1.359 (-3.676)	-3.581 (-2.689)	-5.942[c] (3.316)	2.792 (-2.929)	-2.345 (-3.356)	-3.214 (-3.418)
Percent enrolled in private schools	4.329 (-15.318)	28.41[a] (12.333)	31.57[a] (11.242)	11.434 (-11.185)	0.231 (-11.553)	1.631 (-10.708)
Percent of education revenue from state sources	-7.674 (-6.145)	5.9 (-4.013)	6.133[b] (2.935)	-3.375 (-3.328)	-2.57 (-2.794)	1.695 (-3.704)

TABLE 6.4 (continued)
Results From Logit Regression Models for Charter School Provisions

	Must the charter school application go through the local school district (i.e. no alternative routes)?	In order for a charter conversion to occur, must a majority of teachers approve?	In order for a charter conversion to occur, must a majority of parents approve?	Is there a preference for serving at-risk students?	Do at least some charter schools automatically have more relaxed certification requirements?	Can charters automatically hire and fire teachers without district oversight?
Constant	−2.791	−0.716	−4.854	−0.951	−4.34	4.196
	(−6.472)	(−6.322)	(−6.163)	(−6.268)	(−5.945)	(−7.288)
Adjusted $R2$	0.37	0.15	0.2	0.13	0.13	0.22
N	40	40	40	40	40	40

Notes: Odds ratios and robust standard error reported. Models estimated using the logit command in Stata. Standard errors reported in parentheses. All models use robust standard errors.
[a] Two-tailed significance for $p < 0.01$.
[b] Two-tailed significance for $p < 0.05$.
[c] Two-tailed significance for $p < 0.1$.

beginnings to a more mature, stable system. State legislation will facilitate or undermine the conditions that promote these objectives.

The discussion and empirical analysis in this chapter challenge our conventional notions of charter school laws and their relationship to charter school outcomes. As we have reported, conventional wisdom is that charter school laws are generally either weak or strong, and strong laws will tend to be associated with better outcomes in a state. Our analysis raises two fundamental challenges to this thinking. First, we find that there is as much, if not more, within-state variation as between-state variation. The best comparisons to make, then, may not be between states but between schools and districts within states. Second, not all provisions are created equal. Therefore, we should not expect all provisions, and especially not rough indices, to be accurate predictors of achievement outcomes.

Future research on the relationship between charter school law and outcomes will benefit from new data sources. For instance, adding measures of charter school waiting lists at individual schools and districts can provide additional leverage on how the law is operating to promote charter demand. In addition, we plan to code the rest of the areas of charter school laws to see if other aspects of charter legislation follow the same pattern we have seen here with personnel policy. Future research can also include duration or event history analysis to better capture the dynamic aspects of the policy process.

The most important question, of course, is how to connect the charter law provisions to student academic outcomes. Cross-state achievement comparisons are notoriously difficult since states employ different achievement tests. National exams are not yet available for enough charter schools to allow for significant national comparisons. One method, used by Loveless (2003), is to generate z-scores to facilitate cross-state comparisons of charter schools.

Our analysis suggests that a promising alternative route is to adjust the unit of observation from the state to the district or even school level. Hierarchical modeling might be appropriate, especially where additional legal layers (e.g., district-level collective bargaining agreements) are in play. A multilevel analysis would recognize the complex interactions among state, local, and charter school administration. Future analysis should also improve its measure of union strength.

For state and local policymakers, there are policy implications to derive from our analysis:

- Pay attention to the details of individual provisions in the charter legislation, as they may work at cross-purposes and frustrate the overall growth of the charter movement.
- Recognize that charter school law will have differentiated effects on a state's districts and schools. State lawmakers may consider market segmentation to improve educational offerings more efficiently.

- Acknowledge that the charter movement must be particularly sensitive to the needs of large urban districts, which may be driving policy in many states.

There are lessons, too, for the federal government:

- Continue financial incentives to promote the laboratories of innovation (such as charters).
- Ensure the rights of at-risk children to attend charter schools.
- Provide sufficient support for charters in large urban districts as they face greater challenges in raising student performance.

As our charter legislation and policy database expands and we are able to make connections between legal provisions and tangible charter outcomes, we will be able to offer more specific policy recommendations for multiple layers of government.

REFERENCES

American Federation of Teachers. (1999). Charter schools update. AFT Educational Issues Policy Brief, Number 9, June 1999. Citing: American Federation of Teachers. (1996). Charter school laws: Do they measure up?

Anonymous. (2005). No answers to charter school questions. *State Legislatures,* *31*(2), 8.

Baugh, W., & Stone, J. A. (1982). Teachers, unions, and wages in the 1970s: Unionism now pays. *Industrial and Labor Relations Review, 35*(3), 368–376.

Bibby, J. F., and Holbrook, T. M. (1999). Parties and elections. In V. Gray et al. (Eds.) *Politics in the American States.* 7th ed. Washington, DC: Congressional Quarterly Press.

Buddin, R., & Zimmer, R. (2005). Student achievement in charter schools: A complex picture. *Journal of Policy Analysis and Management,* 351–371, 24(2).

Castelo, S. (2005). Teachers' unions in public education: An assessment of their effects on student performance and the bureaucratization of public schools. Stanford University Public Policy Program. Online: http://www.stanford. edu/dept/publicpolicy/programs/Honors_Theses/Theses_2005/Castelo. pdf.

Center for Education Reform. (2001). Charter school laws: Scorecard and rankings. Washington, DC: Center for Education Reform.

Douglas, W. (2006). Bush addresses NAACP for the first time in his presidency. *McClatchy Newspapers,* July 20, 2006.

Eberts, R. W., & Stone, J. A. (1984). *Unions and public schools: The effect of collective bargaining on American education.* Lexington, MA: Lexington Books.

Eberts, R. W., & Stone, J. A. (1986). Teacher unions and the cost of public education. *Economic Inquiry, 24*(4), 631–644.

Eberts, R. W., & Stone, J. A. (1987). Teacher unions and the productivity of public schools. *Industrial and Labor Relations Review 40* (April 1987), 354–363.

Finn, C. (March 2005). Judging charter schools. Hoover Institution.Henig, J. R., Holyoke, T. T., Moser, M., Brown, H, & Lacireno-Pauet, N. (2002).*The political dynamics of charter school policies.* Paper presented at the 98th Annual Meeting of the American Political Science Association, Boston, MA.

Finn, C. E., Manno, B. V., & Vanourek, G. (2000). *Charter schools in action: Renewing public education.* Princeton, NJ: Princeton University Press.

Frankenberg, E., & Lee, C. (2002). *Race in American public schools: Rapidly resegregating school districts.* Cambridge, MA: The Civil Rights Project, Harvard University.

From, A. (1998). Don't muzzle labor: I may not like all it has to say, but it deserves to be heard. *The New Democrat,* March 1, 1998.

Hardy, L. (2005). Public interest vs. self-interest: Debating reform unionism. *American School Board Journal, 192*(7), 6–8.

Hassel, B. M. (1999) *The charter school challenge: Avoiding the pitfalls, fulfilling the promise.* Washington, DC: Brookings Institution Press.

Hassel, B. M. (2005). *Charter school achievement: What we know.* Charter School Leadership Council.

Henig, J. R. (2004). Washington, DC: Race, issue definition, and school board restructuring. In J. Henig & W. Rich (Eds.), *Mayors in the middle: Politics, race, and mayoral control of urban schools.* Princeton, NJ: Princeton University Press.

Henig, J. R., Holyoke, T. T., Moser, M., Brown, H., & Lacireno-Pauet, N. (2002). *The political dynamics of charter school policies.* Paper presented at the 98th Annual Meeting of the American Political Science Association, Boston, MA.

Hess, F. M., & West, M. R. (2006). *A better bargain: Overhauling teacher collective bargaining for the 21st century.* American Economic Institute.

Howell, W. G. & Peterson, P. E. (2002). *The education gap: Vouchers and urban schools.* Washington, DC: Brookings. Institution Press.

Hoxby, C. (1994). Does competition among public schools benefit students and taxpayers? NBER Working Paper No. 4979.

Hoxby, C. M. (1996). How teachers' unions affect education production. *Quarterly Journal of Economics, 671*–718, 11 (3) August 1996.

Jennings, W., Premack, E., Adelmann, A., Solomon, D. (1998). A comparison of charter school legislation: Thirty-three states and the District of Columbia incorporating legislative changes through October 1998. Washington, DC: U.S. Department of Education.

Keller, B. (2002). Unions turn cold shoulder on charters. *Education Week, 21*(28), 02774232.

Loveless, T. (Ed.) (2000). *Conflicting missions? Teachers' unions and educational reform.* Washington, DC: Brookings Institution Press.

Loveless, T. (2003). *Brown Center report on American education 2003.* Washington, DC: Brookings Institution.

Mauhs-Pugh, T. (1995). Charter schools 1995: A survey and analysis of the laws and practices of the states. *Education Policy Analysis Archives, 3*(13). Available at http://epaa.asu.edu/epaa/v3n13/

Mead, J. F. (2003). Devilish details: Exploring features of charter school statutes that blur the public/private distinction. *Harvard Journal on Legislation, 40,* 349.

Moe, T. M. (2001a). A union by any other name. *Education Next,* Fall 2001.

Moe, T. M. (2001b). Taking on the unions, *Hoover Digest,* 2001(1).

Moe, T. M. (2005). Teachers' unions and school board elections. In W. Howell (Ed.), *Besieged: School boards and the future of education politics* (pp. 254–287). Washington, DC: Brookings Institution Press.

Moe, T. M., & Chubb, J. (1990). *Politics, markets, and America's schools.* Washington, DC: The Brookings Institution.

Molnar, A. (1996). Charter schools: The smiling face of disinvestment. *Educational Leadership, 54,* 9–15.

National Education Association. (2005). Democracy in action. *NEA Today,* September 2005, 45–51.

Palmer, L. B., & Gau, R. (2003). Charter school authorizing: Are states making the grade? Report prepared for the Thomas B. Fordham Institute, June 2003.

Pipho, C. (1993). Bipartisan charter schools. *Phi Delta Kappan, 75*(2), 10–11.

Powell, B. et al. (2000). Do teacher unions hinder educational performance? Lessons learned from state SAT and ACT scores. *Harvard Educational Review, 70* (4), 437–466.

Rofes, E., & Stulbert, L. M. (Eds.) (2004). *The emancipatory promise of charter schools: Toward a progressive politics of school choice.* New York: SUNY Press.

Saltzman, G. M. (1988). Bargaining laws really matter: Evidence from Ohio and Illinois. In R. Freeman & C. Echniowski (Eds.), *When public sector workers unionize.* Chicago: University of Chicago Press.

Shen, F. X. (2003). *Specification uncertainty and model averaging in state policy innovation research.* Paper presented at the Third Annual Conference on State Politics and Policy, Tucson, AZ.

Shen, F. X. (2006). The politics of statutory silence in charter school legislation. Working paper, Harvard University. Online: http://www.fxshen.com/research.

Steelman, L. C., Powell, B., & Carini, R. M. (2000). Do teacher unions hinder educational performance? Lessons learned from state SAT and ACT scores. *Harvard Educational Review 70*(2000), 437–466.

Taylor, L. L., & Fowler, W. J., Jr. (2006). A comparable wage approach to geographic cost adjustment. http://nces.ed.gov/pubsearch/pubsinfo.asp?pubid= 2006321.

Urbanski, A. (2001). Reform or be reformed. Hoover Institution, Fall 2001.

U.S. Department of Education. (1998). A comparison of charter school legislation: Thirty-three states and the District of Columbia incorporating legislative changes through October, 1998. Available for download at www.uscharter-schools.org/pdf/fr/charter_legis.pdf.

U.S. General Accounting Office. (1995). *Charter schools: New model for public schools provides opportunities and challenges.* Washington, DC: U.S. General Accounting Office.

Valletta, R. G., & Freeman, R. B. (1988). The NBER public sector collective bargaining law data set. In R. B. Freeman & C. Ichniowski (Eds.), *When public employees unionize.* Chicago: NBER and University of Chicago Press, Appendix B.

Vanourek, G., Manno, B. V., Finn, C. E., & Bierlein, L. A. (1997). Charter schools in action. Indianapolis, IN and Washington, DC: Hudson Institute.

Wells, A. S. (2000). Beyond the rhetoric of charter school reform: A study of ten California school districts. Los Angeles, CA: UCLA Charter School Study.

Wells, A. S., Grutzik, C., Carnochan, S., Slayton, J., & Vasudeva, A. (1999). Underlying policy assumptions of charter school reform: The multiple meanings of a movement. *Teachers College Record, 100*(3) 513–535.

Witte, J. F. (2000). The market approach to education: An analysis of America's first voucher program. Princeton, NJ: Princeton University Press.

Witte, J. F., Shober, A., & Manna, P. (2003). *Analyzing state charter school laws and their influence on the formation of charter schools in the United States.* Paper presented at the 2003 Annual Meeting of the American Political Science Association.

Wohlstetter, P., Malloy, C. L., Smith, J., & Hentschke, G. (2004). Incentives for charter schools: Building school capacity through cross-sectoral alliances. *Educational Administration Quarterly, 40*(3), 321–365.

Wong, K. K. (1999). *Funding public schools: Politics and policy.* Lawrence: University of Kansas Press.

Wong, K. K., & Shen, F. X. (2002). Politics of state-led reform in education: Market competition and electoral dynamics. *Educational Policy, 16*(1), March 2002.

Yearbook of the American Education Finance Association. (2004). *Political economy of charter school funding formulas: Exploring state-to-state variation in charter school funding formulas,* with Kenneth K. Wong. Sage Publications.

Section 3

Charter School Effects on Student Achievement

DOMINIC J. BREWER AND JUNE AHN

Charter schools, once a radical idea to separate public education financing from public operation, have grown dramatically over the past decade. Their popularity is attributable to parents' desire to choose the kind of schooling their children receive, and to parents' dissatisfaction with conventional public schools in many communities. The "theory of action" behind charter schools is that significantly enhanced school-level autonomy will empower administrators and teachers to use resources to boost student achievement, to be innovative, and to respond to student needs. Charters are released from bureaucratic requirements of state education codes and school district policies. Thus, they are free to run school operations, hire teachers, and implement educational programs as they see fit. The overarching goal is to improve the achievement of students who attend these schools, and, through the "competition" charters provide, also raise student achievement in traditional public schools.

As the number of charters has grown, so too has the number of studies that examine the effects of charters on the students they serve. Studying this question is inherently tricky since it involves a counterfactual—what would students have learned had they not attended a charter school? There are multiple ways to get at this question: by comparing charter school students' scores with those of students who applied to the same schools but lost in an admissions lottery (randomization), by comparing trends in individual students' test scores in charter versus noncharter schools over 2 or more years, or by using individual students' rates of learning before and after entering charter schools. These methods are generally rated excellent or very good by the National Charter School Achievement Consensus Panel (Betts & Hill, 2006).[1]

But the data demands for such approaches are great. For example, since many charters are not overenrolled, the sample that can be used in "lottery" studies is skewed. Any attempt to compare public and charter school students is problematic because unobserved factors are likely to partially explain achievement differences. Using students' learning rates is not possible for students who do not switch schools. Weaker methods, such as looking at school-wide averages and making 1-year comparisons, are more commonly used and appear in studies that have gained national attention, fueled by proponents or opponents of charters out to score political points. Even good researchers may have biases that incline them to search vigorously in complex data for positive or negative effects, and to exaggerate the implications of their findings with broad policy conclusions.

> *Ron Zimmer and Richard Buddin, "Charter Schools in California"; Robert Bifulco and Helen Ladd, "Charter Schools in North Carolina"; Dale Ballou, Bettie Teasley, and Tim Zeidner, "Charter Schools in Idaho"; Mark Berends, Caroline Watral, Bettie Teasley, and Anna Nicotera, "Charter School Effects on Achievement: Where We Are and Where We Are Going"*

The three new empirical studies presented here would be rated "very good" by the consensus panel, as would the methods in Berends and colleagues' proposed National Center on School Choice study. It should not be surprising that the results are mixed in terms of achievement effects, mimicking other work to date. In Idaho, student gains in charter schools appear to be higher than in traditional public schools; in North Carolina, the gains are lower; and, in California, there is not much difference. Charters are creations of state policy. The legal environment within which they operate differs from state to state as do the kinds of students they serve. These three studies contribute to the growing literature through use of student-level longitudinal data and sophisticated econometric modeling, doing their best to cope with student mobility, selection effects, and unobservable factors.

But these studies also demonstrate the limitations of this kind of student achievement research. Charters are designed to be innovative and different, so they are too diverse to be lumped together. Not surprisingly, some schools do well and some less well; *average* effects are not very useful for policymakers or for parents. Absent richer information about how effects differ between school types or how they are linked to what the school is actually doing or the policy regime in which the school operates, reporting gross averages can be misleading. Zimmer and Buddin (2006)

---

[1] Dominic Brewer is a member of this panel, along with Paul Hill, Robin Lake, Julian Betts, Anthony Bryk, Dan Goldhaber, Patrick McEwan, Laura Hamilton, Jeffrey Henig, and Susanna Loeb.

find, for example, differences between classroom-based and non-class-room-based charters, and between conversions and startups. Clearly, as Berends et al. argue, much more information about what the schools are actually doing is needed. Information like this is rarely available in state-wide student longitudinal data, however.

It should also be stressed that even when effects are found, be they positive or negative, they are almost always small. It may well be, then, that other factors—the extent to which charters improve parental satisfaction through the exercise of choice, or whether they increase or decrease segregation—are more important for policymakers. Certainly from a policy standpoint, we need to know more about whether charter schools have competitive effects on traditional schools. Attempting to tease out these effects is extremely difficult, although the chapters here make an attempt. The reality is that there are still too few charters relative to the traditional system to detect competitive effects.

Finally, it is worth carefully considering what to make of charter studies showing that parental choices alter the composition of schools. The results of the studies in this volume are mixed. Zimmer and Buddin find in California, for example, that "charter schools have not created 'White enclaves' or 'skimmed' high-quality black and lower achieving students from TPSs [traditional public schools]," while Bifulco and Ladd suggest that in North Carolina charters have exacerbated racial segregation. The hard question is what to do with results in either direction. If the poor and minority parents are choosing schools with more or fewer students like themselves, it certainly does not seem appropriate for researchers to suggest that this is either good or bad. Society as a whole will have to grapple with how to weigh the desirability of increased choice and parental satisfaction against choices that may not be to the liking of the community as a whole.

REFERENCE

Betts, J., & Hill, P. (2006). *Key issues in studying charter schools and achievement: A review and suggestions for national guidelines.* Seattle, WA: National Charter School Research Project, Charter School Achievement Consensus Panel.

7

Charter Schools in California[1]

RON ZIMMER AND RICHARD BUDDIN

INTRODUCTION

This chapter summarizes a series of studies we have conducted over the last 4 years that evaluate the effectiveness of California charter schools. California has been an important state in the debate over charter schools. It was the second state to authorize charter schools in 1992. More than 210,000 students now attend about 550 charter schools there—the largest charter sector in the nation. Of those, almost 200 new charter schools have opened in the past 5 years. Charter schools are found in most parts of the state, from districts in small, rural counties to large, urban districts (Edwards, 2006).

What also makes California important to the overall charter debate is its variety of charter schools. Some are "conversions" and others are "start-ups." Conversion schools previously existed as traditional public schools; they typically retain an existing facility as well as faculty and students when they become charter schools. Start-up schools, by contrast, are new entities that acquire facilities, faculty, and students at their inception. The motivation to start charter schools may differ between these types, with conversion schools becoming charters to reduce their bureaucracy from the districts and to change specific educational programs, and start-up schools initiating to create a new holistic approach to schools, including curriculum programs, instructional practices, governance structures, and overall mission.

[1] Portions of this research were sponsored by the California Legislative Analyst's Office and the Smith Richardson Foundation. The opinions and conclusions expressed in this research are the authors' alone and should not be interpreted as representing those of RAND or of the sponsors of this research.

California charter schools also use two distinct instructional approaches. Most rely exclusively on instruction in traditional classroom settings, but some make extensive use of nonclassroom settings, such as homeschooling, independent study, and distance learning. Charter schools that use traditional classroom instruction are more likely to have similar curricula and operation than schools that provide a significant portion of instruction outside the classroom.

RESEARCH APPROACH

This study uses information from California to address three key policy questions about charter schools:

- What types of students do charter schools serve?
- Do charters improve the performance of charter students?
- Is charter competition improving the performance of traditional public schools?

These questions address important issues about the effectiveness of charter schools and whether charters are meeting the objective of charter school proponents or causing the adverse effects anticipated by charter opponents. To answer these questions, we rely upon student-level data as highlighted in the following:

- *Statewide student-level data.* The California Department of Education collected individual-level test scores for about 20 million test records between 1997–1998 and 2001–2002. The Stanford 9 achievement test was administered in grades 2–11 in the spring of each academic year. The accompanying administrative data include information on student ethnicity, English learner status, school lunch eligibility, and student mobility. These data do not include an individual student identifier to track individual student progress from year to year. Nevertheless, the file is used to track gains of grade cohorts while precisely accounting for factors that might influence test scores.
- *District student-level data.* We also collected student-level data with individual identifiers from six districts with a large share of charter schools (Chula Vista, Fresno, Los Angeles, Napa Valley, San Diego, and West Covina). These data include the same information as the statewide data, but also include individual identifiers allowing for the measurement of the amount of time spent in different schools, student movement from traditional public schools to charter schools and vice versa, and differences in charter and traditional public school populations.

The remainder of the chapter is divided into three sections (one for each question) and a conclusion. Separate statistical methods are used in each section, so the methods will be described in each section of the study.

WHAT TYPES OF STUDENTS DO CHARTER SCHOOLS SERVE?

Because charter schools are schools of choice, it is important to examine whether they are serving the full range of the student population and whether they are doing so in integrated settings. Charter school critics argue that charter success might be illusory if charter schools are simply recruiting the best students from traditional public schools or if they further stratify an already ethnically or racially[1] stratified system (Cobb & Glass, 1999; Wells et al., 1998). In general, these critics fear that charter schools may not only have negative consequences for the charter students who attend these schools, but if charter schools "skim off" high achieving students, they may also have adverse social and academic effects for students who remain in traditional public schools.[2] However, proponents of charter schools argue that charter schools will improve racial integration by letting families choose schools outside neighborhoods where housing is racially segregated (Finn, Manno, & Vanourek, 2000; Nathan, 1996).

Previous studies have examined the racial makeup of charter schools relative to the average racial makeup of their surrounding districts and states (Frankenberg & Lee, 2003; Miron & Nelson, 2002; Powell, Blackorby, Marsh, Finnegan, & Anderson, 1997; RPP International, 2000). While this research has provided some insights, it does have some weaknesses. First, it has exclusively examined race, ignoring altogether the issue of stratification by ability.[3] Second, it has used cross-sectional snapshots of schools' enrollments, which does not permit examination of the movement of students between schools. Understanding how charter schools affect the mixing of students requires a dynamic model that uses longitudinal data to examine the movements of individual students.

---

[1] For simplicity, we will refer to race/ethnicity as race throughout the rest of the chapter.

[2] The interaction of students with diverse backgrounds and ability levels can have positive social and academic effects for students (Frankenberg & Lee, 2003; Summers & Wolfe, 1977; Zimmer, 2003; Zimmer & Toma, 2000). If charter schools affect the distribution of students both by race and ability, then they may have implications not only for their students, but also for students who remain in traditional public schools. Many fear that charter schools will further racially stratify an already deeply stratified system and will skim off the best students from traditional public schools, reducing the peer effects within the traditional schools.

[3] Sass (2006) does find that students enrolled in "gifted" programs are less likely to transfer to charter schools, but does not consider more general measures like the level of prior test scores.

One exception is a study by Bifulco and Ladd (2006b) in which they examine migration patterns of students of different races as they choose to go to charter schools in North Carolina. They find that black students are more likely to go to charter schools with higher concentrations of black students than those of their exiting schools. These results highlight the importance of using student-level data.

Like Bifulco and Ladd, we use student-level data from the six districts in which we can link students over time to examine the racial makeup of students most likely to enroll at a charter school, and to examine whether charter schools are "skimming" the best students or are actually attracting the lowest performing students. This is presented in a paper entitled "The Effect of Charter Schools on School Peer Composition" (Booker, Zimmer, & Buddin, 2005). The longitudinal nature of the data is used to track student movements from school to school. This data feature allows us to examine the characteristics of students that migrate from a traditional public to a charter school and compare the students' characteristics with the distribution of students at the old and new schools.

Racial Sorting

Do charter school students move to more or less racially integrated schools? Table 7.1 examines the peer environment in both schools for charter transfers. Column two of the table shows the overall results for all students, and columns three through six show detailed results by each racial group. Students are moving to charter schools with a higher percentage of black students and a lower percentage of Hispanic students than the traditional public schools they previously attended.

The effects of charter schools on racial diversity are also examined using a Herfindahl index for each school campus. The index is defined as the sum of the squared shares of each racial group and is scaled from 0 to 1, where 1 indicates total concentration of enrollment in one racial group. The higher the index is, therefore, the less diverse the school is. Students are transferring to charter schools slightly more diverse than the traditional public schools they are leaving.

The results in Table 7.1 show some interesting movement patterns for students in different race groups. The typical black transfer student moves from a traditional public school that is 39% black to a charter school that is 51% black. The Herfindahl measure also shows that black students are transferring to charter schools that are less diverse than the traditional public schools they left. In contrast with black students, white, Hispanic, and Asian students in California tend to go to charter schools that have a lower percentage of students of the same race and that are more diverse than their traditional public schools.

Overall, it appears that black students are choosing charter schools that are less diverse and more "like them." This result is consistent with

TABLE 7.1

Traditional Public School (TPS) and Charter School Peer Environments: Comparison by Student Race

	Total	White	Black	Hispanic	Asian
Number of students	14,210	1,834	5,342	5,641	524
Whites at TPS (%)	14.7	44.9	7.5	11.7	22.5
Whites at charter (%)	14.7	37.5	7.4	13.1	31.7
Difference	0.0	−7.4[a]	−0.1	1.4[a]	9.2[a]
Blacks at TPS (%)	26.1	12.9	39.1	19.5	20.2
Blacks at charter (%)	39.7	18.5	50.8	30.1	22.8
Difference	13.6[a]	5.6[a]	11.7[a]	10.6[a]	2.6
Hispanics at TPS (%)	47.9	28.0	46.0	61.4	36.6
Hispanics at charter (%)	36.0	32.2	25.0	49.4	31.7
Difference	−11.9[a]	4.2[a]	−21.0[a]	−12.0[a]	−5.1[a]
Asians at TPS (%)	11.0	13.6	7.2	7.1	20.3
Asians at charter (%)	9.2	11.0	6.5	7.0	17.2
Difference	−1.8[a]	−2.6[a]	−0.7	−0.1	−3.1
Herfindahl at TPS	0.523	0.442	0.508	0.582	0.409
Herfindahl at charter	0.518	0.347	0.579	0.562	0.336
Difference	−0.005	−0.095[a]	0.071[a]	−0.020[a]	−0.073[a]

[a] Difference is significant at 5% level.

patterns of charter school transfers in North Carolina (Bilfulco & Ladd, 2006b). However, white students are shifting to schools that have a lower percentage of whites than their traditional public schools. Hispanic students move to charter schools with a lower percentage of Hispanics than the traditional public schools they leave.

Ability Sorting

An analysis of ability sorting for charter school movers is shown in Table 7.2. Individual test scores of charter students in the year before their move are shown along with the means of student peers in each student's traditional school. A comparison of the test scores of movers and those of peers left behind shows whether charter schools are skimming the best traditional school students or providing options for students who have not succeeded in traditional public schools.

The results provide little evidence of ability sorting into charter schools. Students moving to charter schools have slightly lower test scores than their traditional public school peers (0.09 and 0.04 standard deviations in

TABLE 7.2
Average Test Scores of Charter Transfer Students: Comparison With Traditional
Public School (TPS) Peers

	Total
Number of students	13,863
Math score of transfer students before transfer	−0.073
Math score of TPS peers	0.013
Difference	−0.086[a]
Reading score of transfer students before transfer	0.022
Reading score of TPS peers	0.059
Difference	−0.037[a]

[a] Difference is significant at 5% level.

math and reading, respectively), which leads us to conclude that California charter schools are not skimming the best students from traditional public schools.

DO CHARTERS IMPROVE THE PERFORMANCE OF CHARTER STUDENTS?

A recent consensus panel on charter schools stressed the importance of analysis that relies on student-level data and a value-added approach to track student progress over time (Betts & Hill, 2006). The panel stressed the biases inherent in school-level comparisons between charter and traditional schools. A key weakness of a school-level analysis is the high degree of aggregation, which masks changes over time in the school's population of students and variation of performance across different subjects and grades. In essence, school-level data may not pick up the nuances of school characteristics and can only provide an incomplete picture of why outcomes vary across schools. Similarly, cross-sectional comparisons of individual student scores in charter and traditional public schools are likely to be misleading, because unmeasured student characteristics (perhaps parental involvement or motivation) may differ across school types and distort the "true" contribution of charter schools to student learning.

The past 4 years have seen several key studies that use longitudinal data to isolate charter school effects. Hanushek, Kain, and Rivkin (2002) found negative effects of Texas charter schools on student achievement during the initial years of operation, but no significant difference in achievement between charter and traditional public schools after about 3 years of operation. Zimmer et al. (2003) found that student achievement in California charter schools was keeping pace with traditional public schools. Booker, Gilpatric, Gronberg, and Jansen (2004a) adjusted for charter-specific mobility effects in Texas and found that charter school students do eventually outperform their traditional public school counterparts. Bilfulco and Ladd (2006a) found that charter students in North Carolina made smaller achievement gains over time than those students would have made in traditional schools. Sass (2006) found that charter students initially had lower performance than traditional public school students, but charter schools produced similar gains to those of traditional public schools as the schools matured.[1]

Our analysis has relied upon a two-pronged approach to assess charter performance in California. The first approach relies on statewide student-level data to examine the patterns in student achievement in charter and traditional public schools and especially to isolate the different effects of alternative charter types (start-up and conversion, classroom- and non-classroom-based instruction). A subset of the statewide data is also used to examine how school operations affect achievement in charters and a matched sample of traditional public schools. The statewide data provide the broadest picture of how charters are doing across the state and do include controls for student background and demographics at each school and over time. A limitation of the statewide data, however, is that they do not include a student-level identifier that would allow the tracking of student progress from year to year. California is planning a statewide student identifier but does not currently have one.

The second approach relies on the district student-level data that do include student-level identifiers. Longitudinal tracking of student progress minimizes the problem of selection bias by examining the academic gains made by individual students over time, factoring out students' baseline achievement levels. Moreover, they permit "within-student" comparisons of achievement gains, examining changes in the achievement trajectories of individual students who move from traditional public schools to charter schools, or vice versa.

Statewide Student-Level Data: Charter Type and Academic Achievement

The statistical model of student achievement in the paper entitled "A Closer Look at Charter School Student Achievement" (Buddin & Zim-

---

[1] Hoxby and Rockoff (2004) also examine four charter schools in Chicago, which provide some evidence that charter students outperform noncharter students. Their analysis capitalizes on the fact that these schools are oversubscribed and used a lottery mechanism to admit students. Presumably, the lottery winners and losers are similar in every way except admission into these schools. Tracking performance of both sets of students then creates an unbiased perspective of performance. However, Hoxby and Rockoff's study has a major drawback in that it may have limited implications for those schools that do not have wait lists. Schools with wait lists may in fact be the best schools, thus it would be surprising if they had the same results as those of other charter schools.

mer, 2005a) is based on a multilevel approach where random effects are estimated for each school and each grade cohort within each school. The school-level random effect allows for unobserved heterogeneity across schools; that is, the learning environment may vary systematically at different schools in ways that have a common achievement effect on the students that attend those schools. The grade-cohort effect is designed to capture the possibility that some groups of students may have a persistent achievement score effect. For example, if third grade students at a particular school score high in math in one year (relative to past cohorts with similar student characteristics), then the next year's fourth grade students at the same school are also likely to excel in math because of unmeasured attributes of students in the grade cohort.

In addition to the random components, the model also adjusts for the individual characteristics of each student taking the test. The key student characteristics available are limited English proficiency, race, gender, and eligibility for the free or reduced-price school lunch program. The California test data also include an indication of the parental education for each student. Finally, the data indicate whether students are in their first year at their current school. Students (and their parents) may have difficulty in making the transition to friends and teachers at a new school, so their test scores in the new school may be lower than those of similar students who remain at the same school (Hanushek et al., 2002).

The formal model describes the relationship between student-level test scores, student and school characteristics, a random school effect, and a random grade-cohort effect within each school. The model includes dummy variables to describe any possible time trend in test scores over the 5 years from 1998 through 2002. The dependent variable is the student percentile test score, T_{ijkt}, observed for student i in school j and grade cohort k at time t. The formal model is

$$T_{ijkt} = x_{it}\beta + w_{jt}\gamma + \theta_j + \Psi_{j(k)} + \varepsilon_{ijkt} \tag{7.1}$$

where

x_{it} and w_{jt} are vectors of measured time-varying student and school characteristics, respectively
β and γ are parameter vectors for student and school effects
θ_j and $\psi_{j(k)}$ represent school and grade-cohort time heterogeneity, respectively
ε_{ijkt} is a random error term that is orthogonal to all other effects in the model

The x_{it} vector includes elements for school type. In particular, we estimated three types of charter school models:

- a basic model that simply compares test scores between charter and traditional public schools
- a model that separates the performance of conversion and start-up charter schools
- a more general model that examines how classroom- and nonclassroom-based instruction affects achievement in conversions and start-ups[1]

Later in this section, we will expand the set of school variables to include survey information on school operations in an analysis of the charters and matched traditional public schools. The regression results in Table 7.3 show that the charter effects for elementary students differ somewhat across alternative types of charter schools.[2] Model 1 results indicate that charter school students are performing the same in reading and 1.44 percentile points lower in math than are comparable students in traditional public schools. Model 2 shows that conversion charter schools have a small, positive effect on reading and a small, negative effect in math compared to traditional public schools. In contrast, start-up students score about 5–7 percentage points lower than do similar students in traditional public schools in reading and math, respectively.

The results from Model 3 show the importance of separating charter schools based on whether they provide classroom- or nonclassroom-based instruction. Students in nonclassroom-based conversion and start-up schools have much lower test scores than do comparable students in traditional public schools. Classroom-based charter schools are keeping pace with traditional public schools—the test scores in classroom-based conversions are one percentile point higher in reading and half a point lower in math, while start-up scores do not differ significantly from those in traditional schools.

The secondary school results in Table 7.4 show that charter students overall are scoring 1.46 and 2.26 percentile points lower than similar students in traditional schools (see Model 1). The results in Model 2, however, show that start-up school students have lower reading and math scores than do comparable students in traditional public schools. The conversion coefficients are insignificant for reading and slightly negative for math.

Finally, the Model 3 results in Table 7.4 show that nonclassroom-based schools are pulling down the average test scores for both conversion and start-up schools. Nonclassroom-based charter schools are performing

---

[1] We should note that not all students that attend a nonclassroom-based charter school receive nonclassroom-based instruction, because many of these schools are actually hybrid schools that include classroom and nonclassroom instruction. In addition, our data do not distinguish whether a particular student uses any form of nonclassroom instruction, but we do know which charter schools offer these programs.

[2] Buddin and Zimmer (2005a) include more specifications of this model, including a comparison of charter effects for new and established charter schools. Tables 7.4 and 7.5 summarize regressions that also control for student demographics.

TABLE 7.3
Stanford 9 Test Regressions for Elementary Students by School Type

Variable	Reading		Math	
	Coefficient	Standard error	Coefficient	Standard error
Model 1: Comparison of charter and traditional public schools				
Charter	0.1315	0.2082	−1.4453[a]	0.2264
R-square	0.5822		0.4736	
Model 2: Comparison of conversion and start up schools				
Charter type				
Conversion charter	0.9785[a]	0.2257	−0.6024[a]	0.2441
Start up charter	−4.6627[a]	0.5346	−6.5341[a]	0.5962
R-square	0.5830		0.4775	
Model 3: Comparison of classroom- and nonclassroom-based charter schools				
Charter type				
Conversion and classroom	1.0123[a]	0.2354	−0.5147[a]	0.2546
Conversion and nonclassroom	−4.325[a]	1.6449	−9.1836[a]	1.843
Start up and classroom	0.9871	0.932	−1.4994	1.0613
Start up and nonclassroom	−7.5771[a]	0.6995	−9.129[a]	0.7723
R-square	0.5848		0.4803	

Notes: Standard errors are in parentheses. The R-square statistic shows the reduction in the variance components for this model relative to an unconditional mean model that only adjusts for the two random effects (Bryk & Raudenbush, 2002). Sample size is 9,114,624 student records.
[a] Associated with coefficients that are significantly different from zero at the $\alpha = 0.05$ confidence level.

poorly compared with traditional public schools. Classroom-based conversion schools have mixed results—the reading score is no different from that in traditional public schools, but the math score is slightly lower. The test scores for classroom-based start-ups are higher than those of traditional public schools, after adjusting for the mix of students attending these schools.

The evidence shows important differences in test score performance across different types of charter schools, but the underlying reasons for these differences are not clear without greater analysis of the operation

TABLE 7.4
Stanford 9 Test Regressions for Secondary Students by School Type

Variable	Reading		Math	
	Coefficient	Standard error	Coefficient	Standard error
Model 1: Comparison of charter and traditional public schools				
Charter	−1.4594[a]	0.2531	−2.2585[a]	0.2752
R-square	0.4045		0.3085	
Model 2: Comparison of conversion and start-up charter schools				
Charter type				
Conversion charter	−0.0062	0.3065	−1.2442[a]	0.332
Start-up charter	−4.5596[a]	0.4469	−4.4677[a]	0.4894
R-square	0.4045		0.3085	
Model 3: Comparison of classroom-based and nonclassroom-based charter schools				
Charter type				
Conversion and classroom	0.1084	0.3094	−1.0962[a]	0.335
Conversion and nonclassroom	−4.3659	2.3507	−8.0897[a]	2.6461
Start-up and classroom	2.7535[a]	0.8936	2.0399[a]	1.0097
Start-up and nonclassroom	−7.2532[a]	0.5486	−6.8754[a]	0.594
R-square	0.4093		0.3123	

Notes: Standard errors are in parentheses. The R-square statistic shows the reduction in the variance components for this model relative to an unconditional mean model that only adjusts for the two random effects (Bryk & Raudenbush, 2002). Sample size is 12,647,295 student records.
[a] Associated with coefficients that are significantly different from zero at the $\alpha = 0.05$ confidence level.

of these schools.[1] In addition, the schools may differ from one another in the types of students that they attract. For instance, nonclassroom-based students may be different from students in traditional public schools in unique ways that are not captured by the demographic factors in the analysis. More explicitly, if nonclassroom-based students have been pulled out of traditional public schools because of problems in traditional settings, then

---

[1] In a paper entitled "Getting Inside the black Box: Examining How the Operation of Charter Schools Affects Performance," we examine how operational features of both charter and traditional public schools are correlated with student achievement. We do not present the results here because of space limitations.

traditional public school students who do not have these problems do not make a good comparison group. With longitudinally linked student-level data, an analysis would be better able to control for these unobservable differences. Nevertheless, the differences in performance among charter schools in our analysis are compelling and underscore the importance of considering these differences when interpreting charter school results.

District Student-Level Data: Statistical Mode

For our analysis of the longitudinal data in the six districts, the statistical model in Equation (7.1) is modified to capitalize on the linkage of individual student records from year to year. Equation (7.2) describes a basic approach for estimating a charter school effect:

$$T_{it} = \mu_i + \gamma C_{it} + x_{it}\beta + \upsilon_{it} \tag{7.2}$$

where

i and t index individual students and years, respectively
T is test score
μ is an unobserved student-specific factor that does not vary over time
γ is an unobserved parameter reflecting the possible effect of charter
        school attendance on T
C is an indicator variable that equals one if the school is a charter school
        and zero otherwise
x is a $1 \times K$ vector of K observable factors affecting s
β is a $K \times 1$ vector of unobserved parameters
υ is a random error term

The model includes observed family background characteristics like race and other demographics that are likely to affect student achievement.

To control for unobservable differences for students that might affect student achievement but are not captured by observable control variable of students, we use a fixed-effect model. A fixed-effect model uses the longitudinal nature of the data to "difference out" the μ for observations on the same individual. To estimate the charter effect through a fixed-effects approach, we average the variables for the ith individual student and subtract this result from Equation (7.2), so the transformed fixed-effects equation is

$$s_{it} - \overline{s}_i = \gamma(C_{it} - \overline{C}_i) + (x_{it} - \overline{x}_i)\beta + (\upsilon_{it} - \upsilon_i) \tag{7.3}$$

where the "bar" above each variable is the corresponding variable mean.

The student fixed effect combines all student-level factors that are invariant over time and affect student achievement, so the results do not include separate parameter estimates for student factors like ethnicity that are invariant over time.[1] The available student background variables do not vary over time, so the x vector consists of a test year variable to detect any trend in scores.

A more general random-growth model is also used to control for the heterogeneity of students attending different traditional public and charter schools (Heckman & Hotz, 1979; Papke, 1994; Wooldridge, 2002). The random-growth specification generalizes the fixed-effects model to allow for individual students to differ with respect not only to a constant factor (μ) but also with the rate of test score growth over time. The basis for the random-growth model is Equation (7.4):

$$T_{it} = \mu_i + \tau_i t + \gamma C_{it} + x_{it}\beta + \upsilon_{it} \tag{7.4}$$

where τ is an individual-specific growth rate. Equation (7.4) is a more general version of Equation (7.2) that allows for individual-specific differences in both the test score intercept and slope. The model is now first-differenced to obtain:

$$\Delta T_{it} = \tau_i + \gamma \Delta C_{it} + \Delta x_{it}\beta + \Delta \upsilon_{it} \tag{7.5}$$

The differencing eliminates the μ, and τ becomes the intercept of the differenced equation.[2] Equation (7.5) is estimated by fixed effects to eliminate τ_i and to obtain estimates of γ and β.

The potential advantage of the random-growth model over the fixed-effect model depends on two factors. First, the random-growth model is more appropriate if the test score trend varies across individual students (remember that the fixed-effects model also controls for an overall test score trend). Second, the random-growth approach is preferred if the student-specific trend is correlated with charter school enrollment or other exogenous variables in the model. For example, if individual students with strong positive trends in achievement were prone to transfer to charter schools, then the fixed-effects approach might suggest a positive charter effect on achievement irrespective of whether those schools did anything

---

[1] In our analysis, we test for serial correlation in the residuals in Equation (7.3). First-differencing is a preferred estimation method if there is strong positive serial correlation in panel data (Wooldridge, 2002). In this case, our test of serial correlation was weak, so the parameters from the fixed-effect model reported later are similar to those from the first-differenced model.

[2] The growth term simplifies because $\tau_i t - \tau_i(t - 1) = \tau_i$. In this specification, the year-to-year change in the trend term is perfectly collinear with the constant and cannot be estimated. The model does include a parameter for the change in the quadratic trend term.

to enhance the learning of the students that transferred from traditional public to charter schools. The estimated parameters γ and β will vary little between these two models if these two factors do not hold.

A limitation of the random-growth model is that it requires at least three successive years of test score data to isolate a test score trend, and this requirement implicitly excludes many students from the analysis. For example, from the cohorts of students enrolled in elementary school in 1998–1999, only second and third graders are observed for three consecutive elementary school years by the end of the observation period in 2001–2002. Similarly, students that enter second grade in 2000–2001 or 2001–2002 are not observed for three consecutive years and are not included in the estimates of the random-growth model in Equation (7.5).

As an extension to these models, we estimate the charter interaction effects by race and by whether the student is classified as limited English proficient (LEP). For the fixed-effects analysis, Equation (7.3) is modified to add interaction terms between the charter school dummy variable and a vector of student characteristics as specified in the following equation:

$$T_{it} - \overline{T}_i = \gamma(C_{it} - \overline{C}_i) + (C_{it}R_i - \overline{C_iR_i})\delta + (x_{it} - \overline{x}_i)\beta + (\upsilon_{it} - \overline{\upsilon}_i) \qquad (7.6)$$

where the charter dummy variable (C_{it}) for student i in time period t is interacted with a vector of demographic characteristics (R_i) of student i, including indicators for black, Hispanic, and LEP, and δ is a 3×1 vector of unobserved effects.

In this formulation of the model, γ represents the effect of charter schools on test scores of students who are not black, Hispanic, or classified as LEP. The coefficients on the interaction terms (δ) indicate whether charter effects are higher or lower for black, Hispanic, or LEP students than for similar students in traditional public schools.

The random-growth model was also modified to add interaction terms that show whether there is a charter effect difference by race or LEP status.

$$\Delta s_{it} = \tau_i = \gamma\Delta C_{it} + \Delta(C_{it}R_i)\delta + \Delta x_{it}\beta + \Delta\upsilon_{it} \qquad (7.7)$$

As in the earlier random-effects specification, this differenced model is estimated by fixed effects to eliminate the individual student effect and derive consistent estimates of γ, δ, and β.

The charter effect in both the fixed-effects and random-growth models is identified from the behavior of students that either switch from a charter to a traditional public school or from a traditional public to a charter school. The differencing approach in both models isolates the student achievement gains associated with these school transitions, while permanent time-invariant factors (observed and unobserved) that affect achievement are held constant. The approaches compare the achievement gains of students in charter schools with those of the same students in traditional public schools and vice versa. The charter effect is the differential effect on student learning of either transferring to a charter from a traditional public school or from a traditional public to a charter school.

The identification of a charter effect from switchers has several potential limitations. First, the approach does not compare the growth in student achievement for students who attend only a traditional or charter school over the 5-year enrollment period. Second, student or family factors may change over time in ways that coincide with the transition to a charter school. For example, parents might provide more homework assistance if they perceive that a traditional public school is low quality and reduce their input after transferring their child to a charter school. If so, the estimated charter effect would understate the "true" effect of charters.

Basic Charter Effect

Table 7.5 shows the coefficient estimates for the fixed-effects and random-growth model across the six districts. The fixed-effects results are reported to add robustness to our results because the results are similar in magnitude and significance across the two models. This suggests that the estimation of the charter effect is not particularly sensitive to the modeling approach. To the extent that the estimates differ, the random-growth model is preferred, since it provides a more complete accounting of differences in the underlying growth trajectory of individual students.

The random-growth estimates in Table 7.5 show that elementary math students in charter schools have test scores 1.64 percentile points lower than comparable students in traditional public schools. At the secondary school level, reading scores are 0.34 percentile points higher in charters than in traditional public schools. School type differences have no significant effect on elementary school reading or on secondary school math.

These results show that achievement in charter schools is largely keeping pace with traditional public schools. The charter effects in the random-growth model are similar to those in the statewide analysis shown in Tables 7.3 and 7.4. The estimates in Table 7.5 are substantially more complete, however, because they implicitly control for unobserved student-level factors that might distort the estimates of the charter effect.

Charter Effects by Demographic Groups

Because many urban leaders, including mayors and school district superintendents, have initiated charter schools as a mechanism to improve learning for disadvantaged students, we also examined the effects of charter schools on urban districts' student achievement generally and on different demographic groups, using data from Los Angeles and San

TABLE 7.5

Fixed-Effects and Random-Growth Models of Student Achievement and Charter Status

	Fixed-effects model		Random-growth model	
	Reading	Math	Reading	Math
Elementary schools				
Charter	−0.0848	−1.2600[a]	−0.2148	−1.6440[a]
	(0.0882)	(0.1056)	(0.1589)	(0.1912)
Trend	1.6107[a]	1.3818[a]	1.6033[a]	1.7558[a]
	(0.0080)	(0.0095)	(0.0135)	(0.0163)
Constant	36.7761[a]	42.2800[a]		
	(0.0251)	(0.0296)		
Observations	1,554,666	1,598,639	816,364	854,899
Secondary schools				
Charter	0.2767[a]	−0.3816[a]	0.3392[a]	−0.1959
	(0.0921)	(0.1021)	(0.1714)	(0.1885)
Trend	0.0323[a]	0.7389[a]	0.2832[a]	0.5099[a]
	(0.0070)	(0.0078)	(0.0138)	(0.0152)
Constant	38.7003[a]	41.6877[a]		
	(0.0224)	(0.0247)		
Observations	1,351,000	1,360,492	749,413	757,760

Notes: Standard errors are in parentheses. As shown in Equation (7.5), the constant term in the random-growth model represents the trend in student achievement, so there is no separate constant term in this equation.

[a] Associated with coefficients that are significantly different from zero at the $\alpha = 0.05$ confidence level.

Diego. The results are based on the analysis from a paper entitled "Charter School Performance in Urban Districts" (Zimmer & Buddin, 2006).

To carry out this analysis, we again used a random-growth model as displayed in Equation (7.2), but added terms that relate the student racial characteristics and LEP status of students with the charter variable. The interaction of charter status with student type is useful for examining whether charter school effects differ for different groups. Black, Hispanic, and LEP students lag behind other students in both of these districts, as is the case in most urban districts. If charter schools reduce student achievement gaps for these groups, then they might pose an important policy option for improving the performance of "at-risk" students.

The interaction terms in the regression specification complicate the interpretation of the charter school effects for different types of students.

TABLE 7.6
Summary of Elementary School Test Results

	Reading test		Math test	
	TPS score	Charter effect	TPS score	Charter effect
Los Angeles schools				
Overall	39.42	−0.61	44.47	−0.30
Student type				
Black and not LEP	34.56	−1.36[a]	34.59	−1.22[a]
Black and LEP	26.95	−1.73	29.16	−2.50
Hispanic and not LEP	33.53	0.11	40.10	1.48
Hispanic and LEP	27.93	−0.26	34.66	0.21
Other and not LEP	51.46	1.91	56.52	−0.16
Other and LEP	43.85	1.53	51.08	−1.44
San Diego schools				
Overall	49.63	−2.10[a]	53.48	−4.97[a]
Student type				
Black and not LEP	42.76	−2.88[a]	43.31	−3.79[a]
Black and LEP	28.81	−0.36	34.22	−4.31
Hispanic and not LEP	44.17	−2.54	47.91	−5.52[a]
Hispanic and LEP	31.22	−0.02	38.81	−6.04[a]
Other and not LEP	57.72	−3.60[a]	60.97	−5.34[a]
Other and LEP	44.77	−1.08	51.87	−5.85[a]

Note: TPS = traditional public school.
[a] Indicates that the coefficient is statistically significant at the 5% level.

Given the complexity of the regression specification, we report summary tables of the charter school effects for different types of students in Table 7.6 (elementary students) and Table 7.7 (secondary students).[1] The tables also show the average test score effect overall and by student type in Los Angeles and San Diego. As expected, the averages indicate that black and Hispanic students lag substantially behind the other racial group. LEP students, who are predominantly Hispanic in California, also have lower test scores than similar students with stronger English skills in each racial group.

The Los Angeles elementary school results in Table 7.6 show that nearly all types of charter school students are doing about the same as they would have done in traditional public schools. Black non-LEP students

---

[1] Zimmer and Buddin (2006) show the complete regression specifications.

TABLE 7.7
Summary of Secondary School Test Results

	Reading test		Math test	
	TPS score	Charter effect	TPS score	Charter effect
Los Angeles schools				
Overall	37.40	−1.15[a]	42.74	1.28[a]
Student type				
Black and not LEP	35.37	−0.33	35.65	0.89
Black and LEP	24.31	−0.90	28.06	−0.46
Hispanic and not LEP	36.53	−1.62[a]	39.51	3.44[a]
Hispanic and LEP	25.48	−2.19[a]	31.91	2.09[a]
Other and not LEP	50.65	−2.35[a]	56.01	0.61
Other and LEP	39.60	−2.92[a]	48.42	−0.74
San Diego schools				
Overall	47.22	1.49[a]	51.48	−1.69[a]
Student type				
Black and not LEP	42.65	1.62[a]	41.55	−2.58[a]
Black and LEP	29.50	1.73[a]	33.10	−2.26[a]
Hispanic and not LEP	44.16	0.70	44.90	−0.20
Hispanic and LEP	31.02	0.81[a]	36.46	0.28
Other and not LEP	56.77	2.71[a]	59.23	−4.15[a]
Other and LEP	43.62	2.82[a]	50.79	−3.83[a]

Note: TPS = traditional public school.
[a] Indicates that the coefficient is statistically significant at the 5% level.

are the only group with a significant charter effect in either reading or math test scores, and these students do worse in charter schools than in traditional public schools.

The San Diego elementary school results in Table 7.6 show that the effects of charter schools are predominately negative with the magnitude of the effects being more negative in math than in reading. Black charter school students have test scores that are −2.88 and −3.79 points lower and statistically significant in reading and math, respectively, compared to comparable black students in traditional public schools. Hispanic students have worse math scores than their counterparts in traditional public schools, but reading scores do not differ significantly across the two types of schools.

Interestingly, the LEP status for Hispanic students (the largest share of LEP students) does not affect the differential achievement of students between charter and traditional schools—LEP and other Hispanic charter school students do no better in reading than their traditional public school counterparts, but both groups of Hispanics do worse in math.

The secondary school charter effects for particular student groups are summarized in Table 7.7. In Los Angeles, the results show charter students performing 1.15 percentile points lower in reading than comparable students in traditional public schools, but charter student math scores are 1.28 percentile points higher than those for students in traditional public schools. The results show that black students are performing at the same level in both charter and traditional public schools. Hispanic and other charter school students are doing worse in reading than are comparable students in traditional public schools. Hispanic charter school students are scoring higher in math than are similar Hispanic students in traditional public schools.

The secondary school results for San Diego show positive reading effects (1.49 points) and negative math effects (1.69 points). The positive reading and negative math effects are dominated by the black and other student effects in both areas. Hispanic students do about the same in charter schools as in traditional public schools.

In general, the results of this analysis suggest that charter schools are having, at best, mixed results for students of different racial categories and LEP students. While there are some cases in which charter schools do improve the performance of blacks and Hispanics, it is clear that they are not consistently creating greater gains than their traditional public school counterparts. We should note that these results are for two large districts in California, and the effects of charter schools may differ in other states and districts, where the charter laws and operational environment differ from those of these California districts.

Other Measures of Student Outcomes

Our analysis, like several recent charter studies, has focused on student achievement in reading and math as the key measure of charter and traditional public school performance. A more complete analysis would include other measures: (1) school factors like safety and learning environment; (2) student achievement in dimensions other than reading and math; (3) noncognitive student measures like self-confidence, motivation, and self-esteem; and (4) high school completion and college transition. These factors are hard to measure objectively, and data availability is scarce. Charter schools may be outpacing traditional public schools in several of these dimensions, but the evidence is not yet available. If charters are making substantial improvements to student safety, the learning environment, or noncognitive student factors, however, we would expect many of these gains to translate into improvement in student reading and math achievement. The broad picture from reading and math scores is that charter schools are keeping pace with traditional public schools, irrespective of changes in other factors related to school type.

IS CHARTER COMPETITION IMPROVING THE PERFORMANCE OF TRADITIONAL SCHOOLS?

While much of the existing research on charter schools has focused on student achievement effects for students who choose to attend charter schools, we argue that this focus may be too narrow. Supporters hope that charter schools can exert healthy competitive pressure on the existing K–12 educational system by giving families alternatives to traditional public schools. In fact, given that charter schools will probably never educate a substantial portion of the nation's student population, charter advocates argue that these schools may have their greatest impact through systemic effects. That is, the competitive effects of charter schools could improve the performance of traditional public schools and enhance the performance of students who do not attend charter schools.

The challenge in evaluating possible competitive effects is in knowing when district or school personnel will perceive a competitive threat. Do charter schools create competitive pressure when they are located near a traditional public school or when they first appear in a district? Do charter schools only create competitive pressure when they start recruiting students away from a particular school, or do they exert pressure when they capture a certain portion of students within a "marketplace?" Additionally, the local environment may influence the competitive pressure that charter schools create. For instance, some districts may have well developed, preexisting choice programs, including magnet schools or open enrollment policies. Also, some districts may be experiencing significant growth or already have overcrowded schools, in which case charter schools may act more like a "release" valve than a source of competitive pressure.

Researchers investigating this issue have made critical assumptions about the competitive process, which could affect conclusions about the competitive effects. For example, Hoxby (2001) defines competition as whether there is minimum market penetration of charter schools within a district; she finds substantial positive competitive effects in Arizona and Michigan. However, Bettinger (2005), using an instrumental variable strategy, also examines competitive effects in Michigan as measured by distance and finds no effects. Using school-level data in North Carolina, Holmes, DeSimone, and Rupp (2003) also look at distance as a proxy for competition and find substantial competitive effects. In contrast, Bifulco and Ladd (2006a) use student-level data in North Carolina and map out the distances of students exiting public schools to enter charter schools. With this mapping, they analyze the effect charter schools have on traditional public schools within concentric distances of charter schools. Their analysis finds no competitive effects.

Sass (2006) and Booker et al. (2004b) also use student-level data in Florida and Texas, respectively, to examine competitive effects. Similar to Bifulco and Ladd, Sass uses concentric circles around public schools and measures whether a charter school is within these concentric circles and what proportion of total students are enrolled in charter schools. Sass finds positive, but small, competitive effects in Florida. Booker et al. use two approaches, which find consistent and substantial competitive effects. First, as in the Hoxby study, the authors use market penetration measures at the district level. Second, they use a campus-level market penetration measure, which is defined by the percentage of students at a traditional campus that leave the school for a charter school.

In a paper entitled "Is Charter School Competition in California Improving the Performance of Traditional Public Schools?" we examine the competitive effect charter schools have on traditional public schools using our survey and district student-level data.[1] Overall, principals surveyed from traditional public schools felt very little competitive pressure; they indicated that they had changed their operations very little in response to charter schools being introduced to the market. Next, we highlight our results from the student achievement analysis, which confirms our results from the survey analysis.

Data Description

The analysis uses several measures to characterize the extent of pressures on a traditional public school to improve its performance in response to competition from charter and other public schools.

- *Distance to charter or other public school.* A nearby charter school may create competition for a traditional public school. The pressure may come from students switching to the charter or from parents demanding higher standards in their current school. Similarly, a nearby traditional public school or magnet school may pressure a school to improve.
- *Presence of charter and other alternatives within 2.5 miles.* This measure resembles the earlier distance measure, but it focuses on the specific area near a school, which could be thought of as an "educational marketplace." Distant charters or magnet schools may have much less effect on competition than the presence of nearby alternatives.
- *Number of charters and other alternatives within 2.5 miles.* More alternatives give parents more opportunities to shop for a school and demand better classroom performance.
- *Share of charter and other students within 2.5 miles.* This measure is a more precise indication of the availability of classroom seats in the

---

[1] A more complete description of the findings is in Buddin and Zimmer (2005b).

neighborhood of a school. If the share of students in the traditional public school is small, then it faces great pressure to keep pace with nearby alternative schools.

- *Students lost to other schools within 2.5 miles.* This is a tally of the percentage of students switching to a nearby charter or other school in the previous year. If transfer rates are high, the school may be pressured to improve its performance relative to nearby schools to avoid the loss of revenue and personnel.[1]

Table 7.8 shows the means for these school-level competition measures for all noncharter schools in California. A key indication of charter importance in California is that 37% of elementary traditional public school students are within 2.5 miles of an elementary charter school. Similarly, 24 and 9% of middle and high school students in a traditional public school are within 2.5 miles of a charter middle and high school, respectively. The charter enrollment shares are small, however, ranging from an average of about 3% for elementary and middle school students to an average of about 1% of high school students. The analysis focuses on whether differences in these competitive measures across schools and over time affect student achievement scores in these traditional public schools.

The last few years have been marked by dramatic growth in charter schools in California. Table 7.9 describes the pattern of charter school growth in the six districts used in our analysis. The results show that the numbers of charter schools and students have more than doubled for elementary, middle, and high schools for the 5-year period from 1998 through 2002. Similarly, the share of students enrolled in charter schools has also doubled over this period. This charter school growth means that more students have opportunities to attend charter schools and that more traditional public schools face competition from charter schools in the local school marketplace.

Model

The model of student achievement in public schools is based on a three-way error component where the three components consist of a student-specific effect, a school-specific effect, and a year-specific effect (Abowd, Creecy, & Kramarz, 2002; Abowd, Kramarz, & Margolis, 1999; Andrews, Schank, & Upward, 2004, 2005). The dependent variable is the student test score, T_{ijt}, observed for student i in school j at time t. Separate test specifications are estimated in reading and math. The formal model is

---

[1] Because our districts are all urban, we use a relatively small radius of 2.5 miles.

TABLE 7.8

Means and Standard Deviations by School Type

	Elementary school		Middle school		High school	
	Mean	Standard deviation	Mean	Standard deviation	Mean	Standard deviation
Student level variables						
Reading percentile	41.0544	19.8642	40.3140	19.6045	37.3366	19.0894
Math percentile	46.0130	21.3198	43.1000	19.3749	45.4319	18.5694
Black	0.1157	0.3199	0.1261	0.3319	0.1214	0.3266
Hispanic	0.6461	0.4782	0.6454	0.4784	0.6071	0.4884
Asian	0.0940	0.2919	0.0922	0.2894	0.1156	0.3197
Limited English proficiency	0.5001	0.5000	0.3056	0.4607	0.2430	0.4289
Free/reduced price lunch	0.7933	0.3583	0.7832	0.3758	0.6382	0.4364
School level variables						
Magnet school	0.1303	0.3366	0.3931	0.4884	0.6448	0.4786
Free/reduced price lunch (%)	78.2648	25.9012	70.2594	20.1507	58.7875	22.7443
English learner (%)	47.5837	24.9659	31.3863	15.3808	25.0839	11.8804
First-year students (%)	17.2755	6.9938	13.6500	5.7903	11.7909	7.0549
School-level competition measures						
Distance to nearest charter	4.0869	2.7763	5.8788	4.1841	8.3725	4.4810
Distance to nearest start-up	6.6162	5.6354	7.1390	5.6389	5.4081	2.9829
Distance to nearest conversion	4.9199	3.0395	8.1329	4.4908	8.8472	4.3847
Distance to nearest TPS	1.3881	0.2190	1.7196	0.6477	1.9861	0.8223
Distance to nearest magnet	2.1193	1.1417	2.3030	1.2989	2.6201	1.2947
Any charter within 2.5 miles	0.3769	0.4846	0.2371	0.4253	0.0911	0.2877
Any start-up within 2.5 miles	0.2183	0.4131	0.1801	0.3843	0.0344	0.1823
Any conversion within 2.5 miles	0.2513	0.4337	0.1260	0.3318	0.0656	0.2475

TABLE 7.8 (continued)
Means and Standard Deviations by School Type

	Elementary school		Middle school		High school	
	Mean	Standard deviation	Mean	Standard deviation	Mean	Standard deviation
Any other TPS within 2.5 miles	0.9976	0.0487	0.9251	0.2632	0.8034	0.3974
Any magnet within 2.5 miles	0.7687	0.4217	0.7330	0.4424	0.6037	0.4891
Number of charters within 2.5 miles	0.8598	1.6283	0.3658	0.7555	0.1353	0.4811
Number of start-ups within 2.5 miles	0.2556	0.5240	0.2005	0.4538	0.0345	0.1833
Number of conversions within 2.5 miles	0.6042	1.4067	0.1653	0.4679	0.1007	0.4324
Number of other TPS within 2.5 miles	15.3580	7.6015	4.1457	2.7874	2.9378	2.3863
Number of magnets within 2.5 miles	1.9090	1.8855	1.5274	1.4335	0.9631	0.9705
Share of charters within 2.5 miles	0.0329	0.0710	0.0276	0.0875	0.0138	0.0581
Share of start-ups within 2.5 miles	0.0042	0.0154	0.0034	0.0146	0.0051	0.0398
Share of conversions within 2.5 miles	0.0287	0.0689	0.0242	0.0842	0.0087	0.0430
Share of other TPS within 2.5 miles	0.8770	0.1072	0.6135	0.2444	0.4504	0.2764
Share of magnets within 2.5 miles	0.1082	0.1190	0.2458	0.2357	0.2573	0.2589
Lost to charter in past year (%)	0.0067	0.0195	0.0067	0.0238	0.0067	0.0238
Lost to conversion in past year (%)	0.0055	0.0183	0.0053	0.0230	0.0011	0.0021
Lost to start-ups in past year (%)	0.0012	0.0057	0.0014	0.0042	0.0024	0.0068
Lost to other TPS in past year (%)	0.2390	0.0755	0.3101	0.0667	0.0445	0.0296
Lost to magnets in past year (%)	0.0810	0.0795	0.1908	0.1073	0.0269	0.0228
Sample size	1,143,375		620,795		512,183	

Note: The competition measures refer to schools of similar type; that is, the share of charter schools within 2.5 miles for elementary schools is based on the share of charter students, grades K–5, relative to all K–5 students within 2.5 miles of the TPS.

TABLE 7.9
Charter School Trends in Six California School Districts

	1998	1999	2000	2001	2002
All schools					
Number of charter schools	27	49	60	69	73
Number of charter students	16,081	26,244	33,310	35,870	38,831
Share of charter students (%)	1.94	3.10	3.86	4.09	4.34
Elementary schools					
Number of charter schools	17	36	41	46	49
Number of charter students	8,299	17,874	19,607	21,110	22,552
Share of charter students (%)	1.88	3.97	4.29	4.55	4.84
Middle schools					
Number of charter schools	11	19	26	35	37
Number of charter students	8,420	11,849	15,577	17,943	20,245
Share of charter students (%)	2.76	3.95	5.10	5.73	6.28
High schools					
Number of charter schools	4	9	11	14	17
Number of charter students	4,735	5,985	8,538	9,338	10,782
Share of charter students (%)	1.93	2.43	3.42	3.70	4.15

Note: Some charter schools span elementary, middle, and high school grades, so the sum of the number of schools by grade exceeds the number of overall number of schools.

$$T_{ijt} = x_{it}\beta + w_{ij}\gamma + \theta_i + \psi_j + \mu_t + \varepsilon_{ijt} \tag{7.8}$$

where

x_{it} and w_{jt} are vectors of measured time-varying student and school characteristics, respectively
β and γ are parameter vectors for student and school effects
θ_i, ψ_j, and μ_t represent unobserved student, school, and time heterogeneity, respectively
ε_{ijt} is a random error term that is orthogonal to all other effects in the model

In many circumstances, a random-effects approach is used to estimate models like that in Equation (7.8). This approach assumes that the student, school, and time heterogeneity terms are orthogonal to the observed student- and school-level variables. In this situation, this seems unlikely because the measures of these variables are incomplete. For example, student motivation and parental support are important determinants of schooling outcomes, but these factors are not measured in test score databases such as those used in this study. Similarly, schools may differ from one another in unmeasured ways that may be correlated with measured factors in the model. As a result, the random-effects estimation of Equation (7.8) is likely to yield inconsistent estimates of the parameters β and γ.

In preliminary statistical regressions, we compared coefficient estimates with random- and fixed-effects models using a Hausman specification test. The results indicated that unobserved student and school heterogeneity was significantly correlated with observed factors in Equation (7.1) for separate runs for reading and math in elementary, middle, and high school. This indicated that a fixed-effect approach was more appropriate for this statistical problem.

Fixed-effects methods produce consistent estimates of β and γ in Equation (7.8). The parameter for time heterogeneity was estimated directly with time dummies because the period of observation consisted of 5 consecutive years. Student and school heterogeneity are more complex. Student test scores are observed over time and, in many cases, across different schools. For a particular student spell at a school, the terms θ_i and ψ_j are both fixed. As a result, student and school heterogeneity can be eliminated from the model by taking spell-specific fixed effects for each student–school combination where:

$$T_{ijt} - \bar{T}_s = (x_{it} - \bar{x}_s)\beta + (w_{jt} - \bar{w}_s)\gamma + (\varepsilon_{ijt} - \bar{\varepsilon}_s) \tag{7.9}$$

This approach means that parameters corresponding to student and school characteristics that are invariant across spells are not identified. The model does eliminate student and school heterogeneity, however, without restricting factors to be orthogonal to measured student and school attributes.

Results

As we noted earlier, researchers have used a variety of measures of charter competition, partially because no one really knows when traditional public schools may actually feel a competitive threat. The results look at various measures of competition for elementary, middle, and high schools in reading and math. After controlling for student and school heterogeneity and measured school variables, little evidence was found that charters are affecting student achievement in other public schools at all.

Table 7.10 summarizes the effects of estimating various versions of Equation (7.9) with alternative measures of student competition. Nearly every measure of charter competition has a statistically insignificant effect on student achievement in nearby traditional public schools. Only one of the measures has a statistically significant effect at the elementary, middle, and high school levels. Even then, the significant factor differs across school types, and the effect does not persist across reading and math within the same school type. Two of the three significant effects have

TABLE 7.10

Effects of Charter School Competition on Traditional Public School Performance

	Reading		Math	
	Coefficient	Standard error	Coefficient	Standard error
Elementary schools				
Distance to nearest charter	0.0148	0.0687	−0.0709	0.1110
Any charter within 2.5 miles	0.3204	0.2927	0.1751	0.4815
Number of charters within 2.5 miles	−0.0840	0.2675	−0.4260	0.3979
Share of charters within 2.5 miles	−15.1273[a]	7.3813	−10.3971	10.8359
Lost to charter in past year (%)	1.6216	8.1507	−9.8795	12.6713
Middle schools				
Distance to nearest charter	−0.0019	0.0421	−0.0784	0.0611
Any charter within 2.5 miles	0.1869	0.5299	1.4088[a]	0.6265
Number of charters within 2.5 miles	0.1099	0.4081	0.7010	0.6627
Share of charters within 2.5 miles	−8.0722	9.3698	−13.7740	24.5579
Lost to charter in past year (%)	−18.4525	35.3818	25.8199	31.7481
High schools				
Distance to nearest charter	0.3033[a]	0.1108	0.2013	0.1387
Any charter within 2.5 miles	−0.1577	1.1209	−0.582	0.5453
Number of charters within 2.5 miles	−0.1477	0.7312	−0.3863	0.6471
Share of charters within 2.5 miles	−29.4159	15.3717	−15.8786	15.4893
Lost to charter in past year (%)	−21.0126	28.1007	10.3569	38.204

[a] Indicates that the coefficient is statistically significant at the 5% level.

the opposite sign predicted by a theory of charter competition. In elementary reading, the regression result suggests that a larger share of charter schools within 2.5 miles *reduces* reading scores at the traditional public school, but it has no effect on math achievement. In high school reading, the distance to the nearest charter school has a *positive* effect on reading scores; that is, reading scores are higher if charter schools are farther away from the traditional public schools. The result for middle school math does show that the presence of a charter school within 2.5 miles of the traditional public school is associated with a higher math achievement score. Overall, these student achievement results suggest that charter schools are not having an effect on the performance of traditional public schools, which is consistent with our survey results from school principals.

Although Table 7.10 does not suggest a competitive effect from charter schools generally, the effects they have on traditional public schools may vary across different types of charter schools, which we examine by looking at start-up and conversion schools separately. Again, we find no competitive effects from either type of charter school (Buddin & Zimmer, 2005). Also, as one further sensitivity analysis, we examine whether the level of pre-existing competition may affect the competitive impacts of charter schools. As we have previously noted, a pre-existing competitive market could blunt the competitive effects of charter schools. Therefore, we also examine the charter competitive effect while adding measures of competitive effects from other traditional public or magnet schools. Again, the measures of competition from charter schools generally indicate no competitive effect. This suggests that competition among the existing public schools cannot explain the lack of competitive effects from charter schools.

The absence of a competitive effect, however, could also be explained by the generally low share of students charter schools represent in any of these districts—never more than 3%—or by the fact that charter schools are acting as a release valve in these growing districts. It is possible that a broader implementation of charter schools than that observed in California would exert pressure on traditional public schools to improve their performance.

CONCLUSIONS

The charter school movement grew out of a hope that by providing greater autonomy to schools, charter schools would be able to cut through bureaucratic frustrations and offer innovative, efficient, and effective educational programs; provide new options to families; and promote healthy competition for traditional public schools. Our results from California show that charter schools generally perform on par with or slightly below the achievement levels of traditional public schools, they have not closed the achievement gaps for minorities, and they have not had the expected competitive effects on traditional public schools. However, in another study not highlighted here because of space limitations (Krop & Zimmer, 2005), we find that charter schools do use fewer resources, which means charter schools have achieved comparable test score results with fewer public resources than traditional schools.

The evidence shows that charter schools have not created "white enclaves" or skimmed high-quality students from traditional public schools. In fact, charter schools have proven to be more popular among black and lower achieving students and may have actually created "black enclaves." In sum, the results suggest that charter schools are not a silver bullet for school improvement, though it is possible that charter schools are having effects on other educational outcomes not captured in this or other studies.

REFERENCES

Abowd, J., Kramarz, F., & Margolis, D. (1999). High-wage workers and high-wage firms. *Econometrica, 67,* 251–333.

Abowd, J., Creecy, R., & Kramarz, F. (2002). Computing person and firm effects using linked longitudinal employer–employee data. Technical paper 2002-06, U.S. Census Bureau. Retrieved September 6, 2005, from http://lehd.dsd.census.gov/led/library/techpapers/tp-2002-06.pdf.

Andrews, M., Schank, T., & Upward, R. (2004). Practical estimation methods for employer–employee data. IAB discussion paper no. 3. Retrieved September 6, 2005, from http://doku.iab.de/discussionpapers/2004/dp0304.pdf.

Andrews, M., Schank, T., & Upward, R. (2005). Practical fixed-effects estimation methods for the three-way error components model. Retrieved September 6, 2005, from http://www.nottingham.ac.uk/economics/staff/details/ru/leed2.pdf.

Bettinger, E. P. (2005). The effect of charter schools on charter students and public schools. *Economics of Education Review, 24*(2), 133–147.

Betts, J. R., & Hill, P. T. (2006). *Charter school achievement consensus panel. Key issues in studying charter schools and achievement: A review and suggestions for national guidelines.* Seattle, WA: National Charter School Research Project, Center on Reinventing Public Education.

Bifulco, R., & Ladd, H. (2006a). The impact of charter schools on student achievement: Evidence from North Carolina. *Education Finance Policy, 1*(1), 50–90.

Bifulco, R., & Ladd, H. (2006b). Race and charter schools: Evidence from North Carolina. *Journal of Policy Analysis and Management, 26*(1), 31–56.

Booker, K., Gilpatric, S., Gronberg, T. J., & Jansen, D. W. (2004a). Charter school performance in Texas (working paper). College Station: Private Enterprise Research Center, Texas A&M University.

Booker, K., Gilpatric, S., Gronberg, T. J., & Jansen, D. W. (2004b). The effect of charter schools on traditional public school students in Texas: Are children who stay behind left behind? (working paper). College Station: Texas A&M University.

Booker, K., Zimmer, R., & Buddin, R. (2005). The effect of charter schools on school peer composition (working paper WR-306-EDU). Santa Monica, CA: RAND Corporation. Retrieved August 21, 2006, http://www.ncspe.org/publications_files/RAND_WR306.pdf.

Bryk, A. S., & Raudenbush, S. W. (1992). *Hierarchical linear models: Applications and data analysis method.* Newbury Park, CA: Sage.

Buddin, R., & Zimmer, R. (2005a). A closer look at charter school student achievement. *Journal of Policy Analysis and Management, 24*(2), 351–372.

Buddin, R., & Zimmer, R. (2005b). Is charter school competition in California improving the performance of traditional public schools? (Working Paper WR-297-EDU). Santa Monica, CA: RAND Corporation. Retrieved August 21, 2006, http://www.ncspe.org/publications_files/OP122.pdf.

Cobb, C. D., & Glass, G. V. (1999). Ethnic segregation in Arizona charter schools. *Education Policy Analysis Archives, 7*(1), 1–20.

Edwards, B. (2006, August). Characteristics and demographics of California charter schools and charter school students. EdSource, Testimony before the California Senate Select Committee on the Master Plan for Education.

Finn, C. E., Manno, B. V., & Vanourek, G. (2000). *Charter schools in action.* Princeton, NJ: Princeton University Press.

Frankenberg, E., & Lee, C. (2003). Charter schools and race: A lost opportunity for integrated education. *Education Policy Analysis Archives, 11*(32). Retrieved, http://epaa.asu.edu/epaa/v11n32/.

Hanushek, E. A., Kain, J. F., & Rivkin, S. G. (2002). The impact of charter schools on academic achievement. Retrieved September 2, 2004, http://edpro.stanford.edu/eah/papers/charters.aea.jan03.PDF.

Heckman, J. J., & Hotz, V. J. (1989). Choosing among alternative nonexperimental methods for estimating the impact of social programs: The case of manpower training. *Journal of the American Statistical Association, 84,* 862–875.

Holmes, G. M., DeSimone, J., & Rupp, N. (2003). *Does school choice increase school quality?* (NBER Working Paper Series 9683). Cambridge, MA: National Bureau of Economic Research.

Hoxby, C. M. (2001, September). *How school choice affects the achievement of public school students.* Paper prepared for the Koret Task Force meeting, Hoover Institution, Stanford, CA.

Hoxby, C. M., & Rockoff, J. E. (2004). The impact of charter schools on student achievement. Retrieved November 15, 2004, http://post.economics.harvard.edu/faculty/hoxby/papers/hoxbyrockoffcharters.

Krop, C., & Zimmer, R. (2005). Charter school type matters when examining funding and facilities: Evidence from California. *Education Policy Analysis Archives, 13*(50), 1–20.

Miron, G. N., & Nelson, C. (2002). *What's public about charter schools?* Thousand Oaks, CA: Corwin Press, Inc.

Nathan, J. (1996). *Charter schools: Creating hope and opportunity for American education.* San Francisco, CA: Jossey–Bass.

Papke, L. E. (1994). Tax policy and urban developments: Evidence from the Indiana Enterprise Zone Program. *Journal of Public Economics, 54,* 37–49.

Powell, J., Blackorby, J., Marsh, J., Finnegan, K., & Anderson, L. (1997). *Evaluation of charter school effectiveness.* Menlo Park, CA: SRI International.

RPP International. (2000). *The state of charter schools: National study of charter schools fourth-year report.* Washington, DC: Office of Educational Research and Improvement, U.S. Department of Education.

Sass, T. R. (2006, Winter). Charter schools and student achievement in Florida. *Education Finance and Policy, 1*(1), 91–122.

Summers, A., & Wolfe, B. (1977). Do schools make a difference? *American Economic Review, 67,* 639–652.

Wells, A. S., Artiles, L., Carnochan, S., Cooper, C. W., Grutzik, C., Holme, J. J., et al. (1998). *Beyond the rhetoric of charter school reform: A study of ten California school districts.* Los Angeles: University of California, Los Angeles.

Wooldridge, J. M. (2002). *Econometric analysis of cross section and panel data.* Cambridge, MA: MIT Press.

Zimmer, R. W. (2003). A new twist in the educational tracking debate. *Economics of Education Review, 22,* 307–315.

Zimmer, R., & Buddin, R. (2005). *Getting inside the black box: Examining how the operation of charter schools affects performance* (working paper WR-305-EDU). Santa Monica, CA: RAND Corporation. Retrieved August 21, 2006, http://www.rand.org/pubs/working_papers/2005/RAND_WR305.pdf.

Zimmer, R., & Buddin, R. (2006). Charter school performance in urban districts. *Journal of Urban Economics, 60*(2), 307–326.

Zimmer, R., Buddin, R., Chau, D., Daley, G., Gill, B., Guarino, C., et al. (2003). *Charter school operations and performance: Evidence from California.* Santa Monica, CA: RAND Corporation.

Zimmer, R. W., & Toma, E. F. (2000). Peer effects in private and public schools across countries. *Journal of Policy Analysis and Management, 19*(1), 75–92.

8

Charter Schools in North Carolina[1]

ROBERT BIFULCO AND HELEN F. LADD

INTRODUCTION

Legislation authorizing charter schools in North Carolina was passed in 1996, and the first charter schools opened in fall 1997. As of 2002, only seven states had more charter schools than North Carolina and, of those, only five had a greater concentration of charter schools: Arizona, Florida, Wisconsin, Michigan, and California. Though its policy is less permissive than that of Arizona and Michigan, North Carolina has taken a moderately permissive approach to charter schools compared to those of most other states, and its program includes many of the elements recommended by charter school advocates.

Because the state has been testing all students in grades 3–8 since the early 1990s, it is possible not only to track students as they move between traditional public schools and charter schools but also to examine their performance on statewide math and reading tests over time. These rich longitudinal data allow for a more careful analysis of the charter school system in North Carolina than in many other states.

This chapter draws heavily on our published research on charter schools in North Carolina (Bifulco & Ladd, 2005, 2006, 2007). As a result, most of the analysis ends in the academic year 2001–2002. The first two sections describe the North Carolina policy context and the administrative data used for this research. Subsequent sections explore the patterns of racial

[1] This chapter summarizes the research reported in three papers by the authors published elsewhere. We thank the Smith Richardson Foundation for supporting that research, and Dallas Stalling and Shana Cook for research assistance.

segregation within charter schools; measure the effects of charter schools on the achievement of the students who attend them; describe the links among segregation, achievement, and test score gaps; and examine how charter schools affect the performance of students in the traditional public schools. We conclude that the North Carolina school system has increased racial segregation, been detrimental on average to student achievement, and has widened the black–white test score gap.

BACKGROUND AND POLICY CONTEXT

Charter schools in North Carolina can be authorized by a local district, the state university, or the state Board of Education, but final approval must come from the state Board of Education. The law caps the number of charter schools statewide at 100 and limits the annual growth in the number of schools per district to five. In addition, local districts have an opportunity to provide input before charter applications are approved. Together, these provisions give the state of North Carolina more control over the establishment of charter schools than is the case in several other states.

Nevertheless, the North Carolina legislation is quite permissive in that it allows any individual or group to apply for a charter and does not require local district approval of a charter application. North Carolina charters operate as independent nonprofit corporations, act as their own employers, and are automatically exempt from several regulations. In addition, they receive operating funding at the same level and are subject to the same testing requirements as those for traditional public schools.[1] The state requires charter schools to develop transportation plans so that transportation is not a barrier to any student who resides in the district in which a school is located. As is the case in most other states, the state provides no funding for start-up costs, but charter schools are eligible for federal start-up funds.

Of the 94 charter schools established before 2002 that served students in grades 3–8, 16 previously were private schools (some of which were quite new) and one previously was a regular public school. Thus, most of North Carolina's charter schools were established from scratch as new schools. The charter school applications filed with the state Department of Instruction indicate that, despite their wide range of programmatic offerings, all follow the North Carolina *Standard Course of Study*, which serves as the basis for the state tests.[2] At least two charter schools that converted from private schools, both located in rural areas, have

---

[1] An independent study of charter school financing in North Carolina found that per-pupil revenues in charter schools were within 5% of revenues in traditional public schools statewide (Speakman & Hassel, 2005), and another found that per-pupil expenditures were about 3% less than traditional public schools in the same districts (Nelson, Muir, & Drown, 2003).

[2] Examples of the range of offerings include art-infused curriculums (eight schools), experiential learning (nineteen schools), and emphasis on African or African-American themes (five schools).

long-standing missions to serve students with special emotional or family problems. In addition, about one quarter of North Carolina applications for charter schools outline specific interventions or recruitment efforts targeted at at-risk students.

Charters can be revoked for a number of reasons, including poor student performance and financial mismanagement. Between 1997 and 2002, the state Board revoked seven charters, and seven more relinquished their charter voluntarily or closed due to low enrollment or financial problems. Overall, about 12% of the charter schools that have been opened are now closed. However, in no case was the decision to revoke a charter or to close due primarily to low student performance (Manuel, 2002). By 2000–2001 there were 90 charter schools and over 15,000 charter school students. Growth has slowed since then, primarily because of the state law capping the number of charter schools at 100. Since 2002, the state Board has approved seven new charter schools.

Charter schools in North Carolina are more likely to be elementary or middle schools than high schools, and most serve at least some students between grades 4 and 8, the grades examined in most of the analysis we describe here. The 93 charter schools in 2001–2002 are spread across 46 of North Carolina's 100 counties. During the 2001–2002 school year, Wake County, home to the state capital of Raleigh, and nearby Durham County had the highest concentrations of charters: 12.4 and 18.2% of public schools, respectively. In Charlotte–Mecklenberg, the state's most populous county, only 6 of 130 public schools were charters in 2002. As of 2006, there were 95 charter schools, of which 14 were in Wake County, 7 in Durham, and 9 in Charlotte–Mecklenberg.

Table 8.1 shows how the mix of students in North Carolina charter schools differs from that in traditional public schools. Charter schools have a larger percentage of black students (40 vs. 31%) and lower percentages of Hispanic (2 vs. 5%) and white (56 vs. 60%) students. At the same time, charter schools serve a higher percentage of students whose parents are college educated and a lower percentage of students whose parents are high school dropouts. Despite the higher education level of their parents, these students exhibit lower levels of performance on end-of-grade (EOG) reading and math tests.

Concerned that charter schools might be established to serve as enclaves for white students, state policymakers have encouraged applications for schools oriented toward serving educationally disadvantaged students, among whom African Americans tend to be overrepresented. In addition, the legislation explicitly requires:

> Within one year after a charter school begins operation, the population of the school shall reasonably reflect the racial and ethnic composition of the general population within the district or of the special population the school seeks to serve residing in the district.[1]

---

[1] See charter school legislation, NSCSG 115C-238, 29F(g)(5) and State Board of Education policy EEO-U-003 for official statement of the state's policy on racial and ethnic balance in charter schools.

TABLE 8.1

Descriptive Statistics on Charter and Traditional Public Schools, 2001–2002

	Charter schools	Traditional public schools
Average enrollment[a]	196	574
Percent female[a]	48.9	48.8
Ethnic compostion[a]		
Percent black	39.9	31.2
Percent Hispanic	2.1	5.3
Percent white	55.5	60.0
Parent education[b]		
Percent less than high school	3.9	10.6
Percent high school grad	34.6	43.7
Percent some college, but did not graduate	4.8	4.1
Percent 2-year college degree	11.6	13.4
Percent 4-year college degree	36.6	22.8
Percent graduate school degree	8.6	5.3
Percent that changed schools in last year[b]	47.4	13.2
Avg. performance on EOG reading[b,c]	−0.057	0.001
Avg. performance on EOG math[b,c]	−0.133	0.002

[a] Figures calculated using Common Core data and are based on entire population of schools.

[b] Figures computed using individual student EOG files maintained by the North Carolina Education Research Data Center, and thus are based only on students in grades 3–8.

[c] EOG test scores converted to standard scores with mean of 0 and standard deviations of 1. Grade specific means and standard deviations were used to make the conversions.

In fact, though, the racial compositions of many charter schools through-out the state have differed significantly from the host district, but not generally in the way initially feared by policy makers. Of the 90 charter schools operating in 2000–2001, 30 were more than 80% non-white and 20 had a higher percentage of non-white students than any traditional public school in the same district. Only eight charter schools had lower percent-ages of non-white students than any traditional public school in the same district (Manuel, 2002).

DATA FOR THIS STUDY

The analysis in this chapter is based primarily on administrative data provided by the North Carolina Education Research Data Center for five cohorts of students. Each cohort contains the universe of students in third grade in North Carolina public schools in 1996, 1997, 1998, 1999, and 2000 and follows them through eighth grade or until the 2001–2002 school year, whichever comes first.

The information available for each student in each year includes scale scores on the EOG reading and math tests; school name; whether the school is a charter; the student's grade, gender, and ethnicity; and the highest level of education completed by the student's parents. EOG reading and math tests are multiple choice and measure the achievement of competencies described in the North Carolina *Standard Course of Study;* they are administered in the spring of each year to students in grades 3–8. Individual results are reported as developmental scale scores, which are designed to measure growth in reading and math, and thus are expected to increase as students move from lower to higher grades. In order to ensure comparability of test scores and test score gains for students in different grades, we use grade-by-year-specific averages and standard deviations to convert the developmental scale scores to standard scores with means of zero and standard deviations of one.

Almost 9,000 of the students in our five cohorts of third through eighth graders are observed at least once in a charter school. We rely on two subsets of this full set of students for various parts of our analysis.[1] First, we use a subset of 6,480 school "movers" to examine changes in the composition of student peers as students transfer from a traditional public school to a charter school. This subset is similar to the full sample of charter school students, except that students in the subset are slightly less likely to be black and have higher average third grade test scores. Second, we use a subset of 5,754 charter school students for whom we observe one or more test-score gains while each was enrolled in a charter school and also in a traditional public school; this helps us identify how charter schools affect achievement. Though comparable in most ways to the full set of charter school students, the students in this subset have higher average third grade test scores, are significantly less likely to have first entered a charter school before grade 4, and are more likely to have left a charter school. Though these differences might generate some bias in our estimates of how charter schools affect student achievement, we have shown in our earlier work that the bias is likely to be small (Bifulco & Ladd, 2006).[2]

---

[1] For more complete descriptive data on these subsets, see Table 1 in Bifulco and Ladd (2007).

[2] Also see later discussion on the extent to which the over representation of movers affects the estimates.

CHARTER SCHOOLS AND RACIAL SEGREGATION

Both black and white charter school students in North Carolina attend more racially segregated schools on average than their counterparts in traditional public schools.[1] Using data from all charter schools in North Carolina for the 2001–2002 school year, we find that the typical black charter school student attends a school that is more than 70% black, while his black counterpart in a traditional public school attends a school that is less than 50% black.[2] Analogously, the typical white charter school student is in a more racially isolated environment than his or her counterpart in a traditional public school: The peers of the typical white charter school student are only 18% black in contrast to about 24% for the student in a traditional public school. In some areas, particularly Charlotte–Mecklenberg and Wake, the cross-sector differences in these racial percentages are even more marked.

Given the possibility that charter schools could be drawing students from predominantly black or predominantly white traditional public schools, these average racial patterns need not imply that charter schools have increased racial isolation. For that purpose, we must examine how the racial mix of a typical student's peer group changes as he or she transfers to a charter school. To that end, we focus on the 6,480 movers in our administrative data set: namely, the students we observe in a traditional public school the year before they enter a charter school. Table 8.2, which compares the characteristics of the other students in the same grade and school during each student's first year in a charter school and during the immediately prior year when the student was enrolled in a traditional public school (TPS), shows that the move to a charter school typically does increase racial isolation.

Specifically, black movers have transferred from traditional public schools that are 53% black on average to charter schools that are 72% black on average. Notice also that black movers are transferring to charter schools with lower levels of average achievement in both reading and math than in the schools they left. White students who transfer into charter schools are making very different choices. First of all, the charter schools they select tend to have lower percentages of black students than the traditional public

---

[1] We focus on the choices made by and the effects of charter schools on African-American and white students. Although Hispanics are a rapidly growing group in North Carolina, the number of Hispanic students and other ethnic groups who have selected into charter schools is too small for most of our statistical analysis.

[2] These percentages and those in the following sentence are based on data from the Common Core of Data from the National Center of Education Statistics for all districts that had at least one charter school in 2001–2002. This data source includes all the charter schools and students in the state. In subsequent analysis based on NC administrative data, we focus on charter school students in grades 3–8.

TABLE 8.2
Changes in Charter School Peer Environment[a]

	Black students			White students		
	Charter	TPS[b]	Average change[c]	Charter	TPS[b]	Average change[c]
N	2,550	2,550	2,550	3,548	3,548	3,548
Percent black	0.718	0.532	0.186	0.175	0.282	−0.107
Percent with college-educated parents	0.290	0.268	0.022	0.473	0.348	0.125
Average lagged EOG reading scores	−0.417	−0.107	−0.310	0.265	0.112	0.153
Average lagged EOG math scores	−0.520	−0.139	−0.381	0.198	0.108	0.090

Notes: "Charter" columns report average characteristics of students in the same grade and school during first year in a charter school; "TPS" columns report same figure for the closest year preceding entrance to a charter school. The sum of black students and white students does not equal the total number of students reported in Table 8.1 because the latter total includes students in other ethnic groups.
[a] Averages for all students observed at least once in a charter school and once in a traditional public school prior to entering charter school.
[b] TPS = traditional public school.
[c] All differences are statistically significant at 0.01 level.
[d] Individual test scores converted to standard scores with a mean of zero and standard deviation of one.

schools they previously attended. Also, in stark contrast to black movers, white movers are transferring into charter schools that provide significantly higher percentages of peers with college-educated parents and higher average levels of achievement. Thus, charter schools in North Carolina clearly increase the extent to which students are racially segregated.

Though not shown in the table, students from families with different educational backgrounds also sort into different types of charter schools. Movers in families with parents without 4-year degrees selected schools in which less than 30% of students have college-educated parents, while those with college-educated parents selected schools in which nearly 60% of students have college-educated parents. For the students with educated parents, the exposure to students with similar educational backgrounds increased by 17 percentage points with the transfer to a charter school.

Thus, students who choose to enroll in North Carolina charter schools tend to end up in schools and grades with higher percentages of students who look more like themselves racially and/or in terms of family background than was the case in their traditional public schools. Moreover, for black students and children of parents without college degrees, this increase in the proportion of students who look like themselves is accompanied by a marked reduction in the average level of achievement among their classmates.

Explaining the Racial Isolation of Charter Schools

As we show next, North Carolina charter school students in general, and black students who move to more racially isolated charter schools in particular, achieve at lower levels than they would have had they remained in traditional public schools. One might reasonably ask why so many black students select into racially segregated charter schools that weaken their academic performance. One possible explanation is simply that, despite the lower academic quality of such schools, black families would prefer to have their children attend racially segregated schools rather than racially mixed ones. If that were the case, policymakers would face a trade-off between promoting academic achievement and providing schools with other characteristics that black families value.

Alternatively, many black families could be choosing racially segregated charter schools because they do not have access to the more racially balanced schools they would prefer. If this were the case, efforts to promote more integrated schooling options might be warranted. In the following analysis we make inferences about the preferences of black and white families for particular mixes of students by race within charter schools and conclude that the latter explanation—namely, that black families end up in racially segregated charter schools despite their preference for more integrated schools—is closer to the truth.

Our analysis is based on the specific choices charter school families made in five North Carolina metropolitan areas. We limit our analysis to these areas because they offer a greater number of charter school options relative to the rest of the state and because the options are characterized by a range of racial profiles.[1] We focus separately on the choices every black or white family made who switched their child to a charter school during the 2000–2001 and 2001–2002 school years and who had at least two charter schools from which to choose within a 10-mile radius of their traditional public school.[2]

Our strategy is to estimate conditional logit models of the choice of charter school, conditional on the student switching to a charter school. Such a model allows us to make inferences about the value that choosers place

---

[1] See Table 6 in Bifulco and Ladd (2007) for information on the characteristics of the choice sets available to charter school students in the five metropolitan areas. Those areas are Durham/Chapel Hill, Forsythe, Guilford, Meckelenberg, and Wake.

[2] The decision to use a 10-mile radius is based on the fact that, for about 90% of the transfers to charter schools, the distance between the charter school in which the student is enrolled and the school the student attended the previous year was less than 10 miles.

on various characteristics of the schools in their choice sets. Although the magnitudes of the parameter coefficients from a logit model are difficult to interpret, the signs of the coefficients have a clear interpretation: A positive sign indicates that the characteristic is valued by the chooser and a negative sign that it is disvalued.

Preferences of Black Charter School Families

Of most interest is the implicit value that black movers place on schools with particular racial profiles. Thus, the key variables in the model are a set of 0–1 variables indicating whether a charter school is 0–20% black, 20–40% black, 60–80% black, or 80–100% black, with the base or left-out category being 40–60% black. In addition to these variables, we include in the basic model two measures of accessibility. The first is the distance between the student's previous traditional public school and the charter school.[1] The second is the number of spaces in the school, specified as the logarithm of the school's enrollment. In a second model, we add additional characteristics for each charter school.

The basic results of the conditional logit analysis for black charter school students are reported in the first column of Table 8.3. The negative signs on all the racial profile variables in that column indicate that, when other factors relating to accessibility held constant, black families are more likely to choose schools with 40–60% black students (those in the base category) over schools characterized by higher or lower percentages of black students. The negative sign on the distance variable indicates that black families prefer charter schools closer to their previous schools to those farther away.

Black families might prefer racially integrated charter schools to those with more racially segregated environments for various reasons unrelated to race, including, for example, a preference for smaller classes or for specific educational programs. Hence, in the second column, we include the pupil–teacher ratio as a proxy for class size and indicator variables for a variety of programmatic offerings. The negative sign on the pupil–teacher ratio indicates that, as expected, black families prefer smaller to larger classes. The programmatic characteristics are derived from the mission statements of each charter school at the time of application. Because of the possibility of collinearity among these programs and the limited availability of some of the programs across charter schools, we are not able to learn much about the value placed on specific programs. Of more interest

---

[1] We would prefer to define this variable as distance from the student's residence but we do not have information on home addresses.

TABLE 8.3
Determinants of Charter School Choice, Conditional Logit Analysis

	Black students		White students	
0–20% black	−3.153[a]	−1.974[a]	2.615[a]	2.809[a]
	(0.305)	(0.483)	(0.663)	(0.797)
20–40% black	−1.603[a]	−1.663[a]	1.852	1.065[a]
	(0.271)	(0.588)	(0.666)	(0.970)
40–60% black (base)	—	—	—	—
60–80% black	−2.064[a]	−2.327[a]	0.429	−2.895[a]
	(0.321)	(0.597)	(0.767)	(1.119)
80–100% black	−1.004[a]	−0.733[b]	−3.060[a]	−4.747[a]
	(0.152)	(0.431)	(0.534)	(1.194)
Distance	−0.231[a]	−0.213[a]	−0.358[a]	−0.369[a]
	(0.025)	(0.029)	(0.036)	(0.046)
Log of enrollment	0.121	0.470[a]	0.890[a]	0.219
	(0.080)	(0.165)	(0.155)	(0.521)
Pupil–teacher ratio		−0.071[a]		−0.110[a]
		(0.014)		(0.046)
Targets at-risk studentsts		−0.137		1.112[a]
		(0.350)		(0.415)
Targets gifted students		1.153[a]		−0.705
		(0.461)		(0.465)
Community-oriented mission		1.799[a]		1.910[a]
		(0.404)		(0.603)
Emphasis on African or African-American studies		0.246		
		(0.378)		
Emphasis on character or moral education		−0.468[a]		0.106
		(0.235)		(0.531)
Emphasis on experiential instruction		−0.182		1.782[a]
		(0.263)		(0.593)
Emphasis on individualized education plans		0.369		−1.145[b]
		(0.227)		(0.657)
Emphasis on alternative assessments		0.336		1.086[a]
		(0.237)		(0.397)
Number of observations	2835	2367	1954	1954
Number of cases	667	629	549	549
Log likelihood	−727.1	−556.5	−251.1	−187
Psuedo R-squared	0.200	0.300	0.614	0.704

Note: Estimated using transfers into a charter school observed during the 2001 and 2002 school years in Durham/Chapel Hill, Forsythe, Guilford, Mecklenberg, and Wake.
[a] Significant at 0.05 level.
[b] Significant at 0.10 level.

is that, even when these variables are included in the regression, the preferred racial mix is still 40–60% black.[1]

Thus, we conclude that the black charter school families who had racially balanced charter schools (those with between 40 and 60% black students) in their choice sets tended to prefer them to more segregated schools. We must be careful, however, not to attribute similar preferences to all black students who made racially segregating moves into charter schools (moves to charter schools that are more than 60% black and with >10% more black students than in the school they left behind). Though they might have similar preferences, we do not know that for a fact, since only 19% of these students had at least one racially balanced charter school in their choice sets. Thus, the substantial majority of black students who made racially segregating moves did not have access to charter schools with racially balanced student profiles—schools that these students might have preferred had they been available.

Preferences of White Charter School Students

If substantial numbers of black charter school students prefer schools that are 40–60% black, why are there so few charter schools available with that racial mix of students? A partial answer to that question emerges from our analysis of the choices white charter school families made. As shown in the last two columns of Table 8.3, these families exhibit their strongest preference for schools that are less than 20% black and, as indicated by the large negative coefficient for the last racial category, they are strongly averse to charter schools in which over 80% of the students are black. Moreover, the patterns are even stronger after we control for the pupil–teacher ratio and programmatic variables. Thus, the models suggest that white charter school families have very different preferences with respect to the racial composition of the school than do their black counterparts.

Given the asymmetry of the preferences of black and white charter school families, it would be difficult to end up with many racially balanced charter schools. Though black families might prefer such schools, the fact that white families prefer schools with far lower proportions of black students sets up a tipping process. Attempts to create racially balanced charter schools are likely to fail as white families looking for

---

[1] At the same time, we note that the negative coefficients at the two extremes of racial isolation—less than 20% black and more than 80% black—are smaller than in Model 1, although only significantly so for the 0–20% black category. One interpretation of the smaller size of these two coefficients relative to the estimates in the first column is that part of the weaker preferences of black charter school families for those schools is attributable to the programs they offer relative to the programs in other schools.

alternatives to traditional public schools choose charter or private schools with more white students when such options exist. The result is the observed pattern in which many black students end up in racially segregated charter schools.

EFFECTS OF NORTH CAROLINA CHARTER SCHOOLS ON STUDENT ACHIEVEMENT

Among the most important and controversial issues in the charter school debate is how charter schools affect the achievement of the students who attend them. This issue is hotly debated in part because the effects are hard to estimate. The most serious problem arises because charter school students are self-selected and are likely to differ in unobserved ways from otherwise similar students who choose to remain in traditional public schools. To address this challenge, we follow the strategy of Hanushek, Kain, and Rivkin (2002) and use repeated observations on individual students to control for individual fixed effects to generate our preferred estimates. In the preferred model, we are essentially comparing the test score gains of students in charter schools to the test score gains of the same students when they attend traditional public schools. (See Bifulco & Ladd [2006], for details.)

For purposes of comparison, we estimate three basic models: a "levels" model, a "gains" model, and a "fixed-effects" model, with the latter generating the preferred estimates. Each of these models is a restricted form of a more general model that we discuss elsewhere (Bifulco & Ladd, 2006, pp. 64–66).

The levels model can be written as:

$$Y_{iGT} = \alpha CH_{iGT} + X_{iGT}B + \eta_{GT} + \varepsilon_{iGT} \tag{8.1}$$

where

Y is a test score for student i in grade G in year T

CH, the variable of most interest, indicates whether that student attended a charter school in year T

X is a vector of individual student characteristics, some of which do not change over time, such as race or gender, and others of which do, such as transferring schools during the year

The η_{GT} are a set of grade-by-year fixed effects

ε_{iGT} is an error term

This model, which we estimate using ordinary least squares and robust standard errors, yields the difference in performance levels between charter school students and traditional public school students, controlling for observable student characteristics and grade-by-year effects. A serious limitation of this model is that it ignores the effects of the student's educational experiences in previous years. Because this and other unobserved factors such as the student's motivation are likely to influence both student test scores and the decision to enroll in a charter school, omitting these variables is likely to bias the estimates of the charter school effect.

A second approach incorporates the prior year's achievement levels by focusing on the achievement gains from one year to the next. This gains model can be written as

$$\Delta Y_{iGT} = Y_{iGT} - Y_{i(G-1)(T-1)} = \alpha CH_{iGT} + X_{iGT}B + \lambda_{GT} + v_{iGT}$$

$$\lambda_{GT} = \eta_{GT} - \eta_{(G-1)T-1)} \tag{8.2}$$

$$v_{iGT} = \varepsilon_{iGT} - \varepsilon_{i(G-1)(T-1)}$$

where the λ_{GT} variables represent fixed effects for the changes from one grade to the next by year. We call this the gains model because it estimates the difference between the average test score gain made by charter school students and traditional public school students, controlling for observable student characteristics and grade-by-year effects. Though preferred to the levels model, this model implicitly assumes no decay from one year to the next in the effects of prior year achievement. In addition, if unobserved student characteristics have additive effects rather than a one-time effect, the estimated value of α from the gains model will be a biased estimate of the effect of attending a charter school.

The fixed-effects model is similar to the gains model except that it includes an individual fixed effect, γ_i:

$$\Delta Y_{iGT} = Y_{iGT} - Y_{iG(T-1)} = \alpha CH_{iGT} + X_{iGT}B + \gamma_i + \lambda_{GT} + v_{iGT}$$

$$\lambda_{GT} = \eta_{GT} - \eta_{(G-1)T-1)} \tag{8.3}$$

$$v_{iGT} = \varepsilon_{iGT} - \varepsilon_{i(G-1)(T-1)}$$

The inclusion of the individual fixed effect means that the coefficients are estimated using only the variation within students (Baltagi, 1995); this eliminates any effects of unobserved differences between charter school students and traditional public school students that remain constant over time. In addition, the X vector now includes only the student-level variables that change over time, with the time-invariant student characteristics incorporated into the student fixed effects. Estimation of this model requires three or more observations for each student, which, with the exception of studies using Texas and Florida data, has not been available in previous quasi-experimental evaluations of school choice programs (Booker, Gilpatric, Gronberg, & Jansen, 2004; Hanushek et al., 2002; Hanushek, Kain, Rivkin, & Brand, 2005; Sass, 2006).

The fixed-effects model provides powerful protection against self-selection bias. However, this protection comes at a cost. Note that the estimated effects of charter schools are based on the experiences of only those students for whom we can observe test score gains at least once in a charter school and at least once in a traditional public school. The estimator could provide biased estimates of the effects averaged across all charter school students if the subsample of students used to identify the charter school effect was not representative of that larger group. We return to this issue later.

Estimated Achievement Effects

The first three columns of Tables 8.4 and 8.5 present our estimates of the three models for math and reading, respectively. The estimated effects of each time-invariant student characteristic in the first two models are generally consistent with expectations. Females exhibit higher achievement levels in both math and reading, and larger annual gains, although the gains' difference is significant only for math. blacks and Hispanics exhibit lower achievement levels than whites. Hispanics, however, make larger annual gains in both reading and math than either blacks or whites. Both the achievement level and annual achievement gains are higher for students with more educated parents. Children of college graduates, for example, score more than one standard deviation higher than children of high school dropouts. Finally, as can be seen for all three models, students who change schools, either because of a move or because they are making a structural change such as to a middle school, make smaller gains during their transition year than students who remain in the same school.

Turning to the charter school coefficients, we find that students in charter schools do less well than their counterparts in traditional public schools. Because the dependent variable is expressed as a standard score with a mean of 0 and a standard deviation of 1, the coefficients in Tables 8.4 and 8.5 can be interpreted as proportions of a standard deviation. In the levels models, charter school students on average score 0.16 of a standard deviation lower in reading and about 0.25 of a standard deviation lower in math than observationally similar students in traditional public schools. From the gains models, we see that students in charter schools also make smaller annual gains on average than observationally similar students. In neither case, however, can we be sure that the lower performance is attributable to being in a charter school; it could reflect unobserved differences in the characteristics of the students who select into those schools.

That alternative explanation does not arise in our preferred third model with student fixed effects. The negative estimates from those models indicate that the smaller gains made by charter school students do indeed appear to be attributable to being in a charter school, given that the student fixed effects control for any time-invariant unobserved differences between charter school students and students in traditional public schools.

TABLE 8.4

Estimated Charter School Impact on Math Test Scores

	Levels	Gains	Fixed effects
Charter school	−0.255[a] (0.073)	−0.076[a] (0.021)	−0.160[a] (0.021)
Gender (male = 0, female = 1)1)	0.036[a] (0.002)	0.009[a] (0.001)	
Ethnicity (reference category Asian and American Indian)			
Black	−0.464[a] (0.023)	−0.019[a] (0.005)	
Hispanic	−0.046 (0.024)	0.020[a] (0.006)	
White	0.155[a] (0.023)	−0.020[a] (0.005)	
Parent education (reference category H.S. dropout)			
High school grad	0.386[a] (0.005)	−0.007[a] (0.002)	
Some college, did not graduate	0.603[a] (0.006)	0.005 (0.003)	
2-Year college degree	0.705[a] (0.006)	0.004 (0.003)	
4-Year college degree	1.076[a] (0.008)	0.029[a] (0.003)	
Graduate school degree	1.404[a] (0.014)	0.058[a] (0.004)	
Change schools in last year	−0.160[a] (0.005)	−0.030[a] (0.004)	−0.027[a] (0.005)
Made structural change in last year	−0.044[a] (0.008)	−0.068[a] (0.008)	−0.061[a] (0.010)
Total observations	1,533,367	1,520,132	1,502,339[b]
Total students	446,855	443,548	425,654[b]

Notes: All models include grade/year fixed effects. Dependent variable is EOG development scale scores expressed as a standard score. Figures in parentheses are robust standard errors calculated using generalization of Huber/white Sandwich estimator and are robust to clustering within schools.

[a] Statistical significance at the 0.01 level.

[b] Sample count includes only those observations of students with at least three valid test score measures, which is the minimum required to identify fixed effects and effect estimates for nonconstant variables.

Based on the fixed-effect models, the negative effects of attending a charter school are large. On average, charter school students exhibit gains nearly 0.10 standard deviations smaller in reading and 0.16 standard deviations smaller in math than the gains they exhibited when enrolled in traditional public schools. Given that the typical charter school student in our sample is observed in a charter school for 1.66 years, the preferred estimates suggest that such a student would score 0.16 standard deviations (0.10 × 1.66) lower in reading and 0.27 standard deviations (0.16 × 1.66) lower in math than if he or she remained in a traditional public school.

TABLE 8.5
Estimated Charter School Impact on Reading Test Scores

	Levels	Gains	Fixed effects
Charter school	−0.158[a] (0.044)	−0.062[a] (0.009)	−0.095[a] (0.014)
Gender (male = 0, female = 1)	0.174[a] (0.002)	0.001 (0.001)	
Ethnicity (reference category Asian and American Indian)			
Black	−0.351[a] (0.023)	−0.029[a] (0.004)	
Hispanic	−0.002 (0.025)	0.041[a] (0.005)	
White	0.235[a] (0.023)	−0.011[a] (0.004)	
Parent education (reference category H.S. dropout)			
High school graduate	0.444[a] (0.005)	0.005[b] (0.002)	
Some college, did not graduate	0.679[a] (0.006)	0.016[a] (0.003)	
2-Year college degree	0.784[a] (0.006)	0.016[a] (0.002)	
4-Year college degree	1.130[a] (0.008)	0.022[a] (0.002)	
Graduate school degree	1.419[a] (0.011)	0.027[a] (0.003)	
Changed schools in last year	−0.133[a] (0.005)	−0.018[a] (0.003)	−0.013[a] (0.004)
Made structural change in last year	−0.048[a] (0.007)	−0.065[a] (0.006)	−0.056[a] (0.007)
Total observations	1,527,157	1,512,587	1,494,885[c]
Total students	445,562	441,863	424,066[c]

Notes: All models include grade/year fixed effects. Dependent variable is EOG development scale scores expressed as a standard score. Figures in parentheses are robust standard errors calculated using generalization of Huber/white Sandwich estimator and are robust to clustering within schools.
[a] Statistical significance at the 0.01 level.
[b] Statistical significance at the 0.05 level.
[c] Sample count includes only those observations of students with at least three valid test score measures, which is the minimum required to identify fixed effects and effect estimates for nonconstant variables.

The difference in achievement growth due to being enrolled in a charter school appears to be considerably larger than the differences in growth between children of high school dropouts and the children of parents with graduate degrees, and between blacks and whites—differences that are the object of considerable concern. The negative impacts of enrolling in a charter school are also substantially larger than the negative impacts of changing schools or making the transition from elementary school to junior high.

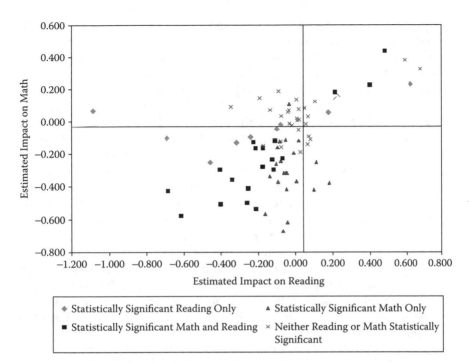

FIGURE 8.1. Distribution of estimated charter school impacts across charter schools.

This finding of a negative average effect need not mean that all North Carolina charter schools are unsuccessful in raising the achievement of their students. Nonetheless, as shown in Figure 8.1, many of them appear to exhibit negative impacts on achievement in both math and reading. The figure depicts our estimates of charter school impacts for each of the charter schools in each of the two subjects. Marks in the southwest quadrant represent schools with negative estimated impacts in both subjects. Those in the northeast quadrant exhibit positive impacts in both subjects. The fact that so many schools are in the southwest quadrant indicates that the negative average impact of charter schools on student achievement is not driven by a few atypical outliers. However, it is also worth noting that a handful of charter schools in North Carolina do appear to provide significant achievement benefits for their students.

Disaggregated Results

In our previous work we have refined and disaggregated these basic results in a number of ways. For example, we examine potential biases from the fact that exiters are overrepresented in our identifying sample;

the possibility that the effects might be less negative for the more established charter schools; the possibility that the effects might vary by the number of years a student has been enrolled in a charter school; and the possibility that the effects may differ based on the race and socioeconomic background of the student. We briefly summarize those results here.[1]

Differences between exiters from and entrants to charter schools. We first disaggregate the results by whether the student is observed exiting from or entering and remaining in a charter school. This disaggregation is driven by the observation that students who leave charter schools to return to traditional public schools are overrepresented in our identifying sample relative to the full set of charter school students. This overrepresentation would make the achievement effects appear more negative than would be the case for the full sample to the extent that these students leave because of a poor academic experience in charter schools. The size of the bias depends both on the extent to which exiters are overrepresented in the sample and on the magnitude of the difference in outcomes between charter school students who exit and those who do not. Based on disaggregated results not shown here for exiters and nonexiters, we find that the estimates reported in the final columns of Tables 8.4 and 8.5 are too negative, but only by 5–6%. Thus, the conclusion remains that on average charter schools in North Carolina have a negative effect on student achievement, at least as measured by performance on the statewide tests.

Differences by age of school. Given the challenges of opening a new school, one might expect that the charter schools operating for longer periods of time would be more effective than those recently opened. To examine this possibility, we estimated the achievement effects of charter schools separately by the number of years the school has been operating. Those results for the fixed-effects model are shown in Table 8.6. Consistent with our expectations, the negative effects are largest for charter schools during the first year. Importantly, however, the effects remain negative and statistically significant even for charter schools that have been operating for 4 or 5 years (and remain negative even after we adjust them for the bias just discussed). This finding that the negative effects persist for older schools differs from those that emerge from comparable studies in Texas and Florida. Although studies for those states also find negative overall achievement effects for charter schools, the negative effects in those states disappear for charter schools that have been operating for 3 or more

---

[1] In our previous work, we have also examined a number of other factors that could potentially bias the results. These include, for example, the fact that our identifying sample underrepresents children entering charter schools in the younger grades within the 3–8 grade range, and the possibility that the students who transferred to a charter school were more likely than others to have been experiencing a downward trend in their achievement prior to the transfer. See Bifulco and Ladd (2006), pp. 71–74.

TABLE 8.6
Estimated Impacts of Attending a Charter School by Years of Operation

	Math	Reading
First-year charter school	−0.312[a] (0.051)	−0.184[a] (0.027)
Second-year charter school	−0.131[a] (0.028)	−0.064[a] (0.019)
Third-year charter school	−0.081[a] (0.027)	−0.056[a] (0.021)
Fourth-year charter school	−0.092[a] (0.030)	−0.064[a] (0.021)
Fifth-year charter school	−0.198[a] (0.060)	−0.159[a] (0.050)
Change in schools	−0.025[a] (0.002)	−0.011[a] (0.001)
Structural change in schools	−0.092[a] (0.001)	−0.044[a] (0.001)

Notes: Both sets of estimates include grade/year and individual student fixed effects. Dependent variables are EOG scale scores converted to a standard score with a mean of 0 and standard deviation of 1.

[a] Statistical significance at the 0.01 level.

years in Texas and 4 or more years in Florida (Hanushek et al., 2005; Sass, 2006).[1]

Differences by years enrolled. An additional extension involves disaggregating the charter school effects not only by the age of the charter school, but also by whether it is the first year a student has been there. The key results, which are not shown here, are that the large negative overall effects appear to be driven largely—but not entirely—by the achievement of students during their first year in a charter regardless of the age of the school (see Tables 8.7A and 8.7B in Bifulco & Ladd [2006.]).

Given that the models separately control for the generic effect of changing schools, this finding means that in the year a student transfers into a charter school, he or she does even less well than if he or she were transferring to another traditional public school. Also, students who choose to remain in charter schools do not continue to accumulate negative impacts after their initial year. This finding is reassuring in that it justifies the decision of many parents to keep their children in charter schools once they are there. However, it is also clear that even this group, which is harmed least by the decision to attend a charter school, has lower levels of achievement as a result of that decision. Finally, the students who ultimately leave charter schools typically exhibit poorer performance in math relative to what they would have done in a traditional public school, both during their first year in a charter school and in subsequent years.

Disaggregation by race and parental education of the student. Here we look at how the achievement effects vary by the race and education level of the

---

[1] Sass (2006) finds that charter schools open 5 years or more in Florida have small positive effects on reading.

TABLE 8.7

Charter School Impacts on Achievement Gains by Student Characteristics

	Mathematics			Reading		
Charter school	−0.160[a]	−0.138[a]	−0.104[a]	−0.095[a]	−0.099[a]	−0.085[a]
	(0.021)	(0.028)	(0.030)	(0.014)	(0.017)	(0.015)
Charter school[b] black student		−0.055[a]	−0.040[b]		0.009	0.016
		(0.025)	(0.024)		(0.019)	(0.021)
Charter school[b] parents no college degree			−0.065[a]			−0.027
			(0.024)			(0.020)
Changed schools in last year	−0.027[a]	−0.028[a]	−0.027[a]	−0.013[a]	−0.013[a]	−0.013[a]
	(0.005)	(0.004)	(0.004)	(0.004)	(0.002)	(0.002)
Made structural change in last year	−0.061[a]	−0.061[a]	−0.061[a]	−0.056[a]	−0.056[a]	−0.056[a]
	(0.001)	(0.002)	(0.002)	(0.001)	(0.001)	(0.001)
Total observations		1,520,238			1,512,688	
Total students		443,553			441,869	

Notes: All models include grade/year fixed effects and are estimated using the "within" student estimator. Dependent variable is annual gain in EOG development scale scores expressed as standard scores with mean of zero and standard deviation of one. Figures in parentheses are robust standard errors calculated using generalization of Huber/ white Sandwich estimator and are robust to clustering within schools.

[a] Statistical significance at the 0.05 level.

[b] Statistical significance at 0.10 level.

parents. Table 8.7 shows the results. In each panel, the first column replicates the results from the preferred model in Table 8.4 or Table 8.5, the second column includes an interaction term that allows us to measure the differential effect on black students, and the third column includes two interaction terms that allow us to differentiate students both by their race and by the educational level of their parents.

The most interesting results emerge for math. As the first entry in the second column indicates, a negative math achievement effect of −0.138 emerges for white charter school students, and an even more negative effect of −0.0193 (−0.138 + (−0.055)) for black students. Thus, the negative achievement effect for black students is nearly 40% larger than that for white students. The third column shows that a student's race and the level of the parents' education have negative and statistically significant, independent influences on the size of the math achievement effect. These estimates imply that black children of less educated parents are most adversely affected by charter schools. Specifically, the negative effect of charter schools on the math achievement of black students whose parents do not have a 4-year college degree is 0.209 standard deviations per year (the sum of all three coefficients), which is twice as large as the 0.104 standard deviation loss experienced by white students with college-educated parents.

The final three columns of Table 8.7 summarize the results for reading. Though the average effects are negative, as was shown in Tables 8.5 and 8.6 and replicated in column 4, they do not differ significantly across racial or educational groups.

Given that North Carolina's black students are disproportionately represented in charter schools relative to white students, the finding that attending a charter school has, on average, had negative effects on student achievement suggests that the introduction of charter schools has increased the black–white test score gap in North Carolina. That the negative effect of charter schools is larger, at least in math, for black students than white students magnifies charter schools' impact on that gap, especially for black children of less educated parents.

THE LINK AMONG SEGREGATION, ACHIEVEMENT, AND TEST SCORE GAPS

In this section we test for a relationship between movement of black students to more racially segregated charter schools and the differentially large negative effect of charter schools on their math achievement. To do so we first identify all the charter school students who made racially segregating transfers into charter schools that are more than 60% black and have >10 percentage points of black students than the traditional public schools they previously attended. Approximately 54% of the black students we observe made such transfers. We then add various interaction terms to our fixed-effect regression model in order to distinguish the effects of charter schools on three groups of students: white students, black students who did not make racially segregating transfers, and black students who did make such transfers.

The results of this analysis are presented in Table 8.8. We focus first on the results for math. The first entry of −0.137 is an estimate of the negative effect of charter schools on white students. The second entry, which is small and statistically insignificant, indicates virtually no difference between the effects of charter schools on the math achievement of white and black students not making a racially segregating transfer. The third entry, in contrast, indicates that the effect of charter schools is significantly more negative for black students who made racially segregating transfers. The point estimates indicate that the negative effects of charter schools on these black students were 51% (0.077/(0.137 + 0.014)) larger than the effects on other black students, and 66% ((0.077 + 0.014)/0.137) larger than the effects on white students. Thus, the relatively large negative charter school effect for black students reported in Table 8.7 is attributable entirely to the experiences of black students who chose charter schools with higher levels of racial segregation than those in the traditional public schools they were previously attending.

TABLE 8.8

Charter School Impacts on Achievement Gains by Student's Race, Type of Transfer, and School Program

	Mathematics		Reading	
Charter school	–0.137[a]	–0.188[a]	–0.099[a]	–0.134[a]
	(0.026)	(0.024)	(0.018)	(0.018)
Charter school × black	–0.014	0.003	0.029	0.019
	(0.033)	(0.030)	(0.029)	(0.027)
Charter school × black × segregating move[c]	–0.077[a]	–0.108[a]	–0.037	–0.028
	(0.037)	(0.037)	(0.032)	(0.032)
Charter school × at-risk[c]		0.173[a]		0.121[a]
		(0.048)		(0.045)
Charter school × at-risk × black[c]		–0.026		0.082
		(0.077)		(0.084)
Charter school × at-risk × black × segregating move[c,d]		0.043		–0.096
		(0.082)		(0.090)
Changed schools in last year	–0.028[a]	–0.028[a]	–0.013[a]	–0.013[a]
	(0.005)	(0.005)	(0.004)	(0.004)
Made structural change in last year	–0.033[a]	–0.061[a]	–0.043[a]	–0.056[a]
	(0.008)	(0.010)	(0.006)	(0.007)

Notes: All models include grade/year fixed effects and are estimated using the "within" student estimator. Dependent variable is annual gain in EOG development scale scores expressed as standard scores with mean of zero and standard deviation of one. Figures in parentheses are robust standard errors calculated using generalization of Huber/white Sandwich estimator and are robust to clustering within schools. Sample counts are the same as in Table 8.3.

[a] Statistical significance at the 0.05 level.

[b] Statistical significance at 0.010 level.

[c] "Segregating move" is an indicator variable equal to one if student transferred into a charter school with more than 60% black and with percent black 10 or more percentage points higher than in the traditional public school from or to which the student transferred, and equal to zero otherwise.

[d] At-risk is a school level indicator value equal to one if the mission and purpose statement in the school's charter application outlined specific intervention or recruitment efforts targeted to students at risk of academic failure, and equal to zero otherwise.

As shown in the third column of Table 8.8, the negative effects of charter schools on reading test scores are also largest for blacks who made racially segregating moves. However, the differences in effects between groups are not statistically significant.

One should not conclude that the relatively large negative effects of charter schools on the achievement of black students who made racially segregating transfers are attributable specifically to the change in the racial profile of their classmates. The racial profile of a charter school is so closely related to its other characteristics—mission, programs, teacher quality, facilities quality—that we cannot distinguish its causal effects from these other characteristics. We do, however, try to look at one such characteristic: whether the school explicitly targets at-risk students. Of the black charter school students who made racially segregating transfers, 34.2% transferred into a school that, according to its mission statement, explicitly targets at-risk students. Perhaps factors such as the peer environment associated with a concentration of students at risk of academic failure, or the curricular focus of at-risk programs, account for the relatively large negative effect of charter schools on black students who made racially segregating transfers.

To investigate this possibility, we estimated a version of our within-student model that allows the effects on each of our student groups to differ for charter schools targeting at-risk populations from those of other charter schools. The results are reported in the second and the last columns of Table 8.8. The large and statistically significant positive coefficients on the variable indicating that a charter school is targeted toward students who are at risk of academic failure (see fourth row) implies that such charter schools have less negative average effects on their students' achievement than do other charter schools.[1] In addition, the estimates in Table 8.8 imply that both types of charter schools—those that target at-risk students and those that do not—generate larger negative effects on black students making racially segregating transfers than on other black students.

To summarize, black students who switch into racially segregating charter schools exhibit even larger negative achievement reductions relative to what they would have achieved in the traditional public schools than do either white students or other black students who transfer into charter schools. Moreover, these larger reductions are not attributable to the fact that about one in three black charter school students selects into schools that target at-risk students. Nor can we conclude that the differentially negative effects are specifically attributable to the racial profiles of the charter schools. Nevertheless, the relatively large negative effects of charter schools on black students who made racially segregating transfers raise a legitimate concern about charter schools that are substantially more segregated than nearby traditional public schools and, as shown previously, are not the preferred option for many black families.

CONCLUSION

The findings in this chapter raise serious concerns about North Carolina's charter school program. One key finding is that charter schools are more racially segregated than traditional public schools in the same district. More telling is that both black and white charter school families tend

---

[1] This coefficient specifically captures the difference in effects on white students. However, the effects of at-risk charters on black students are also much less negative than the effects of other charters.

to choose charter schools with peers who are more racially and socio-economically similar to their own children than were students in their regular public schools. As a result of these choices, the charter school system clearly increases racial segregation. Moreover, many black students have moved into charter schools with higher proportions of black peers than their previous public schools despite lower average levels of student achievement in those schools.

In addition, we find that charter schools have had larger negative effects on the achievement of black students, particularly those with less well educated parents, than on white students. This finding, together with the finding that charter schools have negative effects on average and that black students are more likely to opt into charter schools, implies that North Carolina's charter school program has increased the black–white test score gap.

Whether these outcomes for North Carolina are generalizable to the charter school programs adopted in 39 other states and the District of Columbia is difficult to say. With respect to the segregating effects of charter schools, one might expect larger effects to emerge in a southern state such as North Carolina that has a relatively well integrated public school system compared to many northern or midwestern states, where traditional public schools are more segregated, or to western states where African-American populations are smaller. At the same time, North Carolina is clearly not the only state where charter schools are more racially segregated than traditional public schools (Booker, Zimmer, & Buddin, 2005; Cobb & Glass, 2001; Frankenberg & Lee, 2003). Moreover, other studies have found that when given the opportunity to choose, parents select more racially isolated environments (Henig, 1996; Weiher & Tedin, 2002). Finally, using data and methods similar to those used here, studies of the average effectiveness of charter schools in Texas (Hanushek et al., 2005) and Florida (Sass, 2006) also find that charter schools have negative achievement effects, albeit smaller than those that emerge for North Carolina. Thus, while we cannot say with certainty that our North Carolina results are generalizable to other states, we see no compelling reason to think they are not. More research on the effects of charter school programs on racial segregation, minority achievement, and black–white test score gaps in other states would be useful.

Our results need not imply that efforts to expand parental choice ought to be abandoned. It is hard to argue that only wealthy parents should enjoy the privilege of choosing where their child will go to school. Although charter school students have not benefited academically on average from expanded opportunities to choose, some students undoubtedly have, and even those who have not benefited academically might have benefited in other ways. Thus, it is difficult to argue against the provision of more choice for disadvantaged students. Nonetheless, our results highlight for policymakers the importance of recognizing that any benefits of expanding choice may well come at the expense of other policy goals, such as more racially integrated schools and the reduction of black–white achievement gaps.

REFERENCES

Baltagi, B. H. (1995). *Econometric analysis of panel data.* New York: Wiley.

Bifulco, R., & Ladd, H. F. (2005). The truths about charter schools: Results from the Tar Heel state. *Education Next, 5*(4), 60–66.

Bifulco, R., & Ladd, H. F. (2006). The impact of charter schools on student achievement: Evidence from North Carolina. *Education Finance and Policy, 1*(1), 50–90.

Bifulco, R., & Ladd, H.F. (2007). School choice, racial segregation, and test score gaps: Evidence from North Carolina's charter school program. *Journal of Policy Analysis and Management, 26*(1) (winter), 31–56.

Booker, K., Gilpatric, S. M., Gronberg, T., & Jansen, D. (2004). *Charter school performance in Texas.* Unpublished paper, Texas A&M University.

Booker, K., Zimmer, R., & Buddin, R. (2005). The effect of charter schools on school peer composition. RAND working paper WR-306-EDU. Accessed January 10, 2006, at http://www.ncspe.org/publications_files/RAND_WR306.pdf.

Cobb, C. D., & Glass, G. V. (2001). U.S. charter schools and ethnic segregation: Inspecting the evidence. *International Journal of Educational Reform, 10*(4), 381–394.

Frankenberg, E., & Lee, C. (2003). Charter schools and race: A lost opportunity for integrated education, Education Policy Analysis Archives, *11*(32). Accessed June 1, 2006, at http://epaa.asu.edu/epaa/v1/n32/.

Hanushek, E. A., Kain, J. F., & Rivkin, S. G. (2002). *The impact of charter schools on academic achievement.* Unpublished paper, Stanford University.

Hanushek, E. A., Kain, J. F., Rivkin, S. G., & Brand, G. F. (2005). Charter school quality and parental decision making with school choice. NBER working paper 11252: Cambridge, MA: National Bureau of Economics Research. Accessed June 23, 2006 at http://www.nber.org/papers/w11252.

Henig, J. (1996). The local dynamics of choice: Ethnic preferences and institutional responses. In B. Fuller & R. Elmore (Eds.), *Who chooses? Who loses? Culture, institutions, and the unequal effects of school choice* (pp. 95–117). New York: Teachers College Press.

Manuel, J. (2002). The good, the great, and the struggling: An up close look at charter schools across North Carolina. *North Carolina Insight, 20*(1), 21–55.

Nelson, F.H., Muir, E., & Drown, R. (2003). Financing autonomy: The impact of mission and scale on charter school finance. The State Education Standard, *4*(3) (autumn), 38–44.

Sass, T. R. (2006). Charter schools and student achievement in Florida. *Education Finance and Policy, 1*(1), 91–122.

Speakman, S., Hassel, B., & Finn, C. (2005). *Charter school finding: Inequity's next frontier.* Washington, D.C.: Thomas B. Fordham Foundation. Available at http://www.edexcellence.net/institute/charterfinance.

Weiher, G. R., & Tedin, K. L. (2002). Does choice lead to racially distinctive schools? Charter schools and household preferences. *Journal of Policy Analysis and Management, 21*(1), 79–92.

9

Charter Schools in Idaho

DALE BALLOU, BETTIE TEASLEY, AND TIM ZEIDNER

INTRODUCTION

The emerging picture of charter schools in the United States indicates that, overall, students enrolled in charter schools are performing no better on standardized achievement tests than students in traditional public schools; indeed, studies have shown that in some grades and subjects their performance appears to be worse. Charter school defenders have argued (correctly) that many of these comparisons fail to take into account the self-selected nature of the charter school population and the fact that many students enroll in charter schools because they have not enjoyed success in more traditional settings. However, more sophisticated studies have examined student gains rather than level scores in such states as Texas, Florida, and North Carolina. These studies, too, have concluded that charter schools are not as effective as traditional public schools overall, though there is some evidence that after a charter school's first years of operation (a notably difficult period for many new schools), differences between the charter sector and the traditional sector become insignificant.

In this chapter we extend this literature by examining charter schools in Idaho. In several respects Idaho's experience is at odds with findings from other states. Charter schools in Idaho tend to attract students who have been performing above average in traditional public schools. Newer charter schools appear to be more effective than schools that have been in operation longer. Finally, when we employ the methodology researchers use in other states, we find that elementary students in charter schools have made greater gains than they would have made had they remained in traditional public schools (though the difference in higher grades is reversed or insignificant). However, unlike other researchers, we also find that our conclusion on this point is highly sensitive to methodological assumptions.

We begin with an overview of Idaho charter schools. We then consider two alternative ways of estimating the effectiveness of charter schools, subject to differing biases. Finally, we show that conclusions about charter schools depend on which of the two methods is used. Although we are inclined to trust one of these sets of estimates more than the other, we cannot claim to have settled this matter definitively.

OVERVIEW OF IDAHO CHARTER SCHOOLS

Since the enactment of Idaho's Public Charter Schools Act of 1998, the number of charter schools there has grown at a moderate pace. This may be due in part to the conservative nature of the Idaho Charter School statute, which limits charter growth to six approved schools per year. In addition, no district can add more than one new charter school each year or convert to an all-charter district (Idaho Statute, Title 33, Chapter 52, with 2005 amendments, 2005).

Charter schools are authorized in one of three ways: through the local school board, by the State Charter School Commission, or by appeal to the state Board of Education. In the 1999–2000 school year, eight charter schools were in operation, serving approximately 1,000 students (less than 0.5% of the total student population). By the 2005–2006 school year, there were 28 charter schools, bringing the total students enrolled to 7,400, or approximately 4% of the state's school-age population. An additional three schools were expected to open for the 2006–2007 school year (Center for School Improvement and Policy Studies, 2005).

The wait lists at most charter schools suggest that these statutory restrictions have limited the number of students served by charter schools. As noted in Table 9.1, 8,209 students were enrolled in 2005–2006, with another 4,671 (57% of total enrollment) students on waiting lists. Furthermore, 20 (71%) of the schools started with kindergarten, while only eight (29%) offered grades 10–12. Just one school, Sandpoint, focuses specifically on what is traditionally referred to as middle or junior high school.

Table 9.2 offers a breakdown of the variations of grades served in the study sample. While there is an overall increase of schools across the grades, there are consistently more schools in the lower grades than in the upper grades. Seven schools made changes in the grades offered over the 3 years of data observed. Six of these added grades over time, usually in increments of one per year. The other school scaled back grade offerings, dropping grades 6–8.

Idaho's charter schools are primarily located in three areas: the panhandle, the Boise/Nampa/Meridian region, and the southeast region. The two midstate schools and the one in the panhandle are "virtual" (online) and draw from regions across the state. Two districts, both among the largest in Idaho, serve as host to multiple charter schools. In the Boise District, charter school students make up 2.6% of the student population.

TABLE 9.1
Operating Idaho Charter Schools

Name	Starting year	Grades served	Students enrolled 2005–2006	Waiting list	Authorized by
1. Academy at Roosevelt Center	2005				ID Commission
2. Anser Charter School	1999	K–7	214	300	District
3. Advanced Regional Technical Education Center (ARTEC) Charter School	2005	7–12		NA	District
4. Blackfoot Community Charter School	2000	K–6	100	85	District
5. Coeur d'Alene Charter Academy	1999	6–12	420	90	District
6. COMPASS Charter School	2005	K–8	233	199	ID Commission
7. Falcon Ridge Charter School	2005	K–8	270	75	ID Commission
8. Garden City Community Charter School	2005	K–8			ID Commission
9. Hidden Springs Charter School	2001	K–9	480	471	District
10. Idaho Arts Charter School	2005	K–10	515	200	District
11. Idaho Distance Education Academy	2004	K–12	1000	25	District
12. Idaho Leadership Academy	2002	9–12	150	20	District
13. Idaho Virtual Academy	2002	K–8	1750	0	ID Commission
14. INSPIRE Connections Academy	2005	K–9	146	0	ID Commission
15. Liberty Charter School	1999	K–12	403	1296	ID Commission
16. Meridian Charter High School	1999	9–12	191	Not provided	District
17. Meridian Medical Arts Charter School	2003	9–12	196	30	District
18. Moscow Charter School	1998	K–6	135	20	District
19. North Star Charter School	2003	K–8	265	600	District

TABLE 9.1 (continued)
Operating Idaho Charter Schools

Name	Starting year	Grades served	Students enrolled 2005–2006	Waiting list	Authorized by
20. Pocatello Community Charter School	1999	K–8	296	300	District
21. Richard McKenna Charter High School (formerly Idaho Virtual High School)	2004	9–12	248	0	ID Commission
22. Rolling Hills Charter School	2005	K–8	227	84	ID Commission
23. Sandpoint Charter School	2001	7–9	90	0	District
24. Taylor's Crossing Public Charter School	2005	K–8	Not provided	Not provided	ID Commission
25. Thomas Jefferson Charter School	2004	K–7	270	Not provided	District
26. Upper Carmon Public Charter School	2005	K–6	26	0	District
27. Victory Charter School	2004	K–8	270	576	ID Commission
28. White Pine Charter School	2003	K–7	314	300	District

Sources: Center for School Improvement and Policy Studies (2005); Idaho Charter School Network (2005)

In Meridian, charter schools represent less than a percentage point of the district's student population. The Moscow School District, located in a rural area, has the highest percentage of students served, with 5.3% of students enrolled in the charter school.

Since charter legislation passed in 1998, the charter school system has grown to 28 operating schools as of the 2005–2006 school year. Ten have been in existence for 5 years or more, while another three are in their fourth year. During the past 8 years, two charter schools have had their authorization revoked, and one was discontinued. For the 2005–2006 school year, 10 charter schools were added to the state's roster. This number is greater than the statutory maximum, in part because several charters were approved for the 2004–2005 school year but did not operate until the following year. Seventeen of the 28 charter schools in operation for the 2005–2006 school year received charter authorization from the local school district, while the remaining 11 schools received authorization from the

TABLE 9.2
Number of Idaho Charter Schools by Semester and Grades Offered

Grade	Fall 2002	Spring 2003	Fall 2003	Spring 2004	Fall 2004	Spring 2005
K	7	8	10	10	12	12
1	7	8	10	10	12	12
2	7	8	10	10	12	12
3	7	8	10	10	12	12
4	7	8	10	10	12	12
5	6	8	10	10	12	12
6	6	8	10	10	13	13
7	6	7	8	8	12	12
8	6	7	8	8	8	9
9	4	6	8	9	9	9
10	4	5	6	7	8	7
11	4	5	6	7	8	7
12	4	5	6	7	8	7

Sources: Growth Research Database (2005); U.S. Department of Education, National Center for Education Statistics (2004b)

Idaho Charter School Commission (Center for School Improvement and Policy Studies, 2005).

Distinctive Programmatic Elements in Idaho Charter Schools

The missions and curricula of Idaho charter schools have contributed to the state's diversity of educational practices. The curriculum and instructional method that appears most frequently is the Harbor School Method, with 8 of the 28 schools using it (Idaho Charter School Network, 2005; Harbor Educational Institute, n.d.). Developed by administrators at the Liberty Charter School, this curriculum emphasizes student deportment and character development along with instructional and academic components. The charter schools that employ this method are elementary and elementary/middle schools, except one, which recently extended grade offerings to the 12th grade.

Another frequently utilized instructional method is distance learning, which five charter schools offer. Although all of these schools provide online instruction, curricula vary. Two virtual charter schools furnish resources for parents who homeschool their children; others embrace specific programs like Great Books and the K–12 Program. One of the virtual schools also serves at-risk students both on site and through its online program.

Three of the charter high schools describe themselves as career and college preparatory schools; two are industry/field specific with technology and health care focuses. Two other charter schools have Outward Bound expeditionary learning programs. A few others emphasize the arts. This diversity in curriculum design and philosophy resembles offerings in other states. The heterogeneity of the school design, philosophy, and goals is intended to appeal to parents with distinct preferences for their children's education.

On average, charter schools in Idaho have a higher pupil–teacher ratio of 18:1, compared to a state average of approximately 16:1 (U.S. Department of Education, 2004b). Three charter schools have extended their school year beyond that of the local district and two others operate as year-round schools (Wang, Geiger, & Devine, 2004).

Resources, Financing, and Facilities

Like their traditional public school counterparts, Idaho charter schools rely primarily on state funds (a capitation grant based on average daily attendance) and federal funds. For the 2003–2004 school year, the per pupil expenditure averaged $6,660, ranging from $1,666.50 at Richard McKenna Charter School (formerly Idaho Virtual High School) to $17,105 at Idaho Leadership Academy (Wang et al., 2004). With virtual schools removed from the mix, the range is from $3,205 at Hidden Springs Charter School to $14,274 at Meridian Technical Charter School. Two of the 16 charter schools operating in 2003–2004 also received sizable resources for general management and operations expenditures from undisclosed "other sources." Liberty Charter School and Coeur d'Alene Charter Academy practically matched the state funds allocated to them (approximately $2 million) with revenues from "other sources."

In general, it is unclear how charter schools finance their start-up costs. It appears that new charters minimize expenses by renting or using public facilities and sacrificing certain services (such as transportation). Only 4 of the 16 schools had substantial funds allocated for capital projects, indicating that a permanent facility was being erected. In an evaluation of charter schools during the 2003–2004 school year, the Northwest Regional Educational Laboratory reported that "about 50% of charter schools in Idaho are operating in temporary facilities. It is still an uphill struggle for these schools to find permanent facilities. Some temporary facilities are crowded and limiting to student learning activities" (Wang et al., 2004, p. 5).

Just two charter schools participate in the federal free and reduced-price lunch program (U.S. Department of Education, 2004b), though ten report that they provide lunch (Wang et al., 2004). Six charter schools provide transportation services.

Student Composition

Charter schools in Idaho are less ethnically diverse than the school districts within which they are situated (Table 9.3). This is particularly true with respect to Hispanics, as charters typically enroll a quarter to a third as many as the district enrolls. Furthermore, in the Pocatello and blackfoot school districts, where Native Americans represent 5.3 and 13.6% of the school-age populations, respectively, charter school enrollment of Native Americans is 0 and 2%.

As mentioned earlier, most of Idaho's charter schools do not participate in the free and reduced-price lunch program. Where they do, the percentage of eligible students in 2003–2004 exceeds the rate for the local district (Table 9.4). Where charter schools do not offer the free and reduced-price lunch program, participation in the local district's traditional public schools ranges from 17 to 44%, which is below the percentage of eligible students statewide (54%). With the exception of charter schools in the Boise City Independent School District, most charters serve fewer limited English proficiency students than their local district. However, charter schools do appear to serve special education students at or above the rate of the local district.

Student Mobility

The charter school sector in Idaho is marked by a high degree of student mobility. This in part reflects the growth of the sector. However, there is a lot of movement out of the sector as well as into it. As shown in Table 9.5, more than a quarter of the students attending regular (nonvirtual) charter schools have left the sector at the end of the academic year. While some return to traditional public schools in Idaho, more have left the state or enrolled in private schools. The percentage is even higher among students in virtual charter schools, where the turnover rate has exceeded one third. Within-year mobility is also high, particularly in the virtual schools.

Mobility and Student Achievement

Previous research has exploited this mobility to identify a charter school effect by comparing test score gains of the same students before and after they move between charter and traditional public schools. This is considered superior to comparing the gains of all charter school students to all students in the traditional public sector, inasmuch as charter school students may differ in systematic but unobserved ways from students in regular public schools. Indeed, in Idaho, inferences about charter school effectiveness depend on which of the two methods is used.

TABLE 9.3
Ethnic Demographics of Idaho Charter School Students

Schools and their sponsoring districts	White (%)	Black (%)	Hispanic (%)	Native American (%)	Asian/ Pacific Islander (%)
Blackfoot Charter	90.00	0.00	5.00	2.00	3.00
Blackfoot District[a]	66.29	0.39	18.23	13.57	1.52
Anser Charter	93.60	0.00	1.50	1.50	3.40
Hidden Springs Charter	91.06	0.54	1.62	1.08	0.54
North Star Charter	95.00	0.00	1.00	0.00	4.00
Boise Independent District[a]	87.37	1.95	7.00	0.62	3.06
Coeur d'Alene Charter	96.00	0.50	0.80	0.20	0.80
Coeur d'Alene District[a]	95.29	0.61	2.36	0.64	1.10
Meridian Charter High	97.00	2.00	0.00	0.00	1.00
Meridian Medical Charter	93.50	0.50	2.60	0.00	3.40
Meridian Joint District[a]	91.96	1.38	3.38	0.81	2.47
Moscow Charter	95.00	0.01	0.03	0.00	0.01
Moscow District[a]	90.66	2.00	2.40	1.06	3.88
Liberty Charter	90.00	0.00	7.00	1.00	2.00
Nampa District[a]	72.73	0.72	24.80	0.48	1.27
Pocatello Charter	94.00	0.00	2.00	0.00	0.00
Pocatello District[a]	85.07	1.30	6.55	5.35	1.73
Sandpoint Charter	98.00	0.00	1.00	0.00	1.00
Lake Pend Oreille District[a]	96.17	0.52	1.45	0.73	1.13
Idaho Leadership Academy	100.00	0.00	0.00	0.00	0.00
Snake River District[a]	80.32	0.34	17.63	1.27	0.44
Idaho Virtual Academy	83.00	0.40	1.40	0.80	0.70
Butte County District[a]	93.00	1.00	4.00	0.00	1.00
Richard McKenna	88.00	1.00	7.00	0.00	2.00
Mountain Home District[a]	80.00	4.00	12.00	0.00	3.00
State of Idaho	85.89	0.80	10.85	1.22	1.24

Source: U.S. Department of Education, National Center for Education Statistics (2004a,b)
[a] Districts and state

Figure 9.1 depicts mean levels of mathematics achievement in traditional public schools and charter schools across the nine tested grades. While the data shown are from the spring of 2005, the pattern is the same

TABLE 9.4

Student Demographics by Charter Schools[a]

Charter school name	Free and reduced price lunch[b]	Special education[c]	Limited English proficiency[c]	Percent of schools that are Title[b]
Anser Charter School	N/A	13	1.4	No
Hidden Springs Charter School	N/A	3.8	1.63	No
Boise City Independent School District[d]	0.32	0.11	0.05	0.54
Blackfoot Community Charter School	0.60	0.20	0	Yes
Blackfoot School District[d]	0.46	0.12	0.21	0.79
Coeur d'Alene Charter Academy	N/A	<1	0	No
Coeur d'Alene School District[d]	0.33	0.10	0.00	0.65
Idaho Distance Education Academy	N/A	N/A	N/A	N/A
Whitepine Joint School District[d]	0.44	0.14	0.00	1.00
Idaho Leadership Academy	N/A	4	0	No
Snake River School District[d]	0.39	0.09	0.16	0.83
Liberty Charter School	N/A	7	0	No
Victory Charter School	N/A			
Nampa School District[d]	0.43	0.11	0.17	0.64
Meridian Charter School	0.25	0.1	0	No
Meridian Medical Arts Charter School	N/A	9.6	0	No
North Star Public Charter School	N/A	3	0	No
Meridian School District[d]	0.17	0.10	0.02	0.33
Moscow Charter School	N/A	0.45	0	Yes
Moscow School District	0.19	0.11	0.01	0.43
Pocatello Community Charter School	N/A	17	0	No
Pocatello School District[d]	0.35	0.13	0.01	0.59
Richard McKenna Charter High School (formerly Idaho Virtual High School)	N/A	0	0	Yes
Mountain Home School District[d]	0.33	0.15	0.09	0.70

TABLE 9.4 (continued)
Student Demographics by Charter Schools[a]

Charter school name	Free and reduced price lunch[b]	Special education[c]	Limited English proficiency[c]	Percent of schools that are Title[b]
Sandpoint Charter School	N/A	20	<1	No
Lake Pend Oreille School District[d]	0.42	0.12	0.00	0.83
Thomas Jefferson Charter School	N/A			
Vallivue School District[d]	0.47	0.11	0.13	1.00
White Pine Charter School	0			No
Bonneville School District[d]	0.31	0.10	0.04	0.71
Idaho Virtual Academy (no corresponding district)	N/A	0.06	0	No

Note: Each charter school is followed by its corresponding district.
[a] Percent total of school enrollment.
[b] U.S. Department of Education, National Center for Education Statistics (2004a), 2003-2004 school year.
[c] Information provided by each respective charter school (Wang et al., 2004). School district information for these columns is from U.S. Department of Education, National Center for Education Statistics, 2003–2004 school year.
[d] Name of district.

in all semesters. In charter schools, achievement levels are higher in every grade—the result of positive selection into that sector. In several instances, charter school students even outscore traditional public school students at the next grade level.

For this reason, it is more reasonable to compare charter schools with traditional public schools on the basis of student gains. Figure 9.2 depicts mean gains between fall and spring testing in 2004–2005. In every grade, traditional public school students gain more than charter school students. (Again, the same pattern is evident in other years.) By this simple test, traditional public schools outperform charter schools. However, this conclusion rests on the implicit assumption that charter school students do not differ from traditional public school students in any other way that affects gains. As this may not be true, we consider the change in gain scores as students move between sectors.

Figure 9.3 shows gain scores for students enrolled in fifth grade or lower in 2002–2003. Within-year gains (fall to spring) are shown for 2002–2003 and 2003–2004. The data are longitudinal: The students whose gains are depicted for 2002–2003 are shown one year later in 2003–2004. Because gains tend to diminish with advancing grade level (compare Figure 9.2),

TABLE 9.5
Student Mobility in the Charter School Sector

	Within year			Between years	
	Fall 2002– spring 2003	Fall 2003– spring 2004	Fall 2004– spring 2005	Spring 2003–fall 2003	Spring 2004–fall 2004
Where charter school students went					
Virtual charter schools					
Charter	60	1,063	1,578	425	792
Idaho traditional public schools	2	80	126	118	208
Other	21	158	199	128	273
Leavers as percentage of total	27.7%	18.3%	17.1%	36.7%	37.8%
Regular charter schools					
Charter	986	1,787	2,277	938	1400
Idaho traditional public schools	25	100	87	161	222
Other	54	92	114	204	313
Leavers as percentage of total	7.4%	9.7%	8.1%	28.0%	27.6%
Where charter school students came from					
Virtual charter schools					
Charter	60	1,062	1,576	420	789
Idaho traditional public schools	125	54	104	242	334
Other	486	157	168	639	780
New arrivals as percentage of total	91.1%	16.6%	14.7%	67.7%	58.5%
Regular charter schools					
Charter	986	1,788	2,279	943	1,403
Idaho traditional public schools	37	63	76	616	532
Other	280	84	55	420	543
New arrivals as percentage of total	24.3%	7.6%	5.4%	52.3%	43.4%

Note: Tabulations of unpublished data from Northwest Evaluation Association (2005).

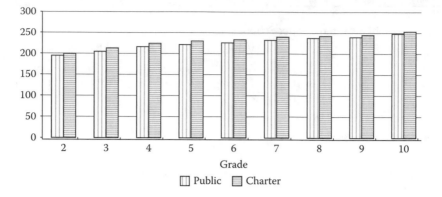

FIGURE 9.1 Comparison of achievement levels: spring 2005.

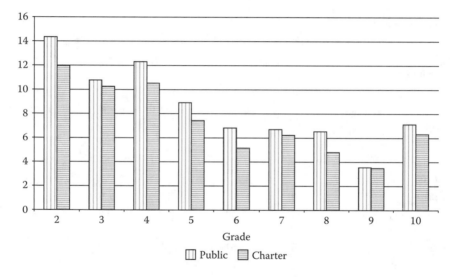

FIGURE 9.2 Comparison of achievement gains: fall 2004 to spring 2005.

2002–2003 gains generally exceed gains in 2003–2004. The middle columns in the graph depict students who changed sectors between these two academic years. Students who moved from traditional public schools in the first year to charter schools in the second year are the only group that experienced greater gains after the move. By contrast, those who moved from charter to traditional public schools saw the greatest decline.

Figure 9.4 shows gains among elementary students for 2003–2004 and 2004–2005. With rare exceptions, these students are different from those in Figure 9.3. However, the same pattern generally holds. The smallest drop

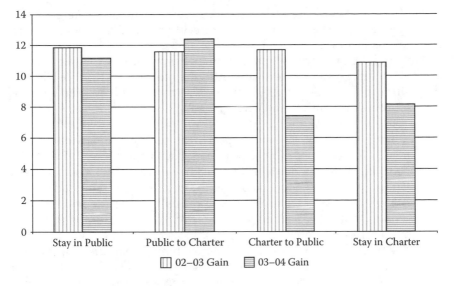

FIGURE 9.3 Achievement gains of students who move and students who stay: elementary school, 2002–2003 and 2003–2004.

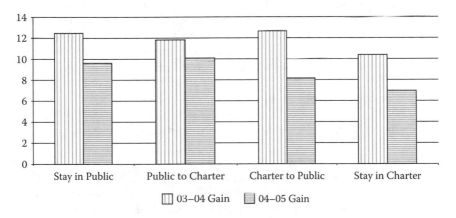

FIGURE 9.4 Achievement gains of students who move and students who stay: elementary school, 2003–2004 and 2004–2005.

in gain scores occurred among students who moved from the traditional public to the charter sector. The largest drop occurred among students who moved in the opposite direction.

The use of longitudinal data (Figures 9.3 and 9.4) as opposed to cross-sectional data (Figure 9.2) leads to different conclusions about charter school effectiveness vis-à-vis traditional public schools at the elementary level. (Graphical evidence at the secondary level is mixed.) Whereas charter schools appear less effective with respect to mean gains, the longitudinal analysis favors charter schools.

Although researchers have shown a marked preference for longitudinal analysis, relying on a sample of students who move can introduce biases if they differ from the larger set of all charter school students. Among possible sources of bias are the following:

- Movers may be atypical with respect to the quality of the student–school match. Although previous researchers have been concerned that students leave a sector due to a poor match, we present evidence later that the reverse has been true among Idaho elementary school students.
- Movers may select a school based on its quality; the result is that schools that are either better or worse than average for the sector are overrepresented among a sample of movers.
- The quality of the student–school match may be a function of a student's prior educational history. For example, as Hoxby and Rockoff (2005) argue, charter schools may be more effective with students who have attended them from the earliest grades than they are with students who arrive after attending traditional public schools.
- Students and their parents may mistake transitory downturns in student performance as evidence about school quality or the student–school match and move between sectors accordingly. The return of performance to a more normal level the following year creates the appearance of a positive charter school effect (if they have moved into the charter sector) or a negative effect (if they have moved out of the charter school sector).
- Serial correlation (trends in achievement) can be confounded with differences in school quality when movers switch sectors.

Whether these biases are worse than selection bias is an empirical question that is difficult to resolve. Accordingly, we present two sets of estimates, one based on a longitudinal analysis of movers and the other based on a cross-sectional comparison of all students in the two sectors. Both analyses employ student gains as the dependent variable. The longitudinal analysis further controls for unobservable student characteristics by including a student fixed effect. The cross-sectional analysis does not. We follow this brief discussion of the evidence favoring one estimator over the other. A more detailed treatment of this question appears in other work (Ballou, Teasley, & Zeidner, 2006).

Analysis of Achievement Gains

Our empirical model takes one of two forms:

$$y_{ijt} = X_{ijt}\,\beta + \Sigma_g\,C_{it}\,\gamma_g\,\psi_g + \alpha_i\,\varphi_i + e_{it} \qquad (9.1)$$

or

$$y_{ijt} = X_{ijt}\,\beta + \Sigma_g\,C_{it}\,\gamma_g\,\psi_g + v_{it} \qquad (9.2)$$

Equation (9.1) includes student fixed effects φ_i while Equation (9.2) does not. C_{it} is an indicator variable for charter schools. C_{it} is interacted with an indicator of grade, γ_g, allowing the charter school effect to differ across grades. X_{ijt} represents student and school covariates. y_{ijt} is a student's fall-to-spring gain, normalized for the number of instructional days between fall and spring testing.[1]

The Northwest Evaluation Association (NWEA) has furnished data for this study. The state of Idaho has contracted with NWEA to provide tests for its statewide assessments in grades 2–10. Participation rates are over 90%. Although tests are administered in reading, language arts, and mathematics, for this study we used only the mathematics results.

We have a limited number of covariates for inclusion in the model. X_{ijt} includes indicators of race (white = 1) and special education, both interacted with grade level.[2] We also included dummy variables for year-by-grade interactions, to control for possible changes in the difficulty of the tests.

The model was estimated using fall-to-spring gain scores from 2002–2003, 2003–2004, and 2004–2005 for students in grades 2–10, when testing is mandatory. Students who switched schools between fall and spring semesters were omitted from the sample. We also dropped observations from Idaho's five virtual charter schools. Although of interest in their own right, these schools are so distinctive (and their combined enroll-

---

[1] Testing dates vary in Idaho. The average time elapsed between fall and spring testing is about 135 school days, with a standard deviation of slightly more than a week. We normalize gain scores by dividing by the approximate number of school days between fall and spring testing, multiplied by 180 to represent a "standard year's" gain. Students with missing test dates (about 10% of the charter school sample and 5% of the traditional public sample) were dropped from the analysis.

[2] Because all covariates are interacted with grade, the model includes no time-invariant regressors. Thus, inclusion of student fixed effects does not cause any other variables to drop out. However, it is still the case that only movers directly furnish information about the effectiveness of charter schools relative to traditional public schools. Observations on nonmovers furnish information about relative effectiveness of instruction at different grade levels within sector (charter or traditional public), but only through this channel do they have any influence on estimates of the difference in average effectiveness between sectors. Accordingly, we will continue to refer to the fixed effects (FE) estimator as an estimator based on a sample of movers, which, though not strictly true here, correctly characterizes the rest of the literature.

ment so large) that their inclusion in the estimation sample would skew the comparison.[1]

Characteristics of the estimation sample are displayed in Table 9.6. Students are classified into three groups: those who remained in the traditional public sector throughout the sample period, those who attended only charter schools, and moved between sectors. Interestingly, more students moved than stayed in charter schools. Observations on movers peak during grades 5–8, suggesting that students are more likely to move in or out of charter schools when they transition from elementary school to middle school.

Compared to students in the traditional public sector, students who spent at least part of this period in a charter school are more likely to be non-Hispanic whites. There are also fewer special education students attending charter schools, though the percentage among movers is virtually the same as among traditional public school students.[2]

RESULTS

Estimates of the charter school effect are displayed in Table 9.7. (A full set of results with coefficients on all the variables in the model is available from the authors.) Models were estimated by ordinary least squares. Standard errors have been adjusted for clustering at the school level using a robust asymptotic covariance matrix.[3] As anticipated, there is a pronounced difference between the models with and without fixed effects. The charter school effect is negative at every grade in the latter. In the former, gains are greater in charter schools in the elementary grades, with the estimates for grades 3, 4, and 5 significant at the 5% level or better. Between columns 1 and 2 there is a discrepancy of about 7 points for third graders, and 4.5 points for fourth graders. These are sizeable differences, given that the mean annual gain in these grades is 12 points.

We have explored a variety of alternative specifications. (Details are provided in Ballou et al., [2006].) The results in Table 9.7 are robust to the inclusion of controls for mobility between schools and districts. The estimates in column 1 are substantially unchanged if we control for initial achievement in fall 2002, assuring us that our negative findings are not

---

[1] Students enrolled in virtual schools account for 35% of the charter school observations.

[2] Because several of Idaho's charter schools do not participate in the free and reduced-price lunch program, data on student eligibility are spotty. Accordingly, we have not included this variable as a control.

[3] In order to compute the robust standard errors, it was sometimes necessary to drop observations where the number of students in a particular grade and school was quite small (e.g., fewer than four). This accounts for some of the discrepancies in sample sizes in Table 9.2. The impact on the coefficient estimates was trivial.

TABLE 9.6
Sample Student Characteristics

	Stayers		Movers
	Traditional public	Charter	
Percentage or mean			
White	84	94	93
Hispanic	12	3	2
Free or reduced price lunch[a]	49	13	32
Special education	10	6	8
School days between fall and spring tests	136	134	136
Percentage of students in:			
Grade 2	11	17	7
Grade 3	11	13	9
Grade 4	11	11	11
Grade 5	11	10	14
Grade 6	11	11	15
Grade 7	12	11	15
Grade 8	12	9	14
Grade 9	11	9	10
Grade 10	10	9	5
No. of observations			
2002–2003	123,209	455	1,256
2003–2004	152,886	1,149	1,228
2004–2005	155,255	1,771	1,307

[a] Eligibility for free and reduced-price lunch is understated in charter schools because some charter schools do not participate in the lunch program.

simply due to the fact that charter school students start at a higher level and therefore show smaller gains.

Studies of charter schools in Texas, North Carolina, and Florida have found that new charter schools are less effective than schools that have been in operation longer (Bifulco & Ladd, 2004; Hanushek, Kain, Rivkin, & Branch, 2005; Sass, 2004). Although consistent with the anecdotal evidence on the difficulties new charter schools face, this pattern does not appear to hold in Idaho. Interactions of charter school age with grade level are negative and usually statistically significant. Controlling for charter school age diminishes the charter school coefficients in the model with student fixed effects when the latter are evaluated at the mean charter

TABLE 9.7
Estimated Charter School Effects

	Baseline model		Controlling for charter school age		Fall-to-fall gains as dependent variable	
	w/o FE	w/FE	w/o FE	w/FE	w/o FE	w/FE
Grade						
2	−3.57	4.28	−3.57	0.21	0.25	4.66
	(0.82)	(3.17)	(0.71)	(1.87)	(0.55)	(1.29)
3	−1.44	5.49	−1.44	3.26	1.12	4.26
	(1.05)	(1.73)	(0.90)	(1.11)	(0.65)	(0.73)
4	−1.97	3.06	−1.97	1.89	0.59	2.11
	(1.34)	(0.78)	(1.24)	(0.76)	(0.57)	(0.60)
5	−1.63	1.5	−1.63	0.66	0.12	0.75
	(1.21)	(0.86)	(1.18)	(0.97)	(0.54)	(0.81)
6	−0.55	0.44	−0.55	−0.23	0.66	0.74
	(1.76)	(1.12)	(1.82)	(1.09)	(0.52)	(0.42)
7	−2.02	−2.11	−2.02	−2.48	−0.57	0.84
	(1.04)	(1.05)	(0.80)	(1.03)	(0.37)	(0.46)
8	−1.87	−0.68	−1.87	−0.82	−0.79	0.82
	(0.57)	(0.67)	(0.38)	(0.72)	(0.38)	(0.45)
9	−0.74	−0.49	−0.74	−0.48	−0.29	0.31
	(0.82)	(0.54)	(0.81)	(0.48)	(0.34)	(0.50)
10	−1.07	−0.24	−1.07	−0.29	0.29	4.66
	(1.03)	(0.91)	(1.00)	(0.84)	(0.34)	(1.29)
Other regressors						
Race × grade	Yes	Yes	Yes	Yes	Yes	Yes
Special education × grade	Yes	Yes	Yes	Yes	Yes	Yes
Year × grade	Yes	Yes	Yes	Yes	Yes	Yes
Years of charter operation	No	No	Yes	Yes	No	No
N	438,516	438,505	438,516	438,516	241,192	241,192

school age for each grade level. However, there continue to be differences of 2 points or more between the charter school estimates for grades 2–5 (columns 3 and 4), depending on the inclusion of student fixed effects.

Finally, our use of fall-to-spring gains as a measure of school effectiveness may be unfair to schools with distinctive programs that reduce summer learning loss. To explore these possibilities, we substitute fall-to-fall gains for the dependent variable.[1] The largest impact is on the model without student fixed effects. Charter school effects are no longer negative in the elementary grades, though the positive coefficients are not statistically significant. However, we still obtain substantially more positive estimates of the charter school effect from the fixed-effects model in the early elementary grades and now, surprisingly, grade 10.[2]

On average, attending a charter school appears to have had a positive impact on mathematics gains for students who moved between sectors during the sample period.

The evidence on nonmovers is much less clear. Nonmovers in the charter sector do not fare better than those in the traditional public sector; indeed, they gain less. But because we cannot compare nonmovers to their own pre- or postcharter experience, it is possible that this gap is an artifact of selection: Students predisposed to lower gains selected charter schools.

One problem with this explanation is that it requires a skewed selection to generate the estimates in column 1 of Table 9.7, if in fact the true effect of charter schools, at least at the elementary level, is represented by the positive coefficients in column 2. In Ballou et al. (2006), we estimate that charter schools would need to recruit more than five below-average gainers for each above-average gainer to turn true effects equal to the median elementary grade estimate in column 2 into apparent effects equal to the median of the elementary grade estimates in column 1. Given how hard it is to predict gains of individual students, it is difficult to see this happening by policy or by chance.

This suggests that we consider other ways in which movers might differ from nonmovers.[3] First, movers are more likely to select newer charter schools (and, as we have seen, in Idaho new schools appear to be more effective than those that have been operating longer).[4] Second, there is a positive association between the number of students moving back to the traditional public sector from a charter school and test score gains the year prior to the move among students who *remain* at that charter school. This

---

[1] The dependent variable was calculated as [(change in scale score)/(elapsed calendar days)](180). The model includes binary indicators for students who switched sectors over the summer.

[2] These estimates rely on only 2 years of data: gains between fall of 2002 and fall of 2003, and between fall of 2003 and fall of 2004. To verify that the differences between columns (6a) and (6b) and the rest of Table 9.2 are not due to this change in the sample, we have estimated the baseline model using the same sample. The results (not shown) are very similar to those in columns 1 and 2.

[3] We summarize a more detailed discussion that can be found in Ballou et al. (2006).

[4] We do not know why Idaho differs from other states in this regard. It may be an historical accident. It may also be that in Idaho newer schools recruit more heavily from the particular clientele the school was established to serve, but that as schools mature, they end up taking more students from the general population to whom the school's instructional program is not as well suited.

does not prove that the schools losing the most students are better (there could be selection effects among the students who stay), but it is suggestive. Finally, premove gains among students who leave charter schools are typically greater than the same-year gains of those who stay at the same schools. That is, not only do the charter schools with high average gains lose more students back to the traditional sector (our analysis controls for school size), but the students they lose had higher mean gains still.

This suggests that we be cautious about drawing conclusions about the average effectiveness of charter schools from such a sample. It also raises questions about the motives of these students and their parents. In Ballou et al. (2006), we report some evidence that students leaving the charter sector with high gains tend also to have lower level scores than their classmates. Students who are benefiting the most from attending charter schools, in terms of learning gains, may nonetheless feel out of place when comparing themselves to their classmates' levels. However, the evidence on this point is not as strong as the other evidence we have cited, and more work needs to be done to understand mobility decisions.

CONCLUSION

Our examination of charter schools in Idaho has turned up several differences between the experience of Idaho and other states, underscoring that generalization about this sector remains hazardous.

Charter schools in Idaho tend to attract students who have been performing above average in traditional public schools. Newer charter schools appear to be more effective than schools that have been in operation longer, though this may in part reflect changes in the mix of students recruited to a school over time. Finally, the analytical method preferred in the literature—a longitudinal analysis comparing gains of individual students before and after their enrollment in a charter school—shows that charter schools at the elementary level have been more effective than traditional public schools in promoting mathematics achievement. However, a simple cross-sectional comparison of gains in the two sectors indicates the opposite.

This is in sharp contrast to findings in Texas, North Carolina, and Florida, where the conclusion that charter schools have been less effective than traditional public schools has not depended on statistical methodology. Though the cross-sectional analysis is subject to selection bias, the longitudinal analysis is sensitive to differences between the sample of students who move between sectors and those who remain in one sector or the other. If biases from the latter source are more important (and there is some evidence to that effect), our qualitative conclusion about charter schools is similar to that reached by other investigators.

REFERENCES

Ballou, D., Teasley, B., & Zeidner, T. (2006). *Comparing student academic achievement in charter and traditional public schools*. Nashville TN: Vanderbilt University, unpublished.

Bifulco, R., & Ladd, H. F. (2004). *The impacts of charter schools on student achievement: Evidence from North Carolina*. Durham NC: Sanford Institute of Public Policy, Working Papers Series SAN04-01.

Center for School Improvement and Policy Studies (2005). Retrieved on July 21, 2006, from http://csi.boisestate.edu.

Growth Research Database. (2005). Fall 2002–Spring 2005 [data file]. Lake Oswego, OR: Northwest Evaluation Association.

Hanushek, E. A., Kain, J. E., Rivkin, S. G., & Branch, G. F. (2005). *Charter school quality and parental decision-making with school choice*. Cambridge, MA: NBER Working Paper 11252.

Harbor Educational Institute (n.d.). General information. Retrieved on July 31, 2006, from www.harborinstitute.org.

Hoxby, C. M., & Rockoff, J. E. (2005). *The impact of charter schools on student achievement*. Unpublished.

Idaho Board of Education (2003). Proficiency levels definitions. Retrieved on August 2, 2006, from http://www.sde.state.id.us.

Idaho Charter School Network (2005). Directory of Idaho Charter Schools, 2005–2006. Retrieved on August 2, 2006, from http://csi.boisestate.edu.

Idaho Statute, Title 33, Chapter 52, with 2005 amendments. (2005). Retrieved on July 26, 2006, from www.sde.idaho.gov.

Sass, T. R. (2004). *Charter schools and student achievement in Florida*. Unpublished.

U.S. Department of Education, National Center for Education Statistics. (2004a). Common Core of Data—Local education agency (school district) universe survey data: 2003–2004 school year [data file]. Available from National Center for Education Statistics Website, http://nces.ed.gov.

U.S. Department of Education, National Center for Education Statistics. (2004b). Common Core of Data—Public elementary/secondary school universe survey data: 2003–2004 school year [data file]. Available from National Center for Education Statistics Website, http://nces.ed.gov.

Wang, C., Geiger, E., & Devine, J. (2004). *Idaho charter schools: Program report, year five (2003–2004)*. Portland OR: Northwest Regional Education Laboratory.

10

Charter School Effects on Achievement
Where We Are and Where We Are Going

MARK BERENDS, CAROLINE WATRAL,
BETTIE TEASLEY, AND ANNA NICOTERA

INTRODUCTION

The debate about charter school effects on student achievement rages on. It seems every study released to the public and picked up by the media fuels the fire of proponents and critics alike. Yet, those who have conducted research on choice issues (and school reform in general) know that analyses are frequently complicated and findings are subject to caveats. Analyses and findings depend on context, methodology, and data availability, among other things. The challenge is to have school, teacher, and student samples sustained over time to see whether—and under what conditions—charter schools are effective or ineffective in increasing student achievement.

A report on charter schools by Henry Braun, Frank Jenkins, and Wendy Grigg (2006) of the Educational Testing Service for the U.S. Department of Education provides more debate fodder for charter school critics and advocates. The report examines fourth grade math and reading achievement differences between charter and traditional public schools in the 2003 National Assessment of Educational Progress (NAEP). The report found that charter school students had lower scores in both subjects when compared with their counterparts in traditional public schools. Although the report has some important descriptive analyses, it also has several shortcomings, some of which the authors are clear in describing.

Nonetheless, it is one more in the increasing number of charter school studies that people are using to help answer the question: Do charter schools work?

The problem is that it is the wrong question. Because charter schools and the students attending them vary, the question instead needs to be: *"Under what conditions* do charter schools work?" That is, what teaching and learning are occurring in charter schools vis-à-vis regular public schools, and what organizational conditions that support positive teaching and learning environments in these schools promote student achievement? Understanding the conditions under which reforms such as charter schools can work is essential for creating better policy and better opportunities for students in our schools.

In this chapter, we review where we are in terms of charter school effects on student achievement and describe where we might go to better understand charter school effects across various studies. First, we look at charter school research on student achievement and assess the reviews of charter school studies. Second, we argue that research is at a point where we can begin to outline a more systematic, rigorous meta-analysis of charter school studies for a clearer understanding of their effects on student achievement. Third, we make the case (along with others) that we need to open up the "black box" of charter schools; that is, we need to gather data on the instructional and organizational conditions that promote achievement as well as unpack the curricular and instructional differences among charter and regular public schools and classrooms.

In short, this chapter describes some of the ongoing research activities of the National Center on School Choice (NCSC) at Vanderbilt and its partner institutions: Brookings Institution, Brown University, Harvard University, the National Bureau of Economic Research, Northwest Evaluation Association, Stanford University, and the University of Indianapolis.[1] The NCSC aims to conduct rigorous, independent research on school choice to inform policy and practice. As such, the Center is conducting several different research projects on vouchers, charter schools, magnet schools, private schools, school transfer options under No Child Left Behind (NCLB), and homeschooling. This volume on charter schools incorporates some of that ongoing research.

WHERE WE ARE: MIXED RESULTS FOR CHARTER SCHOOL EFFECTS

Within the past decade, educational researchers have made progress in understanding the effects of charter schools, though definitive answers about effects on achievement remain elusive. At the time of his review of the school choice literature published in *Educational Researcher* in 1999,

---

[1] The NCSC is funded by a grant from the Institute for Education Sciences in the U.S. Department of Education.

Dan Goldhaber stated that "charter schools are too new for quantitative assessment of the impact they might have on educational outcomes" (p. 19). Since then, many studies have emerged, as have reviews of these studies.

For example, in their recent review of the literature, Hill, Angel, and Christensen (2006) identify five published meta-analyses that examine the impact of charter schools on student achievement.[1] The approaches and rigor of these analyses vary significantly. Specifically, the publications that attempt to synthesize the research on the academic achievement of charter schools vary insofar as the study inclusion criteria (e.g., year of study publication, methodology) and type of analysis (providing qualitative descriptions of the studies or attempting systematically to quantify differences and calculating an effect size). Here, we briefly describe these studies. In the next section, we go on to discuss how systematic meta-analysis may contribute to understanding academic achievement in charter schools.

Miron and Nelson (2001) reviewed research on charter schools' impact on student achievement and ultimately concluded that there was a dearth of "systematic empirical studies" on the topic as of 2001. The authors present an overall impact rating based on the direction and magnitude of the observed impact of attendance at a charter school on student achievement, and weight the impact rating by its methodological quality.[2] Study inclusion was limited to those that analyzed standardized test results and that were relatively recent at the time of their investigation. After examining the 15 studies that met the inclusion criteria, Nelson and Miron contend that the charter impact appears to be mixed or "very slightly positive." However, they also caution that their results may be influenced by the lack of rigorous studies of charter achievement in states that have large numbers of charter schools.

In 2004, multiple high-profile studies were released with conflicting findings regarding the impact of charter schools on student achievement (for example, see American Federation of Teachers, 2004; Hoxby, 2004; U.S. Department of Education, 2004a). Weighing in on the debate, *The Charter School Dust-up* by Carnoy, Jacobsen, Mishel, and Rothstein (2005) presents a reanalysis of the NAEP data on which the AFT report was based, to find that charter school students have test scores the same as or lower than those of traditional public school students in almost every demographic

---

[1] Our review of prior meta-analyses includes those that were identified in the Hill et al. study (2006). Therefore, these studies were not all self-identified as meta-analyses and the authors may not have intended them to be interpreted as such.

[2] The authors concede that a typical meta-analysis would attempt to extract an overall effect size for each study, but this was complicated due to the variety of measures and methods utilized across the studies (p. 12).

category.[1] The authors argue that the data do not support the contention that charter school performance improves as the charter school gains experience or remains in operation over time.

Carnoy et al. (2005) also review various state-level studies of charter school achievement. The researchers report the average performance effect for each of 19 studies conducted in 11 states and the District of Columbia. They provide a description of the controls and methods utilized in each study and find that charter schools have a negative effect. Specifically, the researchers find that the average performance of charter schools falls below that of traditional public schools.[2]

In *Charter Schools' Performance and Accountability: A Disconnect*, Bracey (2005) provides detailed, qualitative descriptions of various studies at the state and national levels. Although the descriptions are thorough, the analysis falls short of properly utilizing meta-analytic procedures that would yield comparable, standardized effect sizes.

Vanourek (2005) examines the status of the charter school movement as of 2005, focusing on the expansion of charter schools, academic performance, accountability, impact, politics, and support of charters. One of the unsurprising findings in the report is that not enough evidence is available regarding the achievement of students in charter schools over time.

In *Studying Achievement in Charter Schools: What Do We Know?* Hassel (2005) summarizes 38 comparative analyses of charter and traditional public schools' performance. Several criteria had to be met in order to be included in the analysis:

- The study had to be recent—all were released in or after 2001.
- The study had to compare charter students' achievement on standardized tests with that of traditional public school students.
- Rigorous methodology had to be utilized in the analysis.
- The study must have examined a significant segment of the charter sector.[3]

The central findings and methodological strengths and weaknesses of each study are delineated in tabular form to allow comparisons across

---

[1] The authors found one statistically significant difference between charter and traditional public school students: African-American charter school students' scores are lower than those of African-American traditional public school students who are not eligible for free or reduced-price lunch in central cities (p. 68).

[2] Some of the studies do show positive gains for students in charter schools relative to students in traditional public schools, but the authors argue that most of the studies do not. Therefore, an argument could be made that their analysis also presents mixed results or findings on the effects of charter schools on academic achievement.

[3] With the exception of two, all studies examined statewide, multistate, or national data.

studies. Hassel finds the methodological quality to vary across charter studies. Hassel argues that 17 of the studies, which utilize data only from one point in time, fail to examine how much progress students and schools are making over time; therefore, they are of limited use in drawing conclusions regarding the effectiveness of charter schools. Of the 21 studies that attempt to examine change over time in student or school performance, nine follow individual students over time.

The Hill et al. (2006) study identifies 41 studies focusing on test scores. These studies involve schools in 13 states: five in California, four in Texas, and three in Florida. Nine of the studies compare student achievement across two or more states; of these, five attempt to discern trends across "studies in single states, using disparate samples and methods" (p. 140). The analyses in this report reveal that results are mixed, with some positive findings for charter schools, some null, and some negative. Any differences are not strong. This study reviews the difficulties encountered in assessing charter school performance and the limits of charter school research (e.g., limited outcome measures, such as test scores, available).

A few trends in these studies are worth noting. First is the growing number of studies available over time. Although there is significant overlap in the analyses, the available literature is expanding. Each of the reviews includes more studies as the charter school sector and associated research increases across more states. Second, it is evident that the charter school research has yielded mixed findings on charter schools' impact on student achievement. Finally, although the previously mentioned articles have provided a start in examining charter school research, they all fall short in utilizing meta-analytic procedures. Due to their strict eligibility criteria, they risk publication bias due to study omission. With the exception of Miron and Nelson's 2001 analysis, the other works are essentially descriptive.

WHERE WE ARE GOING

Charter School Effects on Achievement: Toward a Meta-Analysis

There is a consistent message across the studies discussed earlier: a need to improve methodological rigor and to address the mixed results that frame all charter school research. At a time when the lack of "apples-to-apples" comparisons is a common refrain, the need to form a framework for the standardization of analyses of the current knowledge base is crucial.

This framework can be provided by meta-analysis. According to Lipsey and Wilson (2001), "Meta-analysis can be understood as a form of survey research in which research reports, rather than people, are surveyed" (p. 1). Meta-analysis is a method for aggregating and comparing the findings of different research studies in a systematic manner that allows for meaningful comparison of a particular body of research. The systematic coding of study characteristics allows researchers to examine the relationships between study findings and study elements such as nature of treatment, research design, and measurement procedures.

Meta-analysis synthesizes literature to move to a more cohesive conclusion or conclusions about what we know about a topic. Particularly useful in areas where there are consistently contradictory or mixed impact results, meta-analysis can disentangle impacts by looking across studies. It can identify whether the variance found in the sample of studies is within the studies or between them. Therefore, it can determine whether differences in effect sizes are due to intervention factors or to elements related to implementation, evaluation, or research methods.

Prior attempts in the literature to perform meta-analyses on charter school effects have fallen short of what rigorous meta-analysis standards require. For example, most of the analyses identified as meta-analyses up to this point are more akin to detailed literature reviews. Only one (Miron & Nelson, 2001) has approached the charter school literature with the quantitative methodology required to make conclusions with standardized findings across studies. Another (Hill et al., 2006) makes a first step toward meta-analytic methodology by vote-counting effect direction and cross-tabulating these effects with study methodology. The remaining articles do not rise to the standards of meta-analysis as a stand-alone methodology and serve more to summarize the literature in a qualitative manner.

The aforementioned studies have several shortcomings either collectively or individually where meta-analysis is concerned. First, there is significant publication bias with study eligibility criteria set to include only published studies. The evidence of publication as a proxy for research quality is tentative; meta-analysis methodology literature argues in favor of including both published and unpublished studies to avoid the upward bias found when only published studies are considered (Lipsey & Wilson, 2001). Second, many additional studies written since 2001 may allow for new insights, and refinements can be made to prior reviews that allow for an expansion of eligible studies. These refinements consist of the addition of unpublished studies and the calculation of standardized effect sizes—including the standardization of multivariate results. Third, none of the meta-analyses thus far has attempted to address the statistical significance of the magnitude or direction of charter school effects; this is a needed addition to the literature. Although we propose a charter school meta-analysis that addresses these methodological concerns, challenges remain in the process of standardizing the findings from charter school studies.

Organization of the Proposed Meta-Analysis

According to Lipsey and Wilson (2001) there are four distinct advantages to using meta-analysis: (1) It imposes a discipline on the process of summarizing research findings, (2) it allows key findings to be represented in a more differentiated manner than traditional review procedures such as qualitative summaries or "vote-counting" on statistical significance, (3) meta-analysis reveals relationships that are obscured in other approaches to summarizing research findings, and (4) meta-analysis provides a systematic method to handling information from a large number of studies and findings.

We propose a meta-analysis that will systematically explore the impacts of charter schools so that the mixed results that characterize current literature can be better understood. Additionally, we propose a meta-analysis that will address the methodological approaches used to evaluate charter school effects up to this point. This will capitalize on the aforementioned strengths of the methodology. Each of the charter school effectiveness studies will be systematically coded to capture study characteristics, study design/methodology characteristics, and potential moderator variables of interest. Broad inclusion criteria will be utilized to identify studies. Eligible studies will involve students in grades K–12 in the United States (excluding territories) and the use of charter schools to improve student academic achievement or other learning outcomes. To qualify for inclusion, studies must use standardized test scores (e.g., NAEP scores, state test scores, SATs, or ACTs) as outcome measures. Quantitative data must be reported for at least one qualifying outcome variable. The outcome data may be measured at the student level, the classroom level, the school level, or the state level.

Published and unpublished studies are eligible, including refereed journals, nonrefereed journals, dissertations, government reports, and technical and evaluation reports. Given the purpose of this meta-analysis to summarize the empirical evidence on charter school effects and given the potential upward bias of published studies, all studies are deemed eligible regardless of publication form. Study dates of publication or reporting must be 1991 (the year the first charter school opened) or later.

To conduct broad searches of the charter school research, we used several approaches. We searched various electronic databases, including the Social Science Citation Index (SSCI), ProQuest, Education Resources Information Center (ERIC) database, Dissertation Abstracts, and others. We conducted generalized searches of the World Wide Web (including search engines such as Google). We also searched specific organization and state government Websites, as well as education conference proceedings from 2003 to the present. This exhaustive review has resulted in a count of 122 studies, which we are in the process of systematically reviewing to determine sample overlap and final eligibility.

Proposed Meta-Analyses

Our meta-analysis is designed to include both pre- and post-tests and multivariate analyses. This approach stems from what the literature can offer. Many of the more rigorous, peer-recognized works on charter school effects come from studies that utilize multivariate methods—specifically, regression, student fixed-effects models, and multilevel growth models. Although these methods stand out as rigorous because they include statistical controls, they do not lend themselves as easily to standard effect size calculation as is required in meta-analysis.

To capture the most from the available literature, our analysis will occur in two phases. The first phase requires analysis of the direction of effect, similar to that found in Hill et al. (2006). The contribution of our extension to their work will be the increased literature used as well as the use of different moderator variables to inform our discussion. The second phase is a broader contribution in that we will standardize measures for the magnitude of effect, allowing a standard effect size to be analyzed across studies. We will calculate the effect size using the unstandardized regression coefficient and the standard deviation of the dependent variable. Thus, we can calculate the standardized mean difference effect size for studies using multivariate analysis. This will allow for moderator analysis on the magnitude of effect.

This meta-analytic approach will contribute to the current discussions around inconsistent conclusions about the charter school effect on achievement. However, it is not without its limitations. Although a more quantitative approach will be utilized with the standardized effect sizes of magnitude, our two-step design will still lack the ability to assert statistical significance. A possible third step will include the need for data supplements from many of the study authors so that we can adequately capture multivariate analyses.

Our departure from prior approaches, which we argue is an improvement to the literature, could also be seen as a weakness. Meta-analysis that combines studies using different methodologies can sometimes require oversimplification of study hetereogeneity in order to standardize the variables across studies (Lipsey & Wilson, 2001). Therefore, studies utilizing weak methodological practices must be included in the meta-analysis along with studies of the highest methodological quality. We respond to this potential issue by ensuring that methodological differences are part of our empirical analysis so that the study's rigor can be used as a control in assessing the impact across studies.[1] Also, studies that utilize questionable methodology can be addressed in one of two ways: by correcting the calculation of effect sizes or by removing the questionable studies from the final analysis of impact (Lipsey & Wilson).

We anticipate our meta-analysis will shed light on the question of charter school impacts overall but will be more definitive in exposing the large methodological gaps in the current literature on charter school and achievement relationships. On the one hand, these gaps will likely identify

---

[1] It is known that method variation can produce different if not contradictory effects (see Ballou, Teasley, & Ziedner, 2006).

the need for more rigorous research. This in turn may point to experimental designs where data are collected from randomized field trials.

On the other hand, although random assignment is considered the "gold standard" in research, there may be methodological concerns with too much emphasis placed on it—concerns associated with generalizability in the selection bias of schools studied (Betts et al., 2006). For example, random assignment studies in the charter school literature have thus far utilized natural randomization found in the charter lottery system. There is the potential for selection bias in the school samples studied, since by definition they must be oversubscribed, making them likely to vary significantly from schools that are not oversubscribed; thus, external validity may be affected. Although further random assignment studies will enhance the charter school literature, strong quasi-experimental research designs will also add to our understanding of the differences between charter schools and traditional public schools.

OPENING UP THE BLACK BOX

Charter School Effects in Indianapolis

A growing body of research on charter school effects would benefit from systematic meta-analysis, but additional studies are certainly needed. Few systematically measure what is taking place inside charter schools compared with regular public schools. That is, research has failed to open the black box of charter schools (Betts et al., 2006; Betts & Loveless, 2005; Gill, Timpane, Ross, & Brewer, 2001; Hassel, 2005). As Hess and Loveless (2005, p. 88) state, "Only by understanding how and why these programs work will we be able to replicate their benefits." Moreover, a consensus panel of prominent researchers on choice concluded that researchers should seek to distinguish among schools of choice in terms of effectiveness, and to distinguish the reasons for those differences (Betts et al., 2006, p. 24). They go on to say that such research requires detailed information about curriculum, instruction, organizational conditions that promote achievement, and teacher characteristics and qualifications.

In response to the calls for understanding how charter schools impact student outcomes and what is going on inside the schools, we at the NSCS are conducting a study on charter schools in Indianapolis with our colleagues Drs. Ruth Green and Zora Ziazi of the Center of Excellence in Leadership of Learning (CELL) at the University of Indianapolis. Together, we are focusing on three principal goals. First, we are working toward an impact study that will analyze achievement gains of students who win the lotteries of charter schools and compare them to students who lose the lotteries and attend traditional public schools. Second, we are using a quasi-experimental, longitudinal research design to compare charter schools to a matched control group of traditional public schools over several school years. This provides the opportunity to conduct a process-oriented assessment of the charter schools and matched traditional public schools that will examine organizational conditions that promote achievement, as well as the alignment of curriculum and instructional practices to academic content standards and assessments to open the black box of schooling. As the first two goals are not independent of one another, we will also look closely at how the organizational and instructional practices that we identify are related to student achievement in the two school types.

Finally, we will provide the charter schools and regular public schools in this study with formative assessments that link organizational and instructional practices with student outcomes. Specifically, reports will be created for each school that describe content coverage, cognitive complexity of instruction, and the alignment of instruction with academic standards and assessments. The schools can use this feedback to guide instructional decisions and professional development practices, as well as gauge the impact of school practices on student achievement.

Teaching and Learning Conditions Enabling Student Achievement

It has long been recognized that meaningful school improvement cannot take place without changing the core of teaching and learning (see Gamoran, Porter, Smithson, & White, 1997; Oakes, Gamoran, & Page, 1992). However, today there is a greater understanding that clear standards and strong incentives by themselves are not sufficient to change teaching and learning. Instead, there needs to be a focus on "capacity building"—that is, building those elements needed to support effective instruction (Massell, 1998). To build this capacity, it is critical to support professional development that improves teachers' knowledge and skills, providing appropriate curriculum frameworks and materials, and organizing and allocating resources through school improvement planning. Understanding the key indicators of school improvement is important as schools face overwhelming demands and accountability pressures.

The specific constructs for the organizational conditions that enable student achievement addressed in our research and outlined by Goldring and Cravens in this volume include:

- *shared mission and goals* that establish educational priorities and clear sets of academic activities to fulfill the mission and goals (Newmann, 2002; Newmann et al., 1996)
- *principal leadership* in setting the school's vision and mission and providing instructional direction (Berends, Bodilly, & Kirby, 2002; Brookover, Beady, Flood, Schewitzer, & Wisenbaker, 1979; Edmonds, 1979; Louis, Marks, & Kruse, 1996; Purkey & Smith, 1983; Spillane, 1996)
- *expectations for instruction and focus on student achievement* (see Newmann, 2002; Newmann et al., 1996; Newmann & Wehlage, 1995)

- *instructional program coherence of interrelated educational programs* for students and staff that are guided by a common framework for curricular, instructional, assessment, and teaching and learning environment pursued over a sustained time period (see Newmann, Smith, Allensworth, & Bryk, 2001a, 2001b, Berends, Chun, Schuyler, Stockly, & Briggs, 2002)
- *expert teachers supported by coherent, consistent professional development* (Cohen & Hill, 2001; Darling-Hammond, 1997; Desimone, Porter, Garet, Yoon, & Birman, 2002; Garet, Porter, Desimone, Birman, & Yoon, 2001; Kennedy, 1998; Porter, Garet, Desimone, Yoon, & Birman, 2000)
- *professional community of teachers* who cooperate with, coordinate with, and learn from each other to improve instruction and develop the curriculum (Little, 2002; Louis et al., 1996; Marks & Louis, 1997)

Curriculum and Instruction Aligned to Standards and Assessments

Research suggests that principals and teachers in effective schools are not only dedicated to high standards and expectations, but also spend considerable effort on aligning curriculum content with standards and assessments. Moreover, they reflect critically on their pedagogy and rely on instructional strategies identified in respectable research as effective. In addition, when adopting school and classroom interventions and strategies, staffs in effective schools seek to make the efforts coherent and consistent across the school to support student learning.

Establishing such coherence and consistency across pedagogy and content aligned to standards involves a continuous focus on how the school staff coordinates across and within grade levels. It also involves attention to how the school's common standards are coordinated across subject areas, departments, and the different types of students it serves (Bryk, Lee, & Holland, 1993; Newmann et al., 1996, 2001a). Moreover, schools that aim to align instruction with challenging standards rely on flexible instructional grouping arrangements that provide opportunities for all types of students to be exposed to the standards, learn them, and achieve at higher levels (Gamoran, 2004; Oakes et al., 1992).

In spite of the variation in state standards and the overwhelming amounts of modern knowledge, teachers in effective schools are able to make decisions about what knowledge is substantively worth teaching, provide depth and specificity to the academic standards that guide their instruction, and ensure that their decisions are grounded in respectable research and data-based decision-making. Moreover, when teaching the content—involving facts, theories, concepts, algorithms, question-and-answer sessions, and discussions—teachers in effective schools focus on being accurate and precise. "They emphasize and celebrate 'getting it right'" (Newmann, 2002, p. 30). But getting it right does not imply merely learning isolated fragments of facts. Rather, it moves beyond the facts toward analytic, creative thinking. Students not only reconstruct the knowledge taught in the classroom, but also exhibit in-depth understanding by synthesizing and interpreting knowledge domains.

Our measures of curricular and instructional alignment are based on research that has developed methods for judging the extent and nature of alignment of tests to standards (e.g., Blank, Porter, & Smithson, 2001; Porter, Kirst, Osthoff, Smithson, & Schneider, 1993; Porter & Smithson, 2001a, 2001b; Schmidt, McKnight, & Raizen, 1997; Webb, 1999). Porter (2002) has developed measures of alignment among student achievement tests, content standards, curriculum materials, and instruction with strong measurement properties of reliability and validity.

According to Porter (2002), content is defined as having two major components: topic (e.g., inequalities, vocabulary development) and cognitive demand (e.g., memorization, conceptual understanding). The measure of alignment that we are using is based on data that map a school's standards and assessments along with a teacher's instruction to a "content grid" (see Council of Chief State School Officers [CCSSO], 2002, 2006; Porter, 2002). (For examples of the Surveys of Enacted Curriculum we will administer, see www.seconline.org). The content grid and alignment index have been used in several other studies to predict student achievement gains (e.g., Gamoran et al., 1997) and to describe the consistency of state standards and assessments within and between states (e.g., CCSSO, 2002, 2006).

The main idea behind these tools is to develop a uniform language for describing content—topics and categories of cognitive demand—so that researchers can build useful indices of alignment. These tools have been applied in mathematics, reading/language arts, and science. Table 10.1, for example, illustrates a two-dimensional matrix that uses a language to describe mathematics content (from Porter, 2002). The topic dimension (rows) lists descriptors of mathematics topics: multiple-step equations, inequalities, linear equations, lines/slope and intercept; operations on polynomials; and quadratic equations. The cognitive demand dimension (columns) lists five descriptors of categories of cognitive demand: memorize, perform procedures, communicate understanding, solve nonroutine problems, conjecture/generalize/prove.

The content of instruction is described at the intersection between topics and cognitive demand based on data gathered from teacher surveys. For a target class, teachers report the amount of time devoted to each topic (level of coverage). Then, for each topic, they report the relative emphasis given to each student expectation (category of cognitive demand). These data can then be transformed into proportions of total instructional time spent on each cell in the two-dimensional matrix portrayed in Table 10.1. Across the cells in the content matrix, the proportions sum to 1 (Porter & Smithson, 2001a).

This same approach can be extended beyond classroom instruction to standards and assessments. Thus, we will be able to use the data to analyze the alignment of instruction, standards, and assessments, and to

TABLE 10.1
Content Matrix

Topic	Category of cognitive demand				
	Memorize	Perform procedures	Communicate understanding	Solve nonroutine problems	Conjecture/ generalize/ prove
Multiple-step equations					
Inequalities					
Linear equations					
I ines/slope and intercept					
Operations on polynomials					
Quadratic equations					

Source: Porter, A. C. (2002). *Educational Researcher, 31*(7), 3–14

examine alignment differences in charter and traditional public schools. Such analyses will provide further information about what is going inside the black box of charter schools, beyond the analyses of the relationships between instructional content and student achievement.

Indianapolis Charter Schools

The Indianapolis public schools present a unique educational jurisdiction to examine differences between charter schools and traditional public schools. All but one of the charter schools are chartered through the mayor's office and the Indianapolis Charter Schools Initiative. Each underwent a rigorous and competitive application process and is held responsible to a comprehensive accountability system. In effect, there are similarities between the charter schools that reduce some of the immense variability that can exist and prohibit generalizations. We are focusing on all of the charter schools operating in Indianapolis (18 schools as of the 2006–2007 school year). To meet the demands of a quasi-experiment, we match charter schools to traditional public schools. Through the matching process, we are working toward identifying and including regular public schools in the study as controls. For the 2006–2007 school year, we estimated that there would be about 230 teachers in the 18 charter schools. The matched traditional public schools would have similar numbers of teachers. We anticipated that, of the target sample of about 460 teachers,

368 (80%) would agree to participate in the data collection procedures. All teachers would receive incentives for their cooperation.

With the collected data, we will be able to form a three-level hierarchical database with information on students, teachers, and schools. At the student level, we will collect annual outcome measures of achievement, attendance rates, and continuation rates (e.g., student held back, dropped out, or graduated). These multiple measures will serve as the dependent variables for our analysis that compare students in charter schools to those in matched regular public schools. Additionally, we will collect student demographic data and home addresses. The demographic data are necessary to control for student background characteristics in our achievement models. The home addresses will be used as a control variable that determines how far students travel to school.

The process-oriented analysis will require data collection at the classroom and school levels to understand the organizational and instructional processes of charter and regular public schools fully. The data collection during each year of the 3-year study will involve two surveys for teachers, one survey for principals, and one classroom observation for teachers.

During the spring semester of 2007, we administered the Survey of Enacted Curriculum (SEC) to teachers in the core subjects. The SEC measures the degree of alignment of instruction and curriculum with state standards and assessments. The surveys ask detailed questions about instructional and curricular practices; prior research has shown evidence of reliability and validity (Porter, 2002).

The research team will compensate teachers who take the SEC and provide schools with follow-up technical assistance to make sense of the results. Although the survey is long, its results will provide educators in both charter and traditional public schools with useful information about the degree of alignment within the school. In the era of No Child Left Behind, this information will help schools make data-driven decisions on curriculum and instructional practices that meet the demands of standards-based accountability (Porter, 2002).

During the spring semester of 2008, we will administer a 30-minute survey to all of the core subject teachers and principals who have agreed to participate in the study. The teacher survey focuses on school and classroom climate, professional development activities, and parental involvement. The principal survey focuses on the instructional environment, curriculum and instruction, school improvement efforts, and professional development activities. Additionally, both the teacher and principal surveys include questions about the respondents' backgrounds. The teacher and principal surveys have been designed to measure the parts of the conceptual framework: core components of charter schools, school and classroom contextual factors, and organizational conditions enabling student achievement.

The final components of data collection for the process-oriented analysis are annual classroom observations. The observations will provide a qualitative component to help describe the organizational and instructional practices in charter and traditional public schools. Classroom observations will last 20 minutes and be used to triangulate data collected from surveys of instructional practices.

These quantitative and qualitative data will allow us to conduct a rich set of analyses to understand differences among students, teachers, and schools. The data will permit us to make comparisons to determine if there are differences in the process of schooling between charter and regular public schools. We will also analyze whether student achievement gains are related to teaching and learning conditions, and whether these conditions vary among teachers within and between schools. In addition, these organizational conditions can be examined as dependent variables. For example, we will be able to examine curricular and instructional alignment as a dependent variable to investigate differences among school types, net of other factors.

In addition to our comparisons of charter and matched regular public schools, we are working toward examining students who win and lose the lotteries for the charter schools. Students who win the lottery will be assigned to the treatment group, while students who lose the lottery and attend traditional public schools will be assigned to the control group. The lottery takes care of selection bias because any difference between students who win or lose arises solely by chance (e.g., motivation and ability).

Randomized field experiments using lotteries are not free from all research design limitations. First, generalizations are limited to students whose families decide to enter a charter school lottery. These students may differ significantly from those who did not enter the lottery, limiting the comparisons that may be made. Second, as lotteries occur at the grade level, descriptions of charter school effects must be grade-level specific. Third, students who enter the lottery may not comply with the assignment the lottery gives them. For example, a student may win the lottery and then decide to attend a traditional public school. Additionally, students who do not win the initial lottery may win the lottery on the wait list. Over the course of the study, we will have to consider how to document and analyze participants who do not follow the straightforward assignment process. Fourth, attrition from the treatment groups will likely occur and also will likely not be random, presenting a threat to the internal validity of the study. Although nothing can be done to prevent attrition, researchers can carefully document the students who leave the study and examine the differences in characteristics to determine if differential attrition has occurred.

We are well prepared to track students over time. We have had parents sign study consent forms with their charter school applications so that we can work with the state department of education to gain access to students' achievement records. In addition, we have worked with the charter schools to follow the same procedures for their lotteries and subsequent admission of students.

However, several challenges remain. One challenge is to have sufficient numbers of lottery winners and losers to make our study feasible. Because last year's lotteries show some promise that there is enough oversubscription for this type of randomized study, we remain hopeful. Yet, because there are so many ways that the randomized features can be compromised (e.g., students not returning to traditional public schools, sample attrition, lack of parent consent), we remain circumspect. We anticipate that, in following several cohorts over the next several years, we will be able to have a sample with sufficient power to carry out this study. In the end, the randomized design using lotteries will be complemented by the other data collection strategies to better understand the main effects of charter schools as well as the intervening processes within these schools (see Cook & Payne, 2002).

Opening Up the Black Box in Charters and Other Choice Schools

In another set of studies, the NCSC is working toward understanding teaching and learning conditions in charters and other schools of choice. Goldring and Cravens describe some of this in this volume and we will extend this research to other types of choice schools, including magnet and private schools. Together, we can open up the black box of schools of choice as Betts et al. (2006) suggest and link an array of survey data from principals and teachers to student achievement growth within a quasi-experimental design that is rare in the current state of school choice research.

We have the unique opportunity in the NCSC research agenda to collect the same measures across a wide array of organizational, curricular, and instructional conditions and to examine how schools of choice differ from each other and a comparison group of regular public schools. In addition, we have the opportunity to do what few studies have been able to do: to link measures for these conditions to student achievement growth in reading, language arts, and mathematics across a variety of local contexts with vertically equated assessments administered in the fall and spring across a number of school years.

Working with our colleagues at the Northwest Evaluation Association (NWEA), we hope to extend our surveys of principals and teachers to a larger number of schools and connect them to student achievement gains and growth. In this longitudinal research project, we will address several questions, including:

- How do schools of choice (i.e., charters, magnets, Catholic, other religious/independent schools) compare with matched regular public schools in terms of their achievement growth between 2005–2006 and 2008–2009?
- How do schools of choice differ from regular public schools in terms of organizational conditions that promote achievement?

- How do these school types differ in terms of the content and cognitive complexity of the curriculum and instruction?
- What are the differences in alignment among instruction, curricular content standards, and assessments in schools of choice and regular public schools?
- Are these curriculum, instruction, organizational, and alignment conditions related to achievement growth in reading, language arts, and mathematics?
- Do these relationships differ among schools of choice and regular public schools?

In this 3-year study, we plan to examine achievement gains and growth in schools of choice compared to traditional public schools and to open up the black box of schooling in these different types of schools. That is, we hope to examine schools of choice compared with a matched group of traditional public schools in terms of curriculum, instruction, and school organization.

For the schools that participate in the NWEA growth research database on student achievement, we will rely on a quasi-experimental design to compare schools of choice to a matched control group of regular public schools. We will administer two different principal and teacher surveys in the spring of 2008 and 2009 in 170 charter schools, 60 magnet schools, 27 Catholic schools, 25 other religious and independent schools, and matched regular public schools.

Depending on school participation and participant response rates, we anticipate data on over 400 schools and 8,000 teachers, which we will link to student achievement growth in the fall and spring across years in reading, language arts, and mathematics.[1] Working with NWEA's testing program, our goal is to build a database structure that will allow for multileveling modeling strategies to estimate student achievement growth nested in students nested in teachers nested in schools—a rare quasi-experimental design across districts and schools.

These research questions are embedded in a conceptual framework that aims to further our understanding of what goes on inside schools of choice. (This framework is discussed by Goldring and Cravens in this volume.) All schools of choice share the core components of autonomy, innovation, and accountability (see Bulkey & Fisler, 2003; Gill et al., 2001; Lubienski, 2003; U.S. Department of Education, 2004b). In our conceptual framework, we contend that these components are related to two conditions that enable positive educational outcomes: organizational conditions, and curriculum and instruction (i.e., content and cognitive complexity). The theory is that these practices and conditions within schools and class-

---

[1] If we obtain an 80% cooperation rate from the target 564 schools (resulting $n = 451$) and an 80% response rate for teachers in the cooperating schools (resulting $n = 9,020$), our analysis sample will be larger.

rooms are different across school types and promote differences in student outcomes, particularly student achievement growth.[1]

NWEA Data and Extending NCSC's Research to Other Choice Schools

As a testing and research organization, and a partner in the NCSC, NWEA currently has loaded in its Growth Research Database (GRD) over 4 million students, 36 million test records, and 8,200 schools across 1,800 districts in the subjects of reading, language arts, and mathematics. This will effectively support the NCSC's quasi-experimental program of research and help identify schools to sample for the current proposed research. Currently, we have files cleaned and analyzed for the 2002–2003 through the 2005–2006 school years (e.g., Ballou et al., 2006; Nicotera, Teasley, & Berends, 2006).

NWEA administers computerized adaptive assessments in the fall and spring of each academic year. All the NWEA subject scores in reading, language arts, and mathematics reference a single, cross-grade, and equal-interval scale developed using item response theory (IRT) methodology (see Hambleton, 1989; Ingebo, 1997; Lord, 1980). The mathematics Rasch Unit (RIT) scale is based on strong measurement theory, and is designed to measure student growth in achievement over time. NWEA research provides evidence that the scales have been extremely stable over 20 years (Kingsbury, 2003; Northwest Evaluation Association, 2002, 2003).

In future research, we hope to work with NWEA to draw our sample of schools of choice and matched comparison groups. Schools will be matched according to the following criteria:

- *Test coverage.* All schools will test 95% or more of their students.
- *Grade level configuration.* We will match schools to cover the same grade levels.
- *Geographic proximity.* Using GIS mapping, we will match choice and regular public schools so that they are close to each other (i.e., within a 5-mile radius, a 6- to 10-mile radius, or an 11- to 15-mile radius).
- *District that allows choice.* All schools will be located in districts that allow choice.
- *Baseline achievement scores.* Using previous years of test scores (we have scores dating back to the 2004–2005 school year), we will match schools according to "baseline" student achievement (i.e., school years before the survey data are gathered in spring 2007 and spring 2008).

---

[1] In our research, we will also examine other outcomes, such as parent involvement and teacher turnover. The measures for organizational conditions, curriculum, and instruction will also be examined as dependent measures for understanding differences among school types, net of other factors.

- *Number of teachers.* As a proxy for school size, we will use a count of teachers (full time equivalents).
- *Racial-ethnic composition.* Using information about the percent minority in the schools, we will match schools according to racial–ethnic composition.
- *SES composition.* Using free and reduced-priced lunch information, we will match schools according to SES composition (using free and reduced-price lunch as a proxy).

When we make the matches, NWEA will use a list of options for securing schools' cooperation in the study. Each school of choice may have three to five possible matches. If one of these traditional public schools refuses to participate in the survey, we have other options to pursue. The list of possible matches will be rank ordered for NWEA based on the preceding matching criteria.

*Significance of Understanding Conditions Under Which
Choice Schools Are More Effective*

For years, the usefulness of educational research to policymakers and educators has been challenged by the fact that knowing the characteristics of effective schools does not necessarily translate into creating such schools at scale (see Berends, 2004). The rationale for school choice is that providing autonomy and flexibility will allow schools of choice to operate more effectively vis-à-vis regular public schools. However, we do not know that this is the case. From a policy perspective, as noted by Hess and Loveless,

> Choice-based reform is not a discrete treatment that can be expected to have consistent effects.... While some of the changes produced by choice-based reform are a consequence of choice qua choice, many others are only incidentally related to choice and may or may not be replicated in any future choice-based arrangement. (2005, p. 97)

It may be, for example, that schools of choice (e.g., charter, magnet, private) with certain curricula alignment and data-focused instructional strategies are highly effective, while choice schools without these specific conditions or those that allow teachers to be completely autonomous in their individual classrooms are not very effective.

In addition, because the research on private, charter, and magnet schools is mixed, some schools are likely to be more effective than others. Only by gathering measures of school effectiveness—with a particular focus on classroom instruction—will we be able to understand the conditions under which different school types are related to achievement growth in mathematics, reading, and language arts. Only then will we be able to determine if there is a main effect for choice versus nonchoice schools, or if there are only interaction effects regarding effective school components.

We believe this future research will further our understanding of the context of choice schools, their effects on student achievement growth, and the conditions under which these effects occur. Such understanding will provide useful insights for policymakers and educators alike.

CONCLUSIONS: EFFECTS AND CONDITIONS UNDER WHICH EFFECTS OCCUR

The last decade and the last 5 years in particular have changed the stakes involved in education and its research. Developments in the U.S. Department of Education's Institute of Education Sciences as well as NCLB itself have raised the research bar. Greater demands for rigorous research designs and explicit attention to the importance of basing educational decisions on scientifically based research provide challenges and opportunities for examining school reforms such as school choice. For instance, NCLB includes specific language defining some of the elements of high-quality research, with an emphasis on randomized field trials (see Berends & Garet, 2002). The National Research Council (NRC) has published a volume clarifying the nature of scientific inquiry in education and articulating principles for scientific quality in research (Shavelson & Towne, 2002). Although NCLB and NRC perspectives on the nature of scientific inquiry differ in some respects, both embrace the idea of high-quality research driving practical decision-making in education and emphasize rigor, objectivity, systematicity, and peer review (Towne, 2002).

We believe the further expansion and development of charter schools and the research examining them will provide higher quality studies over the next several years. Our aim is to add to the portfolio of higher quality studies of charter schools and provide systematic syntheses of current and future studies. Certainly, we all agree that more scientific rigor within charter school studies is needed and will likely produce results helpful for both policy and practice. The effectiveness of charter schools remains an open question, particularly when considering the nation's continuing pursuit to create effective schools at scale. Yet, the challenges of developing and sustaining charter school reforms are worthy of pursuit, especially if researchers can have opportunities to conduct rigorous empirical studies that examine the impact of charter schools on achievement and the conditions under which charter schools might be effective.

REFERENCES

American Federation of Teachers. (2004). *Charter school achievement on the 2003 National Assessment of Educational Progress.* Washington, DC: American Federation of Teachers.

Ballou, D., Teasley, B., & Zeidner, T. (2006). *Comparing student academic achievement in charter and traditional public schools.* Paper presented at the Annual Meeting of the American Educational Research Association, San Francisco, CA.

Berends, M. (2004). In the wake of *A Nation at Risk*: New American School's private sector school reform initiative. *Peabody Journal of Education, 79*(1), 130–163.

Berends, M., Bodilly, S., & Kirby, S. N. (2002). *Facing the challenges of whole-school reform: New American Schools after a decade.* Santa Monica, CA: RAND.

Berends, M., Chun, J., Schuyler, G., Stockly, S., & Briggs, R. J. (2002). *Challenges of conflicting reforms: Effects of New American Schools in a high-poverty district.* Santa Monica, CA: RAND.

Berends, M., & Garet, M. (2002). In (re)search of evidence-based school practices: Possibilities for integrating nationally representative surveys and randomized field trials to inform educational policy. *Peabody Journal of Education, 77*(4), 28-58.

Betts, J., Hill, P. T., Brewer, D. J., Bryk, A., Goldhaber, D., Hamilton, L., et al. (2006). *Key issues in studying charter schools and achievement: A review and suggestions for national guidelines.* Seattle, WA: Center on Reinventing Public Education.

Betts, J. R., & Loveless, T. (2005). *Getting choice right: Ensuring equity and efficiency in education policy.* Washington, DC: Brookings Institution Press.

Blank, R. K., Porter, A., & Smithson, S. (2001). New tools for analyzing teaching, curriculum and standards in mathematics and science. Report from Survey of Enacted Curriculum Project (National Science Foundation REC98-03080). Washington, DC: Council of Chief State School Officers.

Bracey, G. (2005). Charter schools' performance and accountability: A disconnect. Retrieved August 20, 2006, from http://www.asu.edu/educ/epsl/EPRU/documents/EPSL-0505-113PRU.pdf#search=%22Charter%20schools'%20pe rformance%20and%20accountability%3A%20a%20disconnect%22.

Braun, H., Jenkins, F., & Grigg, W. (2006). *A closer look at charter schools using hierarchical linear modeling.* Washington, DC: U.S. Department of Education, National Center for Education Statistics.

Brookover, W. B., Beady, C., Flood, P., Schewitzer, J., & Wisenbaker, J. (1979). *School social systems and student achievement: Schools can make a difference.* New York: Praeger.

Bryk, A., Lee, V., & Holland, P. (1993). *Catholic schools and the common good.* Cambridge, MA: Harvard University Press.

Bulkey, K., & Fisler, J. (2003). A decade of charter schools: From theory to practice. *Educational Policy, 17*(3), 317–342.

Carnoy, M., Jacobsen, R., Mishel, L., & Rothstein, R. (2005). *The charter school dustup: Examining the evidence on enrollment and achievement.* Washington, DC: Economic Policy Institute.

Cohen, D. K., & Hill, H. C. (2001). *Learning policy: When state education reform works.* New Haven, CT: Yale University Press.

Cook, T. D., & Payne, M. R. (2002). Objecting to the objections to using random assignment in educational research. In F. Mosteller & R. Boruch (Eds.), *Evidence matters: Randomized trial in education research.* Washington, DC: The Brookings Institution.

Council of Chief State School Officers. (2002). *Alignment study in language arts, mathematics, science, and social studies of state standards and assessments in four states.* Washington, DC: Author.

Council of Chief State School Officers. (2006). *Aligning assessment to guild the learning of all students: Six reports on the development, refinement, and dissemination of the Web alignment tool.* Washington, DC: Author.

Darling-Hammond, L. (1997). *The right to learn: A blueprint for creating schools that work.* San Francisco, CA: Jossey–Bass.

Desimone, L., Porter, A. C., Garet, M., Suk Yoon, K., & Birman, B. (2002). Effects of professional development on teachers' instruction: Results from a three-year study. *Educational Evaluation and Policy Analysis, 24*(2), 81–112.

Edmonds, R. R. (1979). Effective schools for the urban poor. *Educational Leadership, 37,* 15–27.

Gamoran, A. (2004). Classroom organization and instructional quality. In M. C. Wang & H. J. Walberg (Eds.), *Can unlike students learn together? Grade retention, tracking, and grouping* (pp. 141–155). Greenwich, CT: Information Age Publishing.

Gamoran, A., Porter, A. C., Smithson, J., & White, P. A. (1997). Upgrading high school mathematics instruction: Improving learning opportunities for low-achieving, low-income youth. *Educational Evaluation and Policy Analysis, 19*(4), 325–338.

Garet, M., Porter, A., Desimone, L., Birman, B., & Yoon, K. (2001). What makes professional development effective? Analysis of a national sample of teachers. *American Education Research Journal, 38*(3), 915–945.

Gill, B. P., Timpane, P. M., Ross, K. E., & Brewer, D. J. (2001). *Rhetoric versus reality: What we know and what we need to know about vouchers and charter schools.* Santa Monica, CA: RAND.

Goldhaber, D. D. (1999). School choice: An examination of the empirical evidence on achievement, parental decision making, and equity. *Educational Researcher, 28*(9), 16–25.

Goldring, E., & Cravens, X. (2007). Teachers academic focus on learning in charter and traditional public schools. In M. Berends, M. Springer, and H. Walberg (Eds.), *Charter School Outcomes* (pp. 39–59). New York: Taylor & Francis Publishing.

Hambleton, R. K. (1989). Principles and selected applications of item response theory. In R. L. Linn (Ed.), *Educational measurement* (3rd ed., pp. 147–200). New York: American Council on Education, Macmillan Publishing Company.

Hassel, B. C. (2005). *Studying achievement in charter schools: What do we know?* Washington, DC: National Alliance for Public Charter Schools.

Hess, F. M., & Loveless, T. (2005). How school choice affects student achievement. In J. Betts & T. Loveless (Eds.), *Getting choice right: Ensuring equity, and efficiency in education policy* (pp. 85–100). Washington, DC: Brookings Institution Press.

Hill, P., Angel, L., & Christensen, J. (2006). Charter school achievement studies. *Education Finance and Policy, 1*(1), 139–150.

Hoxby, C. (2004). *Achievement in charter schools and regular public schools in the United States: Understanding the differences.* Cambridge: Harvard University, National Bureau of Economic Research

Ingebo, G. (1997). *Probability in the measure of achievement.* Chicago, IL: MESA Press.

Kennedy, M. M. (1998). Form and substance in the in-service teacher education (Research Monograph No. 13). Arlington, VA: National Science Foundation.

Kingsbury, G. G. (2003). *A long-term study of the stability of item parameter estimates.* Paper presented at the annual meeting of the American Educational Research Association, Chicago, IL.

Lipsey, M. W., & Wilson, D. B. (2001). *Practical meta-analysis.* Thousand Oaks, CA: Sage.

Little, J. W. (2002). Professional communication and collaboration. In W. D. Hawley (Ed.), *The keys to effective schools* (pp. 43–55). Thousand Oaks, CA: Corwin Press.

Lord, F. M. (1980). *Applications of item response theory to practical testing problems.* Hillsdale, NJ: Erlbaum.

Louis, K. S., Marks, H. M. & Kruse, S. (1996). Teachers' professional community in restructuring schools. *American Educational Research Journal, 33*(4).

Lubienski, C. (2003). Innovation in education markets: Theory and evidence on the impact of competition and choice in charter schools. *American Educational Research Journal, 40*(2), 395–443.

Marks, H. M., & Louis, K. S. (1997). Does teacher empowerment affect the classroom? The implications of teacher empowerment for teachers' instructional practice and student academic performance. *Educational Evaluation and Policy Analysis, 19*(3).

Massell, D. (1998). *State strategies for building local capacity: Addressing the needs of standards-based reform.* Philadelphia, PA: Consortium for Policy Research in Education, University of Pennsylvania.

Miron, G., & Nelson, C. (2001). Student achievement in charter schools: What we know and why we know so little (Occasional Paper No. No. 41): National Center for the Study of Privatization in Education, Teachers College, Columbia University.

Newmann, F. M. (2002). Achieving high-level outcomes for all students: The meaning of staff-shared understanding and commitment. In W. D. Hawley (Ed.), *The keys to effective schools: Educational reform as continuous improvement* (pp. 28–42). Thousand Oaks, CA: Corwin Press.

Newmann, F. M., & Associates. (1996). *Authentic achievement: Restructuring school for intellectual quality.* San Francisco, CA: Jossey–Bass.

Newmann, F. M., Smith, B. A., Allensworth, E., & Bryk, A. S. (2001a). Instructional program coherence: What it is and why it should guide school improvement policy. *Educational Evaluation and Policy Analysis, 23*(4), 297–321.

Newmann, F. M., Smith, B. A., Allensworth, E., & Bryk, A. S. (2001b). *School instructional program coherence: Benefits and challenges.* Chicago, IL: Consortium on Chicago School Research.

Newmann, F. M., & Wehlage, G. H. (1995). Successful school restructuring: A report to the public and educators by the Center on Organization and Restructuring of Schools. Alexandria, VA: Association for Supervision and Curriculum Development; Reston, VA: National Association for Secondary School Principals.

Nicotera, A., Teasley, B., & Berends, M. (2006). *Examination of student movement in the context of federal transfer policies.* Paper presented at the Annual Meeting of the American Educational Research Association, San Francisco, CA.

Northwest Evaluation Association (2002). *RIT scale norm.* Portland, OR: Author.

Northwest Evaluation Association (2003). *Technical manual.* Portland, OR: Author.

Oakes, J., Gamoran, A., & Page, R. N. (1992). Curriculum differentiation: Opportunities, outcomes, and meanings. In P. W. Jackson (Ed.), *Handbook of research on curriculum* (pp. 570–608). New York: Macmillan.

Porter, A. C. (2002). Measuring the content of instruction: Uses in research and practice. *Educational Researcher, 31*(7), 3–14.

Porter, A. C., Garet, M., Desimone, L., Suk Yoon, K., & Birman, B. (2000). *Does professional development change teachers' instruction? Results from a three-year study of the effects of Eisenhower and other professional development on teaching practices.* Washington, DC: U.S. Department of Education.

Porter, A. C., Kirst, M. W., Osthoff, E. J., Smithson, J. L., & Schneider, S. A. (1993). *Reform up close: An analysis of high school mathematics and science classrooms.* Madison, WI: Wisconsin Center for Education Research, University of Wisconsin-Madison.

Porter, A. C., & Smithson, J. L. (2001a). Are content standards being implemented in the classroom? A methodology and some tentative answers. In S. H. Fuhrman (Ed.), *From the capitol to the classroom: Standards-based reform in the states (100th Yearbook of the National Society for the Study of Education)* (part II, pp. 60–80). Chicago: National Society for the Study of Education; distributed by University of Chicago Press.

Porter, A., & Smithson, J. (2001b). *Defining, developing, and using curriculum indicators.* Philadelphia: University of Pennsylvania, Consortium for Policy Research in Education.

Purkey, S. C., & Smith, M. S. (1983). Effective schools: A review. *Elementary School Journal, 83*(4), 427–452.

Shavelson, R. J. & Towne, L. (Eds). (2002). *Scientific inquiry in education.* Washington, DC: National Academy Press.

Spillane, J. P. (1996). School districts matter: Local educational authorities and state instructional policy. *Educational Policy, 10*(1), 63–87.

Towne, L. (2002). *Scientific research in education and the No Child Left Behind Act.* Paper presented at the National Clearinghouse for Comprehensive School Reform Network of Researchers Meeting, Washington, DC.

U.S. Department of Education. (2004a). America's charter schools: Results from the NAEP 2003 pilot study. Washington, DC: U.S. Department of Education, National Center for Education Statistics, 2005.

U.S. Department of Education. (2004b). Successful charter schools. Washington, DC: U.S. Department of Education, Office of Innovation and Improvement.

Vanourek, G. (2005). State of the charter movement 2005: Trends, issues, & indicators. Retrieved August 20, 2006, from http://www.publiccharters.org/files/543_file_sotm2005pdf.pdf.

Webb, N. L. (1999). Alignment of science and mathematics standards and assessments in four states (Research Monograph No. 18). Madison, WI: University of Wisconsin–Madison, National Institute for Science Education.

11

School Choice
What the NCES Can and Cannot Tell Us

MARK SCHNEIDER AND PETER TICE

INTRODUCTION

The National Center for Education Statistics (NCES) offers a collection of high-quality data that can be used to address many issues of concern to the school-choice community. These data have numerous strengths. First, most—but not all—NCES data are national in scope. Second, much of the data are longitudinal, while others are cross-sectional, repeated at regular intervals. Both types are important: The longitudinal data are vital to studying change, while the repeated cross-sectional data are useful in creating snapshots of educational conditions in the United States that can be compared over time. Another strength of NCES data is that they offer a large amount of information about different stages of choice and how people go about choosing schools.

As we will show in this chapter, the NCES has data about who chooses, what schools they choose from, and the characteristics of the students and teachers in those schools. We will highlight specific NCES datasets that the education research community may find useful to study school choice, including the National Household Education Surveys (NHES) Program, the Common Core of Data (CCD), the Private School Universe Survey (PSS), the Schools and Staffing Survey (SASS), and the Early Childhood Longitudinal Study, Kindergarten Class of 1998–1999 (ECLS-K).

NATIONAL HOUSEHOLD EDUCATION SURVEYS PROGRAM

The NHES is a cross-sectional household survey designed to describe Americans' educational experiences. The survey is repeated at intervals of either 2 or 3 years.[1] For many researchers, perhaps the most important component of the NHES is the Parent and Family Involvement in Education (PFI) survey, which provides descriptive data on the experiences of American households that have school-age children.

The PFI has been surprisingly underused, given the quality of its data and the breadth of its questions about issues that students of choice and their parents care about. Some examples of the types of questions included in the NHES are:

- Do parents choose the public school for their child to attend?
- Do they move to neighborhoods in order to select a school?
- Why do parents exercise their opportunities for choice?
- Who homeschools and why?
- How involved are parents in their children's schools and in the children's educational opportunities in the classroom or in the community?

A note of caution is that NHES data are observational, not experimental. As with any observational data, researchers must consider the influence of unmeasured variables. Nonetheless, NHES data provide opportunities for the school-choice community to study how parents go about choosing schools and choosing to be involved in their children's education. The 2007 NHES collected even more information about schools of choice and why parents have chosen them.

Enrollment Trends

Because the NHES is a repeated snapshot, one can track student enrollment trends by public and private school types. Figure 11.1 shows these trends by school type between 1993 and 2003. The data reveal that, while declining, the enrollment of U.S. students continues to be highest in assigned public schools. Virtually all the observed decline in assigned schools is balanced by growth in public schools of choice (e.g., charter, magnet, and inter- and intradistrict schools), which as of 2003 account for almost 15% of all student enrollments.

One piece of information missing from these particular data is clear: Although we know that schools are chosen or not chosen, extant data cannot tell us what type of public school a parent has chosen. In 2007 this changed. The NHES now collects school names from the parents so that the public release data file will include a derived school type variable. (No actual school names will be released on the data file.) This will enable analysts to distinguish between various types of public chosen schools.

---

[1] Depending on NCES funding levels, the NHES may move to a 4-year cycle.

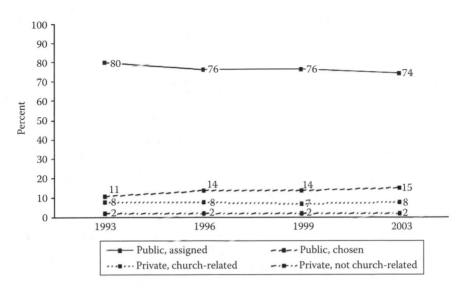

FIGURE 11.1. Student enrollment trends by public and private school type. (From U.S. Department of Education, National Center for Education Statistics, Parent and Family Involvement in Education Survey of the 2003 National Household Education Surveys Program; NHES: 2003.)

Residential Location

The NHES is also useful for understanding school choice because it provides information about residential location. Changing residences, of course, is the traditional way by which parents have changed schools. Figure 11.2 shows the percentage of students whose family moved to a neighborhood so that the student would be eligible for a particular school. A large number of students, 24% in 2003, had parents who said that they had done this. The data also show that this type of choice is significantly lower for blacks (18%) than for any other racial group.

Unfortunately, it is not currently possible to put together trend data. In 1993, the NHES asked parents of students in grades 3–12 whether the school their child was enrolled in was located in the neighborhood where they lived. But neither the 1996 nor the 1999 the NHES asked parents about whether they moved to a neighborhood so that their children could attend a particular school. However, there is census data that suggest that, in the last few years, the extent to which residential mobility is taking place to choose schools has been declining. This decline may be because families have an increasing number of other ways to choose schools without moving location. The 2007 NHES collected data on residential location so that two cross-sectional snapshots will be available.

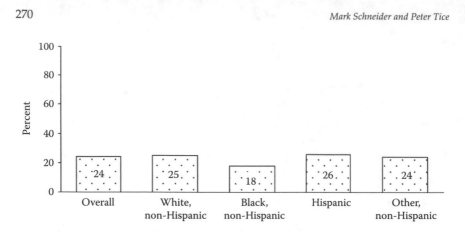

FIGURE 11.2 Students whose families moved to a neighborhood for school eligibility, by race/ethnicity: 2003. (From U.S. Department of Education, National Center for Education Statistics, Parent and Family Involvement in Education Survey of the 2003 National Household Education Surveys Program; NHES: 2003.)

Homeschooling

Recognizing its rapid growth, the NHES began collecting data about homeschooling in 1999, 2003, and again in 2007. This task is difficult because the homeschooling population is small and scattered across the nation. The NHES provides the following data about homeschooling:

- national estimates on the number of homeschooled students
- the education attainment levels of parents who choose to homeschool
- the reasons parents decide to homeschool their children
- the curriculum parents use
- involvement with public schools
- whether students are engaged in distance learning

National estimates. National estimates on the total number of home-schooled students are low, so no subnational data can be reported. In 1999, the NHES estimated that 850,000 students were being homeschooled—about 1.7% of all students in the United States. In 2003, the estimate increased to 1,096,000 students—about 2.2% of students in the United States. Among homeschooled students, about 82% were homeschooled full time in 1999 and 2003, while 18% were homeschooled part time in both years.[1]

The homeschooling population is small compared to student populations in public and private schools; since the NHES sample is randomly

---

[1] Part-time students include those who were homeschooled but were also enrolled in school for 25 hours or less per week.

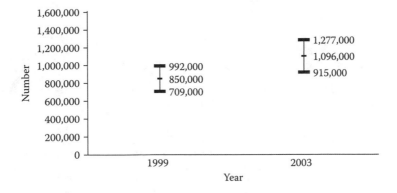

FIGURE 11.3 Estimated number of homeschooled students with a grade equivalent of kindergarten through 12th grade. Note: The estimated number includes 95% confidence intervals. (From U.S. Department of Education, National Center for Education Statistics, Parent Survey of the 1999 National Household Education Surveys Program; Parent and Family Involvement in Education Survey of the 2003 NHES.)

drawn, the sample size of homeschoolers is also small. As Figure 11.3 shows, the standard errors for the homeschooling estimates are large. Improving the precision of the estimates would require a significant and expensive increase in sample size. For instance, to reduce the confidence intervals by 25%, the added data collection costs would be approximately $700,000.

The NCES plans to try other methods to get better estimates. To date, the NCES has not used state administrative records, membership lists, and buyers of homeschooling materials as a means to study homeschoolers because list methods represent only particular populations who appear on the list. Instead, the 2007 NHES included a seeded sample of homeschoolers from commercial mail lists to study response rates among probable homeschoolers and the general population. The dual-frame approach may also be used to study differences in the characteristics of the homeschool list and the random sample and may lead to better estimates.

Education level of homeschooling parents. There is considerable interest in what types of parents choose to homeschool their children, and the NHES provides some information about this population. For example, the NHES has information about the education attainment of parents who homeschool their children. From Figure 11.4, we see that homeschooled children are more likely than all students, on average, to have parents with college degrees. In 2003, some 44% of homeschooled children had parents with college degrees or more, compared to 36% of all children. Since 1999, that spread has become less pronounced. For instance, the percentage of homeschooled students who had parents with a high school diploma or less increased from 19% in 1999 to 25% in 2003. The NHES does not collect information

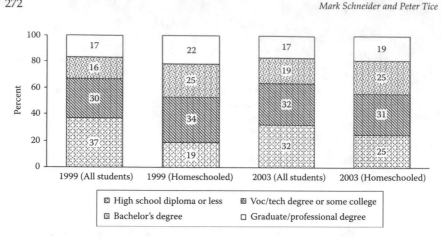

FIGURE 11.4 Parent education level of all students and homeschooled students: 1999 and 2003. (From U.S. Department of Education, National Center for Education Statistics, Parent Survey of the 1999 National Household Education Surveys Program; Parent and Family Involvement in Education Survey of the 2003 NHES.)

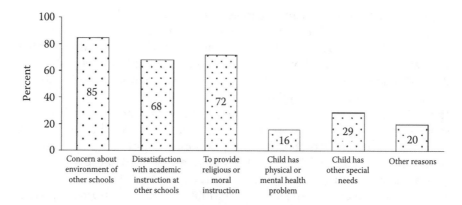

FIGURE 11.5 Reasons parents report for homeschooling their children: 2003. (From U.S. Department of Education, National Center for Education Statistics, Parent and Family Involvement in Education Survey of the 2003 National Household Education Surveys Program, 2003.)

that easily allows researchers to examine reasons for this growth in the low end of the education distribution for homeschooled children.

Why parents homeschool. The 2003 NHES also asked parents why they decided to homeschool their children. As Figure 11.5 shows, the three most frequently cited reasons were: (1) a concern about the environment of other schools (85%), (2) dissatisfaction with academic instruction at other schools (68%), and (3) to provide religious or moral instruction (72%). When asked for the *most* important reason they decided to homeschool,

31% of parents cited a concern about the environment of other schools, while 30% cited the desire to provide religious or moral instruction.

COMMON CORE OF DATA

The Common Core of Data (CCD) annually collects both fiscal and non-fiscal data about all public schools, school districts, and state education agencies in the United States. The CCD also provides a sample frame for many NCES surveys, including the Schools and Staffing Survey (SASS). The 2003–2004 SASS, which as of this writing is the most recent survey, was built upon a 2001–2002 CCD sampling frame. This lag can be a problem for studying the rapidly changing world of school choice. Most notably, as new charter schools are formed and others close, the frame has missed the many charter schools that were created after the 2001–2002 frame was constructed.

The CCD's nonfiscal data come from schools, school districts, and states, while the fiscal data come from districts and states, but not from schools. To date, the NCES has not determined how to collect fiscal data from individual schools. Additionally, the fiscal surveys report on revenues and expenditures from the previous school year, so generally there is a 1-year lag between school finance information and the nonfiscal features of school systems. There is an added challenge of collecting the fiscal data about schools of choice, which has to do with who is recording the data, who is reporting it, and the accuracy of the reported data.

CHARTER AND TRADITIONAL PUBLIC SCHOOL FUNDING

With this caveat in mind, consider the level of comparative funding of charter schools and traditional public schools. A widely cited Fordham Institute report, *Charter School Funding: Inequity's Next Frontier* (Speakman, Hassel, & Finn, 2005), found that charter schools were funded at about 80% of the level of traditional public schools. How do these data compare with the CCD data?

The CCD only collects data from 16 states that have *charter school districts*. Most of these districts are, in fact, single schools in states where a charter school is its own local education authority (LEA) and reports its own fiscal information. In other states, either there were no charter schools, or charter schools did not report data independently of the traditional school districts. The most recent CCD data represent about 335,000 charter school students, which was about one third of the total enrollment in charter schools at that time.

Nonetheless, CCD data do provide some insights into the financing of charter schools. Consider first the range in the ratio of charter school to traditional public school revenues, which is from 0.68 in Arizona (which means that the charter schools are funded 68% of the traditional public schools) to over 1.0 in favor of charter schools in Arkansas, the District of Columbia, Indiana, Minnesota, and Rhode Island. Moreover, while the Fordham Foundation reported a 0.78 ratio overall, the NCES finds that the ratio is 0.92 for current revenues and 0.94 for expenditures—significantly higher than the Fordham Foundation's estimate.

The CCD data in Table 11.1 are 1 year later than the Fordham report, which may explain some of the differences. Still, there are marked disparities in the revenue numbers reported in the CCD and the ratios computed on those numbers for the overlapping states in both the CCD and the Fordham report. For the seven states for which both the CCD and Fordham report data, Fordham reports that the charter schools are funded at 82% of traditional public schools, while the CCD reports 90%.

What accounts for these discrepancies? The short answer is that we do not know. The NCES data are easily and widely available, however, allowing researchers to inspect them carefully and perhaps discover why the discrepancies exist.

Do Schools Ever Die?

This is a question that can be considered with CCD data. It comes from a statement that charter school proponents often make: "Charter schools die, but traditional public schools never do." This observation has often been held up as evidence that school choice "works." That is, if a charter school is not performing, it goes out of business; in contrast, the argument continues, if a traditional public school is not performing, it will not die.

The CCD data (Figure 11.6) show that the closure rate for all schools in the nation is about 1.4%, with the closure rate in 2004–2005 higher for charter schools (about 3%) than traditional public schools (a little over 1%).

The NCES has explored the data to learn why traditional public schools go out of business. One of the reasons, not surprisingly, is the long-term trend of consolidating rural schools. Rural states like Maine, Nebraska, and South Dakota have very high school closure rates. In rural areas nationwide, the closure rate is also higher. Interestingly, closure rates in central cities are higher than in their surrounding suburbs.

At present, we do not know why traditional public schools are closing. Perhaps it has to do with the consolidation of schools and shifting demographics, or with the accountability provisions of No Child Left Behind. Nonetheless, we do know that traditional public schools are not immortal. They disappear at more than a 1% rate per year. On a base of 96,000 schools, that is a lot of schools.

TABLE 11.1
Comparison of Revenues and Expenditures Between Regular School Districts and Charter School Districts, 2003–2004

State	Regular public schools				Charter schools				Ratios	
	Count	Pupils	Mean per-pupil current expenditure ($)	Mean per-pupil revenue ($)	Count	Pupils	Mean per-pupil current expenditure ($)	Mean per-pupil revenue ($)	Current expenditure	Current revenue
AR	301	427,586	6,868	7,375	5	799	6,888	7,576	1.00	1.03
AZ	207	872,903	8,461	10,634	332	78,053	5,796	7,196	0.68	0.68
CA	788	3,167,728	7,970	9,479	6	5,066	6,663	7,079	0.84	0.75
CT	166	552,505	1,0781	13,028	12	2,280	9,502	11,534	0.88	0.89
DC	1	65,099	12,801	16,613	25	10,047	1,3490	17,372	1.05	1.05
DE	16	105,771	9,700	11,090	13	6,257	7,335	8,288	0.76	0.75
IN	292	1,005,587	7,736	9,576	17	2,998	7,814	10,107	1.01	1.06
MI	564	1,669,432	8,345	9,386	171	68,795	7,744	8,429	0.93	0.90
MN	345	822,130	8,020	9,969	88	142,56	8,830	11,100	1.10	1.11
NC	117	1,325,707	7,136	8,252	93	21,915	7,355	8,006	1.03	0.97
NJ	551	1,342,559	12,331	15,488	44	11,695	11,533	12,863	0.94	0.83
OH	612	1,797,666	7,958	9,048	158	45,692	8,290	9,656	1.04	1.03
PA	500	1,756,012	8,725	10,537	95	39,260	8,394	9,443	0.96	0.90
RI	35	145,775	10,184	12,059	5	657	10,949	13,749	1.08	1.14
TX	1,037	4,267,195	8,149	9,914	179	54,441	7,349	7,872	0.90	0.79
UT	39	483,188	6,319	8,234	18	3,205	4,967	6,957	0.79	0.84
Total	5,571								0.94	0.92

Source: U.S. Department of Education, National Center for Education Statistics, Common Core of Data, School District Finance survey, FY 2004 (1a).
Note: Students in special education, vocational education, and education service agencies removed.

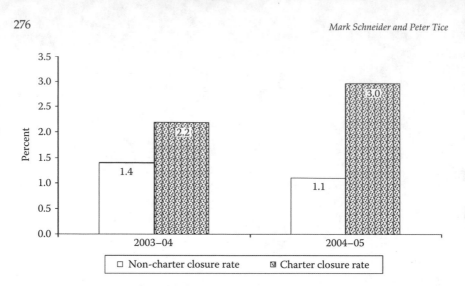

FIGURE 11.6 School closure rates of noncharter schools and charter schools. (From U.S. Department of Education, National Center for Education Statistics, Common Core of Data, Public Elementary/Secondary School Universe Survey, 2003–2004 [la], and Public Elementary/Secondary School Universe Survey, 2004–2005 [la].)

PRIVATE SCHOOL UNIVERSE SURVEY

The Private School Universe Survey (PSS) is a biennial survey that provides data about private schools, including the total number of private schools, teachers, and students. Its target population is all schools in the 50 states and District of Columbia that are not supported primarily by public funds, schools that provide instruction for one or more grades between kindergarten and 12th grade, and schools with one or more teachers. The PSS excludes organizations that support homeschooling and do not provide classroom instruction.

Student Enrollment

The most recently available PSS data from the 2003–2004 school year indicate that there were 28,400 private schools that enrolled 5.1 million students. Figure 11.7 shows the trend in school enrollment between the 1989–1990 and the 2003–2004 school years.[1] The data suggest that there is substantial change going on in the makeup of the private school student population. For instance, student attendance in Catholic-affiliated private schools decreased from 55% in the 1989–1990 school year to 46% in 2003–2004. That decrease has been offset by increases in both other

---

[1] Since data are available on 28 religion-affiliated private school types, it is possible to decompose these estimates into finer detail.

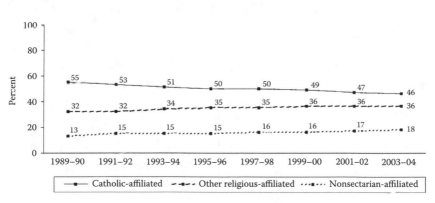

FIGURE 11.7 Private school student enrollment trends by private school affiliation. (From U.S. Department of Education, National Center for Education Statistics, Private School Universe Survey [PSS]: 2003–2004, 2001–2002, 1999–2000, 1997–1998, 1995–1996, 1993–1994, 1991–1992, 1989–1990.)

religion-affiliated private schools (Christian conservative, affiliated, unaffiliated) and nonsectarian private schools (regular, special emphasis, special education). Behind these numbers, we see the following trends.

- The decline in students attending Catholic-affiliated schools took place in the parochial schools, while there was a slight increase in students attending diocesan schools and no increase in students attending private Catholic-affiliated schools.
- The increase in students attending other religion-affiliated schools took place mostly in Christian conservative private schools; student enrollment in these types of schools increased from 11% of all private school students in 1989–1990 to 15% in 2003–2004.

SCHOOLS AND STAFFING SURVEY

The Schools and Staffing Survey (SASS) is a cross-sectional survey that collects data from regular public schools, charter schools, and private schools every 4 years, with much of the data available by state.

Researchers using the SASS can study issues such as teacher and administrator characteristics, teacher demand, and teacher compensation. Information is also available on district hiring practices, and principals' and teachers' perceptions of school climate and problems in their schools. Researchers can also use SASS data on school programs and conditions, and characteristics of the student population.

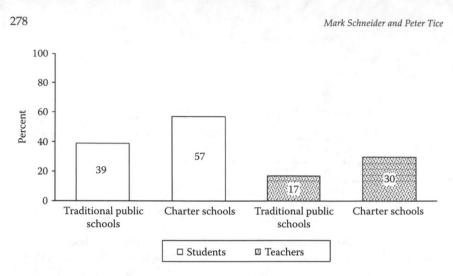

FIGURE 11.8 Minority students and teachers in traditional public schools and charter schools: 2003–2004. (From U.S. Department of Education, National Center for Education Statistics, School and Staffing Survey, 2003–2004 School Year, public school, BIA school, and private school data files.)

Student and Teacher Minority Trends

There are a few interesting patterns to note from the 2003–2004 SASS. First, Figure 11.8 shows student and teacher minority concentrations in traditional public and charter schools. Confirming other studies, SASS data reveal that charter schools have a higher proportion of minority students than traditional public schools. Less well known but also documented by the SASS is that charter schools also have a higher percentage of minority faculty members than traditional public schools.

Teacher Education and Experience

Another pattern worth noting is that the education level of teachers in traditional public schools is higher than that found in charter schools (see Figure 11.9). Teachers in traditional public schools are more likely than teachers in charter schools to have a bachelor's degree or more, and teachers in charter schools are generally less experienced than teachers in traditional public schools. In charter schools, 43% of teachers have 3 or fewer years of full-time teaching, compared to only 18% of teachers in traditional public schools.

DATA SETS ON STUDENT ACHIEVEMENT

Ultimately, parents, researchers, and policymakers want to know what effect schools of choice have on student achievement. The NCES has

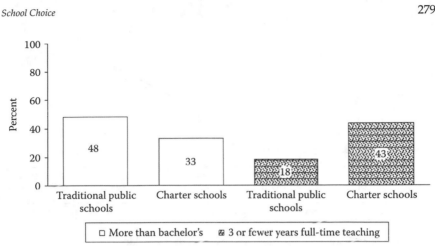

FIGURE 11.9 Select teacher characteristics in traditional public schools and charter schools: 2003–2004. (From U.S. Department of Education, National Center for Education Statistics, School and Staffing Survey, 2003–2004 School Year, public school, BIA school, and private school data files.)

several data sources that help answer that question, two of which will be briefly described here: the Early Childhood Longitudinal Study, Kindergarten Class of 1998–1999 (ECLS-K) and the new state longitudinal data systems.

The Early Childhood Longitudinal Study, Kindergarten Class of 1998–1999

The ECLS-K is an ongoing longitudinal study with achievement data in reading, math, and general knowledge/science. The original sample included about 22,000 children enrolled in public and private kindergarten programs during the 1998–1999 school year. Data are currently available from the fall of kindergarten through the spring of fifth grade, with data collections having taken place during the fall and spring of kindergarten and first grade, the spring of third grade, and the spring of fifth grade. A final data collection occurred in the spring of eighth grade in 2007. Parent and school-administrator interviews can be used to determine the type of school that students were enrolled in (e.g., public or private). Teacher interviews provide data on teacher characteristics and instructional practices.

The ECLS-K data can be used for a variety of things. For instance, Figure 11.10 shows the mean reading scores for students based on the type of school they attended between kindergarten and fifth grade. With this and other ECLS-K information, researchers can examine relationships between school characteristics (e.g., public vs. private schools) and student achievement. They can also map data from the parent and principal interviews and match data from the CCD.

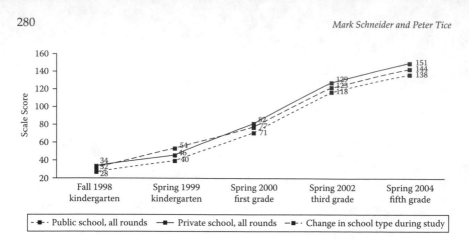

FIGURE 11.10 Mean reading scale scores for fall 1998 kindergartners by time of assessment and school type. (From U.S. Department of Education, National Center for Education Statistics, Early Childhood Longitudinal Study, Kindergarten Class of 1998–1999 [ECLS-K], longitudinal-third grade public-use data file and fifth-grade restricted-use data file.)

Potentially, researchers can take these kinds of data over time to measure growth in student achievement as a function of various conditions and possibly develop various kinds of selection models to better understand observed patterns.

The sister study to the ECLS-K, the Early Childhood Longitudinal Study, Birth Cohort (ECLS-B), collects data beginning with a cohort of children at birth and ending at pre-K. Other NCES longitudinal studies provide data on high school cohorts that are repeated about every 10 years. A useful feature of these longitudinal studies is that they often begin as school based, with samples of as many as 18,000 or more students. However, over time as students start moving, the studies become increasingly student based, which presents a problem for researchers interested in school effects. Still, they are rich datasets that contain information on and assessments of student performance, as well as information about teachers, schools, principals, guidance counselors, and parents. In other words, these longitudinal studies offer a detailed picture of the educational experiences of children and are especially beneficial because the interviews are repeated every couple of years.

State Longitudinal Data Systems

These data represent a coming revolution in the ability to document and understand the condition of American education. Currently, the Institute of Education Sciences/NCES is supporting 14 states as they develop state longitudinal data systems based on administrative records (a number that will grow with future Congressional appropriations).

These systems are intended to enhance the ability of states to efficiently and accurately manage, analyze, and use education data—including individual student records—for the purpose of making data-driven decisions to improve student learning. They are also intended to facilitate research to increase student achievement and close achievement gaps. To increase the value of individual state experiences, the NCES sponsors data conferences where state grantees share experiences and solve problems they have in constructing their longitudinal data systems. The goal is to take the states' data and help link them over time so that they can be used to track student progress from kindergarten through 12th grade and, ideally, the postsecondary years.

The shift from survey data to administrative data heralded by these state longitudinal data systems has profound implications in how researchers will go about understanding the condition of education in the United States. It may open up many new opportunities to better document the effects of school choice on achievement.

CONCLUSION

The NCES offers a wide collection of data that education researchers can apply to many of the school choice issues they care about. This chapter has provided a glimpse into what some of these datasets are and how researchers can use them to investigate what they want to know.

As a federal statistical agency, the NCES's mission is to collect and disseminate information about the condition of education in the United States. Schools of choice are increasingly central to that condition. The NCES hopes that researchers will use our data; that they will figure out what works and what does not; and, finally, that they will help the nation discover what can be done to better measure and understand the ever changing nature of America's schools.

REFERENCE

Speakman, S. T., Hassel, B. C., & Finn, C. E. (2005). *Charter school funding: Inequity's next frontier*. Washington, DC: Thomas B. Fordham Institute, Progress Analytics Institute, Public Impact.

Index